ROUTLEDGE LIBRARY EDITIONS: TRADE UNIONS

Volume 1

WHITE COLLAR WORKERS

WHITE COLLAR WORKERS

Trade Unions and Class

PETER ARMSTRONG, BOB CARTER,
CHRIS SMITH and THEO NICHOLS

Routledge
Taylor & Francis Group

LONDON AND NEW YORK

First published in 1986 by Croom Helm Ltd.

This edition first published in 2023
by Routledge
4 Park Square, Milton Park, Abingdon, Oxon OX14 4RN

and by Routledge
605 Third Avenue, New York, NY 10158

Routledge is an imprint of the Taylor & Francis Group, an informa business

British Library Cataloguing in Publication Data
A catalogue record for this book is available from the British Library

ISBN: 978-1-032-37553-3 (Set)
ISBN: 978-1-032-41040-1 (Volume 1) (hbk)
ISBN: 978-1-032-41045-6 (Volume 1) (pbk)
ISBN: 978-1-032-41044-9 (Volume 1) (ebk)

DOI: 10.4324/9781032410449

Publisher's Note
The publisher has gone to great lengths to ensure the quality of this reprint but points out that some imperfections in the original copies may be apparent.

Disclaimer
The publisher has made every effort to trace copyright holders and would welcome correspondence from those they have been unable to trace.

WHITE COLLAR WORKERS
TRADE UNIONS
AND CLASS

PETER ARMSTRONG
BOB CARTER
CHRIS SMITH
THEO NICHOLS

CROOM HELM
London • Sydney • Dover, New Hampshire

©1986 Peter Armstrong, Bob Carter, Chris Smith and Theo Nichols
Croom Helm Ltd, Provident House, Burrell Row,
Beckenham, Kent BR3 1AT
Croom Helm Australia Pty Ltd, Suite 4, 6th Floor,
64-76 Kippax Street, Surry Hills, NSW 2010, Australia

British Library Cataloguing in Publication Data

Armstrong, Peter
    White collar workers, trade unions and class.
    1. White collar workers – Great Britain
    I. Title
    331.7'92'0941   HD8039.M39
    ISBN 0-7099-0571-8

Croom Helm, 51 Washington Street, Dover,
New Hampshire 03820, USA

Library of Congress Cataloging in Publication Data
Main entry under title:

White collar workers, trade unions, and class.

    Bibliography: p.
    1. White collar workers—addresses, essays, lectures.
2. Social classes—addresses, essays, lectures.
3. Political sociology—addresses, essays, lectures.
4. Trade-unions—white collar workers—addresses, essays,
lectures. I. Armstrong, P.J. (Peter J.)
HD8039.M39W45   1986   331.88'041   85-28806
ISBN 0-7099-0571-8

Printed and bound in Great Britain by Mackays.of Chatham Ltd, Kent

CONTENTS

Acknowledgements

PART TWO : THE POLITICS OF WHITE COLLAR TRADE
UNIONISM

ACKNOWLEDGEMENTS

An earlier version of Peter Armstrong's chapter 1 first appeared in Sociology 17, 3, and thanks are due to the editor for permission to reprint it here. The data on which the study is based were obtained during an ESRC sponsored project directed by Professor J. F. B. Goodman, to whom thanks are also due. Peter Armstrong would also like to thank the management and workers at MoFoL, the officers and members of NUFLAT and the supervisors who, as part-time students, cooperated with his survey. Bob Carter thanks the AUEW convenor and foremen at Browns Ltd and the National Executive members, full-time officers and rank and file members of ASTMS who took time to discuss their union with him. Chris Smith thanks the BAe workers he interviewed, BAe management for allowing him access to them, TASS divisional organisers and convenors, and, for their continued interest and insights, Bob Murdock, Terry Rogers, Harry Blair, Mike Cooley and Ron Whitely.

All the contributors wish to acknowledge their very great debt to Pauline Tilley for her excellent work in producing this book.

INTRODUCTION

Theo Nichols

    An entire history of political sociology could be
written on the theme of the 'new middle classes'. As Ross
has put it: 'Whether in the guise of the "managerial
revolution", "white collar", the "new working class", or the
"new petite bourgeosie", the emergence of intermediate strata
in advanced industrial societies has been rediscovered more
often than the wheel' (1978, p.163). What holds for
political sociology, conventionally defined, is no less true
for Marxism. Throughout this century the undulations of
class struggle have triggered the re-examination of
capitalist class relations by Marxists, anti-Marxists and
revisionists alike. The fact that there have been certain
times when particular strata have been inspected for what
contribution they may make to continuity and change is not
surprising. It is no cause for surprise, either, that debate
within Western Europe has burgeoned in different countries at
different times in accord with particular national
developments. It is no mere coincidence, for example, that
interest in the <u>mittelstanden</u> figured so prominently in
Germany in the inter-war period. In addition to the need to
understand the social bases and political economy of fascism,
it had become apparent as early as the 1920s that the ratio
of salaried to manual workers in Germany was particularly
pronounced (as can be seen from Carter, 1985, p.16).
Similarly, the much more recent discussion of <u>couches</u>
<u>intermédiares</u> in France can be partly attributed to the
relatively late development of these strata in that country.
    Of course, a secular decline in manufacturing and an
apparent increase in 'mental' rather than 'manual' labour has
provided a much more general impetus to the theorisation of
'intermediate strata' in most advanced capitalist societies.
Over the last decade, however, analysis of these questions in
Britain, especially Marxist analysis, has been greatly
influenced by works which have come from elsewhere in Europe
and which have been overwhelmingly theoretical in nature
(Carchedi, 1977; Poulantzas, 1975). Perhaps it is as a

1

consequence of this that British work has contributed rather
little to the actual examination of the active interrelation
of classes in Britain. At any rate, and with few exceptions,
empirically based investigations have been sorely lacking. A
leading purpose of this book is to make some contribution to
the rectification of this situation.

This Introduction is intended to situate the
empirically-based studies which constitute the body of this
book in the light of a discussion of the theoretical work of
Poulantzas, Carchedi and other writers and in the context of
the state of class analysis today. To begin with, though, it
briefly re-visits the important contribution that
sociologists in Britain had made to the analysis of social
stratification (Lockwood) and class relations (Dahrendorf)
prior to the arrival of the new Marxist theories of the
middle class in the 1970s. It also makes due acknowledgement
to the view which, up until that time, many people had
regarded as the authentic Marxist one - that which posited
the existence of a capitalist class on the one side and of
one big (and ever increasing) proletariat, or waged labour
class, on the other. As will be seen later, the effects of
the earlier social stratification analyses and of the
two-class view are clearly evident in two apparently quite
different but for practical purposes rather similar
tendencies - toward synthesis and simplification - that
characterise some of the most recent work in this field.

Lockwood was primarily concerned with the question of
how the class consciousness of clerks was determined. But
what is of crucial importance about his work in the present
context is that in the process of exploring this question he
made use of a three-dimensional approach (Lockwood, 1958).
In practice it is arguable that Lockwoods' own perspective
derived in good part from much earlier work in Germany
(Weber) and the more contemporary American work of Wright
Mills, 1953. But there can be no question that Lockwood's
three-fold distinction between 'market situation' (source and
size of income, job security, mobility chances), 'work
situation' (position in the division of labour at work) and
'status situation' (position in terms of prestige) had an
enduring influence on the thinking of several cohorts of
British sociologists, a later work giving this line of
analysis yet greater currency (Goldthorpe et al, 1969). The
work of the German sociologist, Dahrendorf, which appeared in
Britain at more or less the same time that Lockwood's did,
has never had anything like the same direct impact, perhaps
because Dahrendorf eschewed the British tendency to focus
attention on occupations (so-to-speak 'within' the class

structure) and distanced himself also from the study of social stratification. He insisted that class should always be a category for the purpose of analysing the dynamics of social change and its structural roots (1959, p.76), and he located these structural roots in authority relations.

Dahrendorf's own particular attempt to marry Marx and Weber (the idea of conflictual class relations deriving from a perverse re-working of what Marx really meant - or what, according to Dahrendorf, he would have meant had he not died - and his preoccupation with authority having some affinity with Weber) soon became subject to a standard criticism: that logically his analysis pointed to the existence of as many ruling and subservient 'classes' as there were what he called 'imperatively co-ordinated associations', whether in industry, churches or even cricket clubs etc (Giddens, 1973). Like all two-class theorists Dahrendorf also had difficulty in arriving at any satisfactory analysis of the middle class. Whatever Dahrendorf's theoretical difficulties however, and they were considerable, for not the least of them was his conception of capitalism itself (Nichols, 1969), his work merits notice here for a particular reason. The very aspect of class relations that so pre-occupied Dahrendorf himself - authority - brought to the fore a problem which theorists of the middle class have continued to wrestle with since. It might very well be said, indeed, that a good deal of the re-theorisation of class over the past decade has been devoted to the task of finding a correct sequence of conceptual development into which to insert the authority relations which, it is generally agreed, Dahrendorf erroneously took as his point of departure.

Authority is itself an aspect of 'condition', and whether recent theorists of the new middle class have been British (Abercrombie and Urry, 1983; Giddens, 1973), American (Wright, 1977, 1978) or located elsewhere in Europe as the most influential of them have been (Carchedi, 1977; Poulantzas, 1975), it has been part of their project to attempt to incorporate an analysis pitched at this level of condition - Lockwood's work, status and market situation, if you will - into a prior analysis of place. (For a definition of these terms, together with an indication of how Giddens deals with them, see Nichols, 1979.)

The attempt to cope with the various aspects of condition by locating these within what, in all cases, is regarded as a theoretically prior analysis of the capitalist mode of production, took different forms in the works of Carchedi, Poulantzas and Wright. Since their works have set the context for most subsequent developments they will be considered shortly. But despite the clatter that these new middle class theories made in the 1970s it is useful to recall at this point that another, much simpler, strand of Marxist thought both pre-dated these new theories and has lived on since. This is the idea that the working class can be defined by the performance of wage labour.

By 'proletariat', Engels wrote in the English version of the Manifesto of the Communist Party in 1888, is meant 'the class of modern wage-labourers who, having no means of production of their own, are reduced to selling their labour-power in order to live'. Almost a century later an attempt by Cohen to subject historical materialism to the power of modern analytical philosophy arrived at a very similar definition. 'The proletarian', according to Cohen, 'is the subordinate producer who must sell his labour-power in order to obtain his means of life' (1978, p.73). And whilst Cohen admits in Karl Marx's Theory of History that his definition is not free from defects, he makes no attempt in that work to repair them. For as Cohen sees it, his definition is 'of the right type'. It defines the class 'with reference to the position of its members in the economic structure, their effective rights and duties within it' – and not, this being prohibited by Cohen's own self-declared 'austerely structural' analysis, in terms of 'consciousness, culture and politics' (1978, p.73, my emphasis).

Now there is something to be said for Cohen's position in so far as he wished to counter-pose it to another – the subjectivist kind of analysis in which class itself is defined in terms of consciousness. It is necessary to concede also that his definition is not quite as straightforward as it might appear at first sight. His concern is with matters de facto rather than de jure and his proposition 'in order to obtain his means of life' permits those who own some means of production to be included in the proletariat, provided they cannot 'live by' the possession of these except under 'capitalist aegis' (1978, p.72). These things said however – and ignoring here the question of whether Cohen's two class analysis was also Marx's, which has been eloquently and effectively discussed by Hall, 1977 – two further comments are in order. That Cohen's rigorous analytical philosophy is of very little help in interpreting (let alone changing) the politically and ideologically infused relations within his 'proletariat' as it actually exists in given societies, and that his reference to 'economic structure' itself lacks detailed elaboration. On the first point it is perhaps sufficient to note that, for some purposes at least, analytical philosophy has its limitations. But in connection with the second point it is useful to consider the work of another theorist, Carchedi. The promise of Carchedi's work is that it does seek to provide a further elaboration of the economic, thereby to permit a further distinction within the category of waged/salaried labour, within which of course the new middle class, unlike the old petty bourgeoisie, is formally situated.

Carchedi's analysis is conducted at a high level of abstraction but, put simply, it rests on a distinction between three aspects of capitalist relations of production. In addition to distinguishing between ownership and non-ownership, and thus owners/non-owners, Carchedi distinguishes between labourers/non-labourers and between producer/non-producers. (The latter distinction is between those who produce surplus value and those who expropropriate this surplus from their unpaid labour. In the case of those employed in spheres like banking where, on the labour theory of value, no surplus value is actually produced, so that there is no 'exploitation', the term 'oppression' is applied to the analagous expropriation of unproductive workers' labour.) It is on the basis of these distinctions that Carchedi then specifies the capitalist and working class. Those in the capitalist class are characterised as owners, non-producers and non-labourers: the working class as non-owners, producers and labourers.

In order to insert the new middle class into his analysis, Carchedi then takes account of a double movement. In the one movement, following Marx, he sees the early stages of industrial capitalist development to have taken the form of a merely 'formal' subordination of labour to capital. Under this, workers were brought together in the factory for the purpose of extracting surplus from them, but with the technical conditions in which production took place remaining much the same. Later on, however, a 'real' subordination took place. The labour process was subjected to continuous revolution, it became complex, and labour was socialised, with the product itself now resulting from the labour of many interdependent collective workers, some engaged in predominately manual labour and some not. Carchedi then sees these changes within the labour process to have been complemented by another movement, by similar transformations in the functions hitherto performed by the individual capitalist. In and of itself the production process would require 'co-ordination and unity'. But complex organisational forms have emerged to subject it to 'control and surveillance' for the exploitation of surplus value (or, by logical extension, oppression).

It is, according to Carchedi, as a consequence of these two developments that a category of non-owners has emerged which performs both 'the function of the collective worker' and 'the global function of capital'. Indeed, he emphasises: 'This fact, that the new middle class performs the global function of capital even without owning the means of production, and that it performs this function in conjunction with the function of the collective worker, is the basic point for an understanding of the nature of this class' (1977, p.89). On this schema, the 'old middle class' were typically exploiters. They had strategic control over the means of production, were the real owners, and the dominant function that they performed was that of capital. The 'new middle class', by contrast, do not have strategic control, are not the real owners, and since the global function of capital is not necessarily dominant, their fundamental function is not necessarily that of exploiters (or oppressors). Even when they are on the side of capital, they are both exploiters (or oppressors) and oppressed.

Carchedi identifies the global function of capital in terms of 'control and surveillance'. There is some similarity here with Dahrendorf's analysis of authority relations (as other writers have observed: Abercrombie and Urry, 1983, p.64; Parkin, 1979, p.23). Even so, Carchedi's analysis rests on a very different theoretical base to that of Dahrendorf's 'imperatively co-ordinated association'. It 'works' through a recognition that capitalist production entails both the production of use values and of surplus value. Carchedi's new middle class is specified in terms of labour and capital functions, and the process of proletarianisation in terms of a shift from the performance of capital to labour functions. In fact, it is this very distinction between labour and capital functions that has attracted one of the most frequently made criticisms of Carchedi's work. It has been argued for example that it is highly problematic whether Marx himself thought that the function of labour could be separated out from the function of capital, with the latter conceived as external to the production process, for the period after which labour had been socialised (Cottrell, 1984, pp.85-6). In much the same vein Poulantzas insists, following Marx's own discussion of the 'double-nature' of supervision, that to co-ordinate and unify is to engage 'simulanteously' in the process of exploitation (Poulantzas, 1975, p.226). Many other critics have claimed that it is difficult to apply Carchedi's distinction because of the problem of distinguishing which work tasks are composed of which functions (e.g. Johnson, 1977, p.206). This last criticism and those which precede it command respect. But they scarcely mean that Carchedi's conceptual work has nothing to offer to the analysis of class dynamics.

However, it is quite obvious that since Carchedi's attempt to provide a further elaboration of the economic as it enters into class determination deliberately excluded the political and ideological his analysis remained a partial one only. This may account in part for the more widespread influence of Poulantzas. Poulantzas has been the leading figure who has attempted to theorise class relations at the political and ideological as well as economic levels. The key assumption upon which Poulantzas constructs his theory is that the performance of productive labour is a necessary condition for working class membership ('productive labour' itself being defined, in contrast to Marx, in terms of the reproduction of 'material elements' in 'material production': cf. Poulantzas, 1977, p.216; Marx, 1969, p.401). With this as his starting point, Poulantzas then proceeds to introduce relations of a political and ideological kind in order to determine further the class relations that pertain <u>within</u> the general waged/salaried labour category. Those who perform productive labour are excluded from the working class if they occupy a dominant place in political relations or ideological relations (i.e. those which deprive the working class itself of real or imaginary knowledge through their association with 'mental labour'). For Poulantzas, these agents - engineers, technicians etc. - are then consigned to a 'new petty bourgeoisie', along with the broad spectrum of all those who perform unproductive rather than productive labour.

Initially, the 'class map' to result from this exercise may not appear to differ very much from some features of one that many British sociologists had in their heads well before the new Marxist theorisation of class took-off in the 1970s. The importance attributed to the mental/manual labour division conspires to suggest just this; so does the stress on political relations, for conceptions of 'work situation' always have taken account of these, at least in their face-to-face (authority) dimension. But there is at least one important respect in which Poulantzas's theorisation of class relations leads him to break company with a previously common sociological assumption. In his determination of classes Poulantzas accords place in the division of labour primacy over condition. For him, therefore, no matter how closely the immediate 'work situation' of those who perform unproductive labour conforms to that of manual workers, they remain irredeemably new petty bourgeois. In this respect Poulantzas also differs from some of his fellow marxists, for whom deskilling is seen to constitute proletarianisation. For Poulantzas, a deterioration in the work/market/status situation of those who perform 'white collar' salaried labour can only make for a 'proletarian polarisation': it cannot make them proletarians proper. Even if they are 'clearly objectively polarised in the direction of the working class' their 'class determinations place them in the petty-bourgeois camp' (1977, p.314).

As for what is to be made of this, it has been repeated <u>ad nauseum</u> that Poulantzas's formulations yield a very small working class. They most certainly do. But this observation is in no way relevant to an assessment of the consistency and coherence of his theory. More pertinent here is the observation that, although Poulantzas insists that 'social classes do not firstly exist as such, and only then enter into a class struggle' (1977, p.14) his actual analysis is such as to suggest that, locked in place in class struggle, they quite literally remain in 'place' ever after. Poulantzas's functionalist leanings have been criticised amongst others by Clarke, 1977. Other critics have challenged the Marxist credentials of his concept of productive labour, and its relevance for the determination of class. Some have held his analysis to be flawed because it is economistic (Abercrombie and Urry, 1983, p.73). Yet others (like Wright, 1977, 1978), claimed it to be flawed because it does not accord primacy to the economic, but invokes political and ideological relations in an inconsistent way. Both views have something to be said for them, depending which features of Poulantzas's theory are considered. Rather than pursue this apparent conflict of opinion here, however, it is more fruitful to turn to Wright's analysis, for in addition to advancing the claim that contradictory class relations exist (which is anathema to Poulantzas) Wright <u>does</u> promise us a coherent and consistent class analysis, and one moreover in which primacy <u>is</u> accorded to the economic.

Central to Wright's analysis is the distinction he draws between 'economic ownership' (control over investment and resource allocation: cf. Carchedi's 'strategic decisions') and two sorts of 'possession' - control over the physical means of production and control over labour-power. Such a distinction is by no means original (Bettelheim, 1976), but the use to which Wright puts it is. He defines the capitalist class by its controlling position with respect to all three of these relations, then (although he does not use this term himself), he effectively defines the working class as a class that is 'dispossessed' - which lacks control over economic ownership and both types of possession. Contradictory class locations are then specified within the sphere of waged/salaried labour in cases where the relations are 'mixed'. Foremen, for example, are seen to occupy a contradictory class location because, although lacking control at the level of economic ownership and over the physical means of production they none the less have control over the labour-power of others. Employees who have a certain degree of autonomy with respect to the physical means of production (a polyglot category in which Wright includes laboratory researchers, some highly skilled craftsmen and a 'professor in an elite university'), are seen to occupy another contradictory class location, this time between the proletariat and the (traditional, self-employed) petty bourgeoisie, whose position entails economic ownership.

As stated already, Wright's analysis grew out of a critique of Poulantzas. As a critique, it makes some effective points. Thus Wright is able to show that Poulantzas introduced economic, political and ideological criteria in an inconsistent way. In the case of the bourgeois class for example, Poulantzas included those who stand in a dominant place in economic relations (employers) and those who stand in a dominant place in political and ideological relations (like heads of state apparatus). In the case of inclusion in the working class, by contrast, Poulantzas down-graded the importance of political and ideological criteria. He held that the performance of productive labour was a necessary (if not sufficient) condition for inclusion in this class. Taking Poulantzas's analysis to its logical conclusion, Wright has no trouble in showing that, in much the same fashion as Poulantzas argues with respect to the working class, it could be argued that unproductive capital also lies 'outside the dominant capitalist relation of exploitation' and thus, to be consistent, 'agents occupying the place of unproductive capital [e.g. bankers, insurance chiefs, T.N.] should not be regarded as members of the capitalist class'.

The trouble is that similar problems of consistency also beset Wright's own analysis. Wright's problems become particularly evident when he considers the case of some of those agents who are situated outside of production, in the state apparatus for example. Consider the police. For Poulantzas, the police would stand in a dominant <u>political</u> relation to the working class. In economic terms, as unproductive labour, they are paid out of revenue produced by the labour of that class. The 'deskilling' of their jobs or the freezing of their pay (should this happen) might perhaps lead them to militancy or to support for that of the working class - but there is no way that they could stand in that class place as policemen. For his part, Wright accepts that police have no control over the labour power of others and relatively little control over their own labour power, and no economic ownership. As Wright himself observes, this would mean that 'at the level of economic relations alone, police are waged labourers' (1976, p.40). However, Wright is not really happy to consign police to the working class. And he seeks to grasp some of the same aspects of the place in which the police are located that Poulantzas did, but at the expense of abandoning his own major theoretical proposition; namely that 'the extent to which political and ideological relations enter into the determination of class position is itself determined by the degree to which these positions occupy a contradictory location at the level of social relations of production' (Wright, 1976, pp.39-40). Police, he ends up telling us, 'occupy a contradictory class location defined principally by a non correspondence of economic <u>and</u> political relations' (Wright, 1976, p.40, my emphasis). A similar slippage occurs in Wright's treatment of top positions in the state apparatus. 'In terms of economic relations alone', he tells us, 'it would be hard to characterise the heads of various state apparatuses as being unambiguously bourgeois' (Wright, 1976, p.41). It certainly

would.   For according to a previous table of Wright's (Table
9, p.25) they are characterised under the heading 'Economic
Criteria' as lacking legal ownership, economic ownership and
possession;   that   is   as   unambiguously   proletarian,   not
bourgeois at all.   It is, Wright claims, in seeking to cope
with this problem, 'only at the top levels of the state
apparatus [that it is] plausible to argue that ideological
and   political   factors   are   sufficiently   strong   to   neutralise
the   contradictory   quality   of   class   relations'   (Wright,   1976,
p.41).   But   here   of   course   a   contradiction   appears   in
Wright's own theory.   For according to this, it was to have
been contradictions at the level of the economic which were
to   have   specified   the   extent   to   which   political   and
ideological   relations   entered   into   the   determination   of   class
position.   To make his theory work, Wright has to shift the
meaning of 'contradiction' from that which pertains <u>within</u>
the economic to that which pertains <u>between</u> the economic and
the   political.   Like   Poulantzas,   he   does   not   in   practice
consistently accord primacy to the economic.
    There are further difficulties.   As Carter has observed:
'researchers and technicians may have a limited control over
how they perform their tasks but there is no doubt about who
defines their ends' (1985, pp.80-1).   To depict these groups
as   'residual   islands   of   petty-bourgeois   relations   of
production within the capitalist mode of production' may
therefore be to unduly minimise the extent to which their
active relations are between them and the working class on
the one hand and capitalists on the other.   Then again, the
analytical distinction between the two sorts of possession,
control over physical means of production and control of
other people's labour-power, may prove difficult to apply in
practice.   Very often control over the former will entail a
measure of control over the latter.

    Two broad tendencies have resulted from the frequently
made   claim   that   the   analytically   distinct   functions   that
Carchedi proposed in his work on economic identification are
in fact difficult to identify, from the recognition, amongst
other things, that Poulantzas's stress on productive labour
is   theoretically   unproductive,   and   from   recognition   that
Wright's analysis of contradictory class location is itself
not free from contradiction.   One of these tendencies is
toward <u>simplification</u>, the other toward <u>synthesis</u>.
    A recent work by Cottrell provides an example of
simplification.   As Cottrell sees it, the attempt by Marxist
theorists to arrive at a 'correct' definition of the new
petty bourgeoisie/middle class has pushed them into 'a kind
of conceptual gerrymandering'.   Not only this, but he notes
another feature of the theories that Marxists were wont to

develop in the 1970s which has been much remarked upon by other writers – that it is not possible, even on some of the leading theorists' own admission, to draw any definite political conclusions from their analyses. Faced with this, Cottrell concludes: 'Better to admit that the divisions within the working class, in the broad sense, are not such as to permit a conceptual segregation at the level of the "capitalist mode of production", or even "modern capitalism", but have to be investigated more specifically in the context of particular social formations' (1984, p.91). Cottrell's way forward is, in short, first to go back to basics, to define the working class as that class whose members do not possess any means of production and who are therefore constrained to sell their labour-power, and then, second, to get on with the work of actually investigating social and cultural collectivities and political forces. Cottrell's second, more practical prescription, necessarily follows from his definition of the working class in terms of waged labour. Both this, and his minimalist conception of what theory can do, quite clearly implies that a mass of empirical work remains to be done.

The theories of the new middle class were pitched at such a level of abstraction that they most certainly left large and empty spaces which cried out for empirical investigation. To some degree Abercrombie and Urry, the two authors who best exemplify the tendency towards synthesis, have attempted to provide this. At least, this is so to the extent that their work centres on a particular society, Britain. The weight of Abercrombie and Urry's work remains on the theoretical side however. From Marxism, they take the notion of capital 'functions', refining this beyond Carchedi's usage to refer not only to 'control' but also to 'reproduction' (of labour-power) and to 'conceptualisation' (of the labour process). From Weberian sociology, they take the familiar notions of 'work' and 'market situation', extending their analysis to take particular account of 'credentialism'; that is, the attempt to sustain or enlarge the educational credentials that control access to particular places in the social division of labour.

Synthesising these elements, Abercrombie and Urry hold that the distinctive market and work situation and hence, as they see it, the class position of the capitalist class is being transformed through the depersonalisation of property ownership; that its functions are becoming 'somewhat indistinguishable' from those of what they term the 'service class'; and that alongside the siphoning into the service class of the functions of capital – reproduction, conceptualisation and control – there is occurring a 'proletarianisation' of 'deskilled white collar workers' (a claim that they qualify by noting that the 'residual functional separation between white collar workers and manual workers reinforces the differentiation within the working class which makes the notion of proletarianisation difficult to apply in any straightforward way': 1983, p.125, 152-3). The upshot of their analysis as it applies to the formal category of waged/salaried labour is: one, that a service class exists, which can hardly be called a 'middle class' since there is no readily distinguishable class above it; and, two, that a much larger category of deskilled white collar workers exists below this which, given its 'proletarianisation', cannot be properly considered middle class either.

Abercrombie and Urry reject the view that classes possess 'essences', which inexorably emerge as history unfolds, and they take the view that classes are not reducible to the objective determinants which are seen to generate them (cf. Poulantzas). The position that they adopt on the nature of classes - that they possess 'causal powers', by which they mean that they have powers 'to generate empirically observable events' (1983, p.131) - paves the way for the stress they put on 'credentialism'. This is perhaps a little odd, in the British context, given the historic influence that ascriptive (and not simply technical, or even suposedly 'technical') criteria have had on recruitment to the higher and middle levels. Their claim that the 'policing' of those who have attained professional places in the 'service class' is 'carried out according to the associations' code of ethics' (1983, p.121) is also rather thin. At the very least more evidence to support such a generalisation is required. There is one important respect, however, in which Abercrombie and Urry's work may help to generate more interest in a matter that has long been unduly neglected, in part because not only has much recent writing on class been conducted at such a high level of abstraction, but so has that on the state. Broached long ago in the work of one of Britain's outstanding students of social policy, and returned to more recently by Gould (see Titmus, 1958; Gould, 1980), this concerns the disproportionate degree to which those who Abercrombie and Urry assign to a 'service class' are privileged through their relation to the British state - through tax reliefs on school fees, mortgages, private medical and other insurance. These benefits are not confined to those in Abercrombie and Urry's 'service class' of course. But they are historically generated and empirically observable benefits that are enjoyed disproportionately by members of the 'service class' and the political implications of this, in contemporary Britain, is that they represent a fetter on the sort of ideal free-market trajectory that some members of the present Government would seem to want to follow. If we are interested in the politics of class (and, if not, why bother?) it is highly pertinent to take such considerations seriously (for needless to say,

Introduction

Abercrombie and Urry's 'service class' is also a blockage to socialism).

An important part of Abercrombie and Urry's project was to pose new questions, or to uproot questions that had been posed within different problematics and co-ordinate these into a new way forward – in a different and more dynamic way from that which had as its hallmark the <u>classification</u> of individuals and groups (which is very often what class theory has been, the denials notwithstanding). A certain lack of precision can be justified because of this. For instance, their statement that the functions performed by the service and capitalist class are 'somewhat indistinguishable' or that 'proletarianisation' is 'difficult to apply in any straightforward way' can be justified in large part by their desire to point to processes and active class relations, rather than to engage in the sterile manufacture of brittle class categories. It remains the case, however, that even though these authors seek to put forward a more dynamic analysis they manage to tell us relatively little about the active interrelation of classes, least of all within the process of production. It is notable that just as some of the empirical material they use to greatest effect is American, so some of their assumptions about Britain derive, not from their own original observations but from novelistic accounts by the likes of H. G. Wells, George Orwell and Margaret Drabble. In itself, there is nothing 'wrong' with this of course. Indeed, compared to the preposterous prose of so much 'class analysis' such excursions are cause for pure joy. But, there does seem to be a case for original research that is actually based on closer observation.

One particular recent contribution (Crompton and Jones, 1984) does not fall neatly into either of the two lines of development referred to so far, i.e. simplification or synthesis. And it does report original empirical work. One of its main objectives is to examine the non-manual labour process in order to ascertain the extent to which de-skilling has actually occurred. Based on studies in three large white collar bureauacracies – a local authority, a life assurance company and a major clearing bank – it argues that much clerical and administrative work has been deskilled, that the notion this does not apply to men because of their greater mobility out of clerical work is less well founded and less relevant to the thesis of proletarianalism than often thought (cf. Goldthorpe 1980; Stewart, Prandy and Blackburn, 1980), and that, in any case, the class situation of men cannot be comprehended without a consideration of the role of women in the social and technical division of labour – not least because gender itself contributes to the social definition of jobs. Dealing in specifics, the work of Crompton and Jones is necessarily limited. Specific details matter though, and such work is not to be lightly dismissed, least of all in a

13

field in which the production of a predominately theoretical literature has threatened to become an end in itself.

None of the contributors to this book would want to argue against the importance of examining the underlying assumptions upon which theories are based, the investigation of their internal consistency and so on. But all of them also believe that theoretical work needs to be allied to empirical work, and that processual observational studies have some part to play in furthering our knowledge of the active interrelation of those who differ in their place/function and condition. Noting, therefore, that there is in fact very little reportage of <u>active relations</u> even in the work of Crompton and Jones - and this despite the fact that their study is by far the most grounded empirical account of all those referred to above - the present book has the modest purpose of bringing together several case studies that, it is hoped, will help to rectify the present imbalance and thereby make a small step toward the development of more realistic theory.

The book is in two parts. Part One presents material that focusses on the actual interrelation of supervisory, manual and technical workers. Part Two focusses on white collar trade unionism. The idea is to discuss these matters side by side, for as the contributors see it white collar trade unionism has been as ill-served by the mechanical analyses of some industrial relationists as by the <u>ex-cathedra</u> pronouncements of some Marxists. (Armstrong introduces the relevant literature on white collar trade unionism at the beginning of chapter four.) The case studies in Part One all centre on work relations, and yet more specifically, and in contrast to Crompton and Jones, on work relations within manufacturing. Work is not of course the only site of class struggle but it is an extremely important one and no excuse is therefore offered here for concentrating upon the point of production in Part One. As for the focus on manufacturing, this is no more than a function of the case studies we have to hand - cases that it is hoped are worth bringing together because they do provide at least some insight into active relations in a way that the great bulk of the discussion of class relations over the past decade has not. Concerning other features of the case studies, it should be noted that the absence of an explicit treatment of gender and ethnicity is not a result of deliberate policy but is once again much more a function of the cases studied. In chapters two and three, for example, the supervisors, technical workers and manual workers who figure in the case studies are overwhelmingly male; in chapter one women are represented amongst both supervisors and supervised.

These points about manufacturing, gender and ethnicity may all conspire to suggest that the case studies presented below are located in relatively 'uncomplicated' situations. This is not entirely so. For example the case presented in chapter one is set in factory that employs men, women, and some members of ethnic minorities. But to the extent that it is true that the situations studied are not cross-cut by immediate gender and ethnic differences this is in some ways an advantage. It enables some other 'complications' that have often been neglected hitherto to be unravelled. In chapter three, for example, which is concerned with technical workers, Smith is able to demonstrate at some length that this term conceals an often unrecognised diversity, and suggests on the basis of his study, which includes what is probably one of the biggest concentrations of such workers in Britain, that it is difficult to understand technical and other workers without giving due recognition to their own experience of craft work and the residues of craft ideology.

Certain other more general propositions – which may well apply irrespective of workplace gender and ethnic distinctions – also emerge the more clearly. On the basis of his observations in chapter one, for example, Armstrong argues amongst other things that the deterioration in the market and work situations of the supervisors he studied – as evidenced by their lack of decision-making power, by piece-workers in their charge sometimes earning up to twice as much as they did and the de-skilling of the supervisors' own jobs – did not lead them to change sides between capital and manual labour. In fact, it had the opposite effect. Dealing with a shop floor that was particularly vulnerable because it was weakly organised, the foremen responded by driving those under them yet harder. Given the circumstances that prevailed it might not be outlandish to surmise that a similar outcome might have been expected whether all of those supervised had been women – and even if they had been supervised by women. In passing, though, it is perhaps worth noting that the supervision of women by women remains under-researched. A flotilla of recent books and articles on the problems of female managers has generally failed to explore the question of whether and how the politics of gender operate in such contexts.

The conclusion to emerge from chapter one – that 'proletarianisation of condition' is not synonymous with a changed place in class relations, no matter how much it may be resented – has direct relevance for more conventional sociological analyses of social class, and also some Marxist ones. This piece also provides some concrete reasons to explain why Abercrombie and Urry were correct to conclude that the notion of proletarianisation is difficult to apply in any straightforward way (1983, p.125). Other contributions suggest that the trade unionism espoused by white collar workers can display certain distinctive features, again notwithstanding some aspects of proletarianisation. In chapter four, for example, which reports one of the few enquiries that have actually been conducted into the question of what supervisors want from their unions, it is suggested that what they want is not simply to further their interests as 'employees', but to secure and enhance their role as employees whose particular function is to act as controllers of other employees. Chapter two, which is set in a factory where shop floor organisation was relatively well developed, and yet more particularly in the context of a factory sit-in, underlines the need to take account of a further consideration. Read in conjunction with chapter one it suggests that the production politics of white collar workers are a product of the capital and/or labour functions that they perform, as mediated, amongst other things, by the strength of manual labour. It is difficult to find any Marxist contribution to the theoretical analysis of the new middle class (however defined) that does not stress that class relations always exist in class struggle. Remarkably enough, there is a real dearth of observational studies like this one - which shows how in the midst of heightened conflict supervisors did 'go over' to manual labour, but only up a point, and in a particular way. Limited as the case studies are by the sectors in which they are located, by the specific characteristics of the workforces and by the particular trade unions that they examined, there is much to be said in support of them in so far as, with respect to the above and other examples, they add substance to some of the most high-flown theory ever to be produced in the social sciences, and bring it down to earth, or, substantially fault it.

The case studies gathered together in White Collar Workers, Trade Unions and Class should be of interest to those who have come to wonder what use can be made 'on the ground' of new middle class theories like those of Poulantzas and Carchedi. They should be of no less interest to those who, suspicious of the over-theorisation of class, are drawn to the simplicity of an economic (waged labour) definition of the proletariat. The latter position, as noted earlier, leaves all the work to be done - if, that is, the analysis of class relations is ever to lead us any closer to a consideration of likely real-world outcomes - and it is with the examination of such outcomes in specific contexts that the case studies which follow are concerned.

PART ONE

CLASS RELATIONS AT WORK

Chapter One

CLASS AND CONTROL AT THE POINT OF PRODUCTION - FOREMEN 1

Peter Armstrong

On the Marxist view, the fundamental class division is between the buyers and sellers of labour power, in which conception of class, white-collar workers are, at first sight, 'objectively' proletarian (see, for example, Allen, 1973). For Lockwood (1958) and the many empirical researchers who have followed his basic approach, the problem then became one of explaining why some white collar workers did not see their class situation in these terms (Lockwood, 1966; Child, Pearce and King, 1980), or why they did not manifest such supposedly appropriate forms of action as joining trade unions (Prandy, 1965). On this latter point the assumed association between unionisation and proletarianisation has been heavily criticized, partly on the grounds that trade union recruitment can be adequately explained by reference to institutional factors alone (Bain, 1970; Bain, Coates and Ellis, 1973), and partly because the characteristics and aims of white collar unions may be such as to call into question any association between unionisation and class action (Blackburn, 1967; Weir, 1976; Reynaud, 1983).

More fundamentally, Lockwood's work, and by implication the tradition of empirical research deriving from it, was later criticized by Crompton (1976) on the grounds that although the basic problem may have derived from Marxist theory, the search for structural bases for the variations in white collar workers' consciousness and unionisation led Lockwood to concentrate on such matters as income differentials, the bureaucratisation of the work place, blocked promotion channels and so forth, all of which have more to do with the market situation of white collar workers (within the employing organisation as well as external to it) than with their relationship to the productive process. In that sense, the operational conception of social class in Lockwood's work was Weberian rather than Marxist, since his conclusion, effectively speaking, was that in terms of consciousness and action, the market situation of white collar workers could outweigh the influence of their position as the sellers, rather than the buyers, of labour power. With the advantage of 27 years' hindsight, one might then ask why the latter distinction should have been considered to be fundamental enough to generate the problem in the first place.

Lockwood's Weberian emphasis on social action, in which class action was linked, in the first instance, to class perception, has arguably distorted much of the subsequent literature, some of which seems to be based on the idea that the question of class position ends with that of class perception. Thus volume three of the 'Affluent Worker' studies (Goldthorpe, Lockwood, Bechhofer and Platt, 1969), whilst entitled - 'The Affluent Worker in the Class Structure', is actually concerned almost entirely with the workers' views on the class structure and on their own place in it. Though possessing the advantage that attitude surveys are easier to perform than observational studies, the rather obvious problem with this approach is that action, particularly for working class people, may. be structurally constrained.

Within the 'perceptions' approach, the Weberian spirit has also frequently manifested itself in the treatment of class as a category rather than as a relationship (see, for example, Roberts, Cook, Clark and Semeonoff, 1977), which is odd considering the prominence given to the 'relational' aspect of class in the 'Affluent Worker' studies, and is certainly inconsistent with the Marxist view that the antagonism of class interests, deriving from different positions in the social relations of production, is integral to the definition of class itself. A recent exception to this generalisation is the work of Stewart, Prandy and Blackburn (1980) which, however, like the 'Affluent Worker' studies views the relational aspect of class as a matter of sociability outside the workplace. The approach of this chapter differs in two respects: class relationships are viewed as questions of antagonism or identity of interests and they are examined within the workplace rather than outside it. Whilst it is perfectly true that the process of production is not the whole of the total process of reproduction of capitalist social relations (cf. Poulantzas, 1978, p.180), it is certainly a fundamental part of it.

In an approach very different from the Weberian attitude surveys reviewed so far, Crompton set out to explore, in a more thoroughgoing fashion, the implications for white collar unionism of a consistently Marxist conception of class. Basing her discussion on the theoretical analyses of Carchedi (1977), Poulantzas (1973) and Wright (1979a), she argued, in effect, that the distinction between the buying and selling of labour power had been misconstrued; that although white collar workers were certainly the sellers of their own labour power, the actual role of some of them in relation to the productive process was to perform some of the functions of the buyer of other people's labour power. There were therefore two respects in which white collar work could become proletarianised. Firstly it could become less concerned with the process of buying labour power and more concerned with the actual process of production. Secondly the position of white collar workers within the process of buying labour power could be progressively de-skilled, routinised and subject to bureaucratic controls, a process described by Braverman (1974, Ch.14) and Wright (1979b) amongst others. Although, as will be argued later, this second supposed aspect of proletarianisation is not really consistent with Crompton's basic approach, her attempt to test, in the case of insurance clerks, the thesis that unionisation is most likely when proletarianisation occurs in both of the senses outlined above (Crompton, 1979), and her later study of a wider range of white collar workers (Crompton and Jones, 1984), though ultimately flawed, remain amongst the few attempts to operationalise a conception of class which focusses on the <u>function</u> of white collar work rather than the degree of privilege associated with it. Though later workers have displayed an interest in this view of the matter, the consensus seems to be that the difficulties of operationalising the question of the economic function of white collar work rule out its use in empirical research (see, for example, Child, Pearce and King, 1980, p.366) which, perhaps partly for this reason, has continued to utilize the relatively easily scaleable variables associated with the Weberian conception of class. This has meant that, whether consciously or unconsciously, most empirical work on the class position of white collar workers has had little to say about, and has certainly not been a test of, Marxist theorising on the subject.

Apart from Crompton's work, two further exceptions to this generalisation should be mentioned. Carter, in chapter two of this volume, shows how, in a factory sit in, supervisors responded by taking on 'collective worker' functions whilst their role in the 'global function of capital' was in abeyance. Although concerned with an atypical situation, this study interestingly demonstrates the role played by economic interests in conditioning class allegiances. Of less immediate relevance, Wright (1979c) attempted to demonstrate that variations in manager's salaries could be accounted for by the varying extents to which they performed the control functions of capital, though this work was later criticised by Stewart, Prandy and Blackburn (1980) on the grounds that the operationalisation of managerial control (the level of manager's education) was unsound. Clearly it is important to add to the scanty empirical backing which underlies the considerable Marxist theorising on the class position of white collar workers. This is the first object of the present chapter.

The prevailing Weberian emphasis on market situation has had a further effect on the literature: many studies of white collar workers are, as Kelly (1980) has pointed out, very vague on the <u>kind</u> of workers which are under consideration and especially on the actual tasks which they perform. If, however, we are interested in the distinction between buying and selling labour power rather than in rankings of privilege, the question of the content of white collar work is clearly critical. To put the matter crudely, white collar work which is unambiguously part of the productive process will be, in the Marxist sense, proletarian, whilst any which is contained entirely within the administrative apparatus concerned with the buying of labour power will lie within the bourgeois apparatus of control. In Carchedi's (1977) terms, this is the distinction between the 'collective worker' and the 'global function of capital'. Of course there will be intermediate cases, and this matter will be discussed presently.

From the point of view of work content in relation to class position, it is important, at least at the level of consciousness and action, that the present study is concerned with the direct supervisors of labour, for whom issues of control, however they interpret them, are immediate, rather than with, say, the kind of clerical workers studied by Crompton (1979) and Crompton and Jones (1984), for whom the origins of the wages and surplus which they are paid to move about may be the subject of considerable mystification. In this connection, it is disappointing, to say the least, that Crompton's own latest study of clerical workers (Crompton and Jones, 1984) has nothing at all to say about the economic function of their tasks, in contrast to her earlier theorising on the topic.

Of course the more specific literature on industrial supervisors is much concerned with issues of control, though, with the exception of authors such as Prandy (1965) and Child, Pearce and King (1980), this is often not explicitly related to class position. In the literature which does relate control to class situation, the consensus appears to be that the bureaucratisation and/or mechanisation of white collar work amounts to a decisive loss of control for supervisors so that their situation now differs little from that of shopfloor workers (see, for example, Braverman, 1974, Ch.14; Edwards, 1975; Child and Partridge, 1982).

There are important points at issue here. In the first place the argument tends to equate the subjection of white collar workers to increased managerial control with a loss of control by them of the shopfloor workforce. Thus Carchedi (1977) observes that the proletarianisation of white collar workers involves their becoming the objects rather than the subjects of control and surveillance, whilst Wright (1979c, p.4) extends the argument to claim that the class location of managers is contradictory because, as well as exerting control over the labour force, they are themselves subject to control. In the same way, Crompton and Jones' latest study of white collar workers confuses a loss of decision-making scope with a loss of the control function (1984, p.57 et seq). It is important in this connection to appreciate that the transmission of management orders - even unmodified - may be an essential part of the control apparatus. Thus Runciman (1967) observes that although low level white collar workers are just as much the recipients of orders as manual workers, their location in the process of production remains fundamentally different. From the point of view of analysing the class position of supervisors, loss of autonomy in the control function of capital should not be confused with exclusion from the control function itself. As with the 'pissing pots' observed by Hill (1973) and as will appear in the present paper, supervisors may well be held accountable for implementing or policing decisions made by their seniors. Where this is the case, the situation of a 'subaltern of capital' (Nichols and Beynon, 1977) however lowly, cannot be equated with that of a 'private'.

Related to this confusion, there is a tendency, perhaps understandable in non-Marxist writing but surely inconsistent with a Marxist approach, to equate loss of control generally with exclusion from the control function of capital. Thus Carchedi (1977) argues that the de-skilling and fragmentation of clerical work is an aspect of its proletarianisation, despite his simultaneous insistence that it is fundamentally a matter of its economic function.

Later in this chapter, there will appear an instance in which, through the introduction of complex new machinery, supervisors have lost technical control of the production process whilst retaining the function of containing labour costs, with perhaps predictable consequences for their relationships with shopfloor workers. In other words they have lost a form of control which is arguably part of the productive process whilst retaining a relatively unambiguous control function of capital. Often, however, and especially where survey rather than case study methodologies are employed, it can be very difficult to distinguish between these two aspects of control, paticularly since these are characteristically combined in single jobs and ideologically obscured by blanket concepts of 'efficiency'. This again may be a reason why empirical researchers have avoided trying to operationalise a Marxist conception of class.

Looking more closely at class in relation to the question of loss of control, we find a divergence within the Marxist approach itself. Thus Carchedi (1977) argues that proletarianisation is a progressive process in which supervisors gradually take on 'worker' functions as they lose the control function of capital. In the work of Wright (1979a, p.76), control is conceived of as having three aspects: economic ownership, control over the physical means of production and control over the labour power of others, thus allowing for 'contradictory' class locations which possess some of these aspects of control, but not others. Both of these conceptions of class, in their different ways, allow for intermediate positions in the class structure. For Poulantzas (1978, p.228), however, matters are more clear cut: any position which involves a significant part of the control function of capital is, for him, located within the bourgeois administrative apparatus.

All three of these views of social class depend upon a distinction between the technical division of labour (a particular allocation of the physical and intellectual work necessary for the process of production to be carried out, whatever the system of ownership) and the social relations of production (a structure of domination and subordination deriving, in capitalism, from ownership or non-ownership of the means of production and which is directed, amongst other things, at ensuring that the value added in the production process exceeds the sum total of wages and other costs and that this surplus goes to capital). Though such a distinction is clear enough in principle, many managerial, technical or supervisory positions which play a part in the functions of capital within the social relations of production (for example, by ensuring that the pace of work is high enough to ensure a surplus) also involve a role within the technical division of labour (for example, by co-ordinating work-flows so that the workers' efforts are not wasted). Whereas for Carchedi and Wright this means that the class positions of such occupations are ambiguous or contradictory, for Poulantzas, it does not. Explicitly rejecting such conceptions of intermediate or overlapping class membership (1978, p.228), he makes it clear that, for him, the question of class membership is dominated by the question of whether or not an occupation involves significant capital functions within the social relations of production. If it does, the occupation is considered to be within the bourgeoisie.

As was pointed out in the introduction to this volume, Poulantzas' formulation has been heavily criticized for implying too restrictive a definition of the working class – for example Wright (1979a, pp.53-58) estimates that, on the strictest interpretation of Poulantzas' criteria the proletariat in the USA comprises only about 20% of the economically active population. Without endorsing Poulantzas' rather puritanical view of what constitutes productive labour, the evidence presented in this chapter should nevertheless serve as a warning against his critics' easy theoretical generation of contradictory or intermediate class locations. In fact the case material strongly suggests that the supervisors' role in assisting the productive process was far less relevant for their relationships with the workforce than the part which they played in the control function of capital, minor as that was. The study further suggests what might be a criterion for deciding whether or not a role in the control function of capital is, or is not, 'significant': it is significant to the extent that the interests of the persons involved depend on its adequate performance.

Despite their differences, the perspectives of Carchedi, Poulantzas and Wright all point towards a common conclusion in one important and seldom remarked respect: that the question of the class position of white collar workers, being a matter of the economic functions of their tasks, can only be resolved by empirical investigation. This means, for instance, that the attempt by Abercrombie and Urry (1983) to assign all professional and managerial workers to a 'service class' which performs functions for capital, in sharp contrast to the subordinate, de-skilled - and hence proletarian - white collar worker, is clearly premature. Despite a certain suspicion of empirical work on the part of some Marxist writers, there would appear to be no substitute for the piecemeal investigatory slog. It is in this spirit that the studies in this chapter, and in the rest of the book are offered.

THE NECESSARY EVIL

Moulded Footwear Limited (MoFoL) is a shoe factory in the Greater Manchester Area which, in 1978, employed about 300 men and women. The data for this study were obtained over four months' full-time observational fieldwork, during which period the author was given access to all parts of the factory.

In the shoe industry small suppliers must compete against each other and against cheap imports for the favours of large retailing chains so that when the managing director received a complaint that the latest delivery had contained batches of poor quality, the complaint had to be taken seriously. 'I would have thought', he wrote, amongst the routine apologies, 'that there were enough white coats buzzing around the place to ensure that this could not happen'. It was this statement which later caught the eyes of his (white coated) supervisors when a copy of the letter turned up in their tea-room. 'Buzz, buzz' they chanted in a feeble attempt at ridicule, but it was clear that the managing director's attitude worried them; it reminded them that they had to justify their existence in terms of results. 'He said once that foremen were a necessary evil' explained the personnel manager, 'that's his attitude.'

The same conditional loyalty towards supervisors surfaced when one of them returned after a long illness and attempted to re-impose the previous practice for booking batches of work. When this attempt culminated in two walkouts, the news leaked that 'he's been told that he needn't feel that he'd be letting the company down if he resigned'. The response of the foreman himself was explosive. 'They can bloody stuff their annual dinner' he shouted, when a colleague asked, not so innocently, if he would be attending that celebration.

In MoFoL 9 men and 9 women between them supervised the labour of about 250 manual workers. Nominally speaking, 3 of the men were departmental managers but their work and their conditions of employment were similar to those of the other supervisors and they have all been considered together. On the whole they faced little organised opposition from the workforce. Although the shoemakers' union, NUFLAT, had a closed shop in MoFoL, this in no way implied union strength since it had been granted by a Central Arbitration Committee ruling that MoFoL must conform to the union membership agreement which existed between NUFLAT and the employers' federation (of which MoFoL was not a member). Within the firm, apart from a few localised pockets of solidarity amongst the male workers, trade union organisation was actually very weak, partly due to the individualism with which shoemakers, in common with garment workers, have traditionally reacted to piecework payment systems (Cunnison, 1966, p.63) and partly due to the precarious state of an industry slowly falling apart under the impact of competition from low wage countries. There was plenty to remind the workers of the company's uncertain future. Short-time working was a regular fact of life for some of the women workers and one department of the factory had been recently closed.

As much as in any industry it also made sense for senior managers to ask themselves what they were getting in return for the salaries of the supervisors, who they described, somewhat ominously, as 'unproductive workers'. This attitude, evidenced by the earlier quotations, implies that senior managers interposed a psychological distance between themselves and their supervisors, that they regarded them, not as part of 'us', the agents of capital, but as labour which must continually justify its purchase by contributing in some way towards profitability. Such an attitude means first of all, that the labour of supervisors, just as much as that of other workers, will be subjected to rational scrutiny, leading to the processes of fragmentation and de-skilling which have been claimed as one of the aspects of the proletarianisation of white collar workers in general (e.g. Braverman, 1974, Ch.14). The work of MoFoL's supervisors was unexceptional in this respect: there was a separation of conception and execution in that much of their work consisted of implementing the decisions of senior managers and the supervisory task was further fragmented in that the records pertaining to the workers and to the productive process itself were handed over to specialised clerical departments.

MoFoL's senior management also demonstrated a determination to get value for money out of their supervisors in quite a traditional way. Sitting down to their mid-morning coffee one day, the supervisors were disgusted to find a fresh note from the works manager pointedly restating the exact times of the breaks they were allowed. They were even more disgusted a couple of weeks later when they noticed that the firm's security officer was taking an unusual interest in their comings and goings. Apart from their immediate anger at the security officer himself ('that bloody Algernon! What's it got to do with him?') what shook them was to find themselves 'the subjects rather than the objects of surveillance', another change which has been considered under the heading of proletarianisation (Carchedi, 1977, p.191). 'All the hours I've put in for this firm!' mourned one of the foremen in unrequited loyalty. Though the time discipline imposed on these supervisors was much less onerous that that experienced by the shopfloor workers, they felt it with considerable poignancy: 'When you come down to it, your life's governed by noises. An alarm clock to get up, a buzzer to get your tea, another to go back to work and one to go home'.

To some extent, senior managers' doubts about the utility of their supervisors were assuaged by the very low level of outlay involved. In an atmosphere of secrecy and furtive private negotiation, the salaries of the female supervisors, for example, had been eroded to the point where they were very near the adult minimum wage of £38 (1978 prices) in an industry which is 'a notoriously low payer of female labour' (EOC, 1977, p.11). Foremen took home about £50 per week but, for this, the four who supervised the moulding presses worked an arduous three shift system. Nearly every supervisor in the place could reckon that there were pieceworkers in their charge earning between one and a half and twice as much as themselves.

The response to this decisive proletarianisation of 'condition' (cf Nichols, 1979) had remained latent until the firm 'had to pay out considerably more in order to replace a supervisor who had left in disgust at the rise he had been offered. The existing supervisors had gathered around the newcomer like white corpuscles and he, innocent in the ways of MoFoL, had readily divulged his salary. The ensuing shared sense of outrage swept away the tradition of secrecy and the supervisors, for the first time, had approached senior management as a group with a common grievance. The response was a recitation of the terms of the current government's pay policy whereupon the one or two secret members of ASTMS 'came out' and rapidly recruited the rest. Recognition and procedure agreements followed, much to the disgust of the managing director. 'OK there was an incomes policy' said the personnel manager with the wisdom of hindsight, 'but he could have used some of that year's profits to top up the pension fund'.

Besides holding salaries down, senior management's determination to economise on 'non-productive' labour also resulted, as has already been mentioned, in the four press foremen having to cover three floors of the factory for 24 hours a day, five days per week. Apart from imposing a considerable strain in the form of lost sleep, this meant that a single night foreman had to cover three floors of the factory for 11 hours at a stretch, an arrangement which did little more than provide someone to take the blame if things went wrong (cf Hill, 1973). 'They say they don't understand the problem' said one of them, 'quite honestly, I think they don't <u>want</u> to understand.'

There is one further potential aspect of proletarianisation to consider: the question of how far the supervisors' task has become part of the function of the workforce (to produce surplus value) rather than part of the function of capital (to appropriate surplus value). To put the question another way; are the supervisors mainly assisting the workforce in the technical or administrative senses or are they primarily assisting management in the task of extracting a profit from the workforce? A good many writers acknowledge the relevance of this question but for Poulantzas (1978) in particular it is right at the heart of the question of class membership. One problem with this approach is that it can be difficult in practice to disentangle the ends to which supervisory activities are directed. Nevertheless the difficulties can be exaggerated. As will appear later, there are aspects of supervision which are clearly profit-directed, just as some of the co-ordinating work performed by MoFoL's press foremen was clearly, and literally, labour. Charged with the task of ensuring that the flow of materials to the moulding presses should be uninterrupted, these foremen had fallen victim to senior management's quite rational concern to reduce the number of labourers paid to perform this 'unproductive' task. Left with no option, the foremen hauled trolleyfulls of raw material and bagfulls of stitched uppers from sometimes remote departments in order to keep up with the appetite of their machines. Not that this direct participation in production made them 'feel' proletarian. In fact the foremen resented their situation, not as exploited labourers, but as foremen 'degraded' (as one of them put it) by the imposition of labouring work. Nor did their visible usefulness gain them any credit with their men or, more crucially, with senior management ('glorified labourers is all they are' was the personnel manager's view), and this is very important. It means that the foremen were still judged, and found wanting, as foremen and that the new labouring work therefore represented no security at all.

Arguably then, the MoFoL supervisors could be considered to be proletarianised in four senses; their work, in common with that of most industrial supervisors, was fragmented and de-skilled, they had become the subjects rather than the objects of surveillance, their incomes were actually lower than some of the workers they supervised and some of them clearly performed worker, rather than managerial, functions. Yet the burden of this chapter is that, in terms of their relationships with management and the workforce, the MoFoL supervisors were not actually proletarianised at all. To see why this is so, it is necessary to look more closely at the content of the managerial surveillance of their activities, bearing in mind that the supervisors' sense of insecurity made this a matter for the closest scrutiny. Rather than assume a mechanical association between surveillance and proletarianisation, the question is one of how the manner and matter of surveillance structured the supervisors' interests.

The Surveillance of Supervision

In the first instance the surveillance of supervision involves a straightforward scrutiny of the supervisors' own behaviour and this, it will be recalled, was the case with the treatment of the MoFoL supervisors' time-keeping. However this is trivial. The distinctive feature of supervision is that its worth logically depends upon its effects on the workforce. Accordingly it is through this medium that the main effort of surveillance is logically made.

In this respect the intensified division of white collar labour presents management with certain opportunities - indeed that is arguably part of its purpose. As writers such as Friedman (1977) and Edwards (1980) have pointed out, there has occurred an historical shift from 'personal control' of the workforce to the techniques of bureaucratic administration. For supervisors this has meant not only a fragmentation of their task but also that information relating to their control of the workforce now passes out of their hands to be analysed by specialist staff and there to be made available to senior managers as a means of checking on the supervisors themselves. In practice this long-term trend towards bureaucratisation should be understood as a relative matter. At MoFoL, as in many other workplaces, it was still supplemented by senior managers' personal invigilation of the supervisors' part in the productive process.

Before considering the supervisors' reaction to these two modes of surveillance (the bureaucratic and the invigilatory) it is necessary to mention a further consequence of the division of white collar labour; that as with shopfloor work it has meant a separation of the conception from the execution of supervision. For example the length of the working day for most of MoFoL's employees was set by a nationally negotiated agreement, though for a few this had been supplemented by senior management's insistence that they must contract to work nights and overtime as required. In either case, the supervisors' task in relation to the working day was largely limited to achieving predetermined targets. On the machines which moulded the soles onto the slippers, the same was true of production rates. Here senior management had determined the maximum machine speeds which would allow the moulds to fill properly. The supervisors' task then became one of achieving production figures as near as possible to those calculated from the machine speeds, rather than one of simply increasing production as much as possible. The point is that, where such a separation of conception and execution has taken place, the tendency is for the only possible variation from pre-determined targets to be on the side of failure. In such a situation the reaction of supervisors to any mode of surveillance is likely to be a defensive one, and certainly this was the case in MoFoL.

Surveillance by personal invigilation   One of the processes by which soles were moulded onto the slippers made use of automatic presses which represented a considerable capital investment. 'I'd like to set those machines running and keep them running for months' explained the Managing Director. To that end his daily patrols around the factory and the more frequent excursions of the Works Manager concentrated disproportionately on these machines. If the foremen allowed them to stop for any reason they knew that they would be closely questioned. In the terms used previously, senior management, by their presence and the actions they took, imposed an implicit target of zero down-time for the automatic presses and any deviation from that target constituted a failure for the foreman concerned. The intent was obviously to maximise the return on the capital investment represented by the machines rather than to ensure that the operatives' labour was efficiently organised. In other words the invigilation by senior management in this respect constrained the actions of the foremen so as to maximise the return to capital rather than to maximise their assistance in the process of production. By a process of operant conditioning the foremen learned to keep the machines running at all costs.

In fact this reaction, however understandable, went some way towards negating the object of the surveillance since the even progression through the factoy of batches of various sized slippers depended on periodical mould changes on the automatic presses, an operation which involved stopping the machines for at least half an hour. It was generally possible, however, for the foremen to delay mould changes by building up a backlog of the sizes not currently being produced. If mould changes could be delayed in this manner until the next shift, the next foreman would then become responsible - and so on. This tendency resulted in foremen prematurely and surreptitiously removing from the machining room bags of stitched uppers of the sizes currently being moulded (despite a rule forbidding this) so as to feed the remorseless appetites of their machines. The end result was a series of pile-ups in the warehouse, frantic rushes to complete customers' orders which lacked certain sizes and, in some cases, the total loss of orders. Analogous to the goal displacement which will be discussed in relation to bureaucratic surveillance, the invigilatory mode can encourage the dramaturgical representation of efficiency rather than its substance.

In this spirit, supervisors may also feel it necessary to act out their personal involvement in the production of a busily engaged workforce rather than rely only on their formal responsibility for it. Thus on the occasion of management patrols, MoFoL supervisors could be seen 'instructing' their operatives or at the very least, standing near the productive process as if to draw the mana from it. However, in these efforts the moulding press foremen in particular faced a problem common in the acting profession: that of being upstaged.

Competition for the supervisors   If the arrival of senior managers provoked a dramatic representation of profit in the making, it also offered opportunities for other performers. As Dalton (1949) has noted, staff formally in advisory positions may also feel the need to justify themselves in terms of the productive process, and their consequent attempts at intervention may provoke conflicts with line management. In MoFoL the Quality Control Manager had no formal authority at all over the production process but, as he put it, 'someone's got to take a decision' and, as a result, he believed that he'd 'saved this firm thousands'. Indeed with major customers insisting on very high quality standards, the managing director had little choice but to listen - unless he was prepared to back his own judgement against that of the Quality Control Manager.

Understandably perhaps, the supervisors were unconvinced. 'He'll come down here, pick up a slipper, pull a face and show it to the Managing Director. "I <u>don't</u> like that Mr. X". Now anyone could do that, but it makes him look like an important fellow.' Besides undermining the supervisors' authority over their operatives ('Never mind what Y told you. <u>I'm</u> telling you to do it like this', bellowed one frustrated foreman), these interventions could only demonstrate the indispensability of the Quality Control Manager by emphasizing the dispensability of the supervisors as technical experts. In other words, their contribution to the productive process was being systematically undermined in the eyes of senior management, leaving only the disciplinary control of labour as the justification for their presence. The competition represented by the quality control manager tended therefore to reduce the basis on which the supervisors could claim survival. To the extent that senior management believed them incapable of contributing to the productive process in a technical sense, they would have to stand or fall on their contribution to the control function of capital. Meanwhile the career of the quality control manager waxed and he was eventually promoted to the Managing Directorship of a small subsidiary. 'There's a <u>lot</u> of jealousy' he confided. And indeed there was.

For the moulding press foremen, the fitters posed an additional problem. Whereas most of the tools and machinery used in MoFoL were simple, the automatic injection moulding machines were an exception. Although the foremen could operate these machines they were unable to deal either with breakdowns or with routine mould changes. As in Crozier's influential study (1964), control of these 'crises' had passed to MoFoL's two maintainance fitters. Moreover, since the adjustment of the machines after maintenance or mould changes required trial production runs, the fitters had acquired the expertise to check on the production process itself, whereas the fitters' skills were not of a kind that the foremen could hope to pick up on a casual basis. If the process ran out of adjustment therefore, the men were just as likely to ask a fitter for help as a foreman, particularly since it would often be the fitter who had to perform the actual adjustment in any case. As far as relations between the foremen and the operatives were concerned, the result was that the 'co-operative' aspect of the supervisory task - that of providing technical assistance (to a pieceworker, anxious to keep the process going) - fell to the fitters. The foremen were left with the 'conflict' issue of arguing with the operatives over how much time could be booked for each stoppage. In terms of class relationships the role of the foremen in the control function of capital (that of holding down wage costs) was left ideologically exposed to the workforce since they had lost the 'worker' function of technical assistance.

As far as senior managers were concerned - and stoppages on this key operation invariably attracted an 'ice-cream convention' (the MoFoL term for an array of white coats) - they saw the fitters working away to get the process back on line, whilst the foremen could only stand and watch. 'I've seen 'em walk away from a broken down machine' said the chief engineer, who took pride in the competence of his fitters, 'that's not a foreman to me.' As with the interventions of the quality control manager, the end result was that the foremen had little prospect of justifying their position by demonstrating a contribution to the productive process itself.

Though the detail of these threats to the foremen's position was, of course, specific to MoFoL, the potential for similar threats appears to be rooted in features of the division of white collar labour which are characteristic of modern capitalism. Thus the development of specialist staff positions creates the potential and the incentive for interventions in the production process of the type practiced by MoFoL's quality control manager. Again it is common for the technology of production to progress to the point where de facto control of it passes into the hands of experts. In both cases, as has been noted, the effect is to reduce the extent to which the supervisor contributes, or appears to contribute, to the productive process so that his or her position now depends more on demonstrating a contribution to the control function of capital.

The bureaucratic mode of surveillance   In MoFoL the main channels of information through which bureaucratic surveillance could be exercised were the workers' clock cards, the 'time sheets' on which they recorded their work, and the records of the quality control department. The first point to be made is that, although management determine the type of information to be recorded, the information itself does not then unambiguously decide the nature of the pressure on supervisors: that depends also on the uses to which the information is put. For example the operatives' time sheets contained a record of the batch numbers and sizes of the uppers which they had moulded. This information could have been used, in conjunction with the order sheets (which specified the number of each size in a customer order), to trace any delays in moulding certain sizes belonging to otherwise complete orders. This, as has already been mentioned, was a recurring problem in MoFoL.

This use of the information would therefore have made sense both from the point of view of co-ordinating the workers' efforts and of assisting profitability. Instead, after the wage office had finished with the operatives' time sheets, both sets of data were sent off to an outworker whose painstaking job it was to check through the records for fictitious and double-booked batch numbers. Eventually, it is true, a certain amount of skullduggery <u>was</u> discovered but even then the management failed to recover the comparatively trivial sums involved, after the union's full-time official got wind of their attempts to do so. In other words, senior management's instinct was to use the information to check on the (certainly suspect) honesty of their operatives, to minimise wage costs that is, rather than to solve the sometimes pressing problem of co-ordinating work flows. The choice was a clear one: where the requirements of co-ordination and profitability seemed to diverge, senior management, mistakenly as it happened, opted for the latter. This choice, in turn, affected the nature of the pressure exerted on the supervisors through the medium of the recorded information. Rather than being pressed to improve the co-ordination of work flows and thereby assist in the productive process, they were, occasionally, taken to task for failing to police the manner in which their subordinates booked their work. In the terminology of Carchedi (1977) the written records were used to ensure that the supervisors performed their role in the 'global function of capital' rather than any 'collective worker' functions.

The same tendency was apparent in the use made of the records of departmental 'losses'. As Batstone (1979) has pointed out, management accounting systems constitute vocabularies of motive, sometimes in the form of particular linguistic usages, which can effectively legitimise the demands made by one manager on another. This was decidedly the case with the calculation of departmental 'losses' at MoFoL. These arose in the first place because pieceworkers who were stopped or who were transferred onto alternative work were supposed to receive certain fractions of their average hourly earnings. Whenever this occurred, it was virtually certain that the amount of these allowances would exceed the piecework price of any work produced, and it was in this sense that a 'loss' was supposed to exist. The operatives' time sheets were used to calculate aggregate departmental 'losses' on a weekly basis, which figures were known to be closely monitored by senior management. At the very least supervisors had a strong incentive to avoid registering 'losses' which were in any way out of line. Beyond this however, the use of such a tendentious term to describe an otherwise unexceptional feature of the piecework payment system, enabled senior managers to legitimise a sustained drive against 'losses' as such. One by one supervisors were interrogated over payments made for stoppages or transfers, sometimes a considerable time in the past. 'They shouldn't <u>be</u> waiting, they should be on piecework' was the repeated comment of one senior manager at these inquisitorial sessions. Not surprisingly supervisors became extremely reluctant to allow waiting time after these experiences. 'That's it - no more time to be booked. Mr. X's orders', was the message as relayed to the workforce by one forelady. Faced with a more refractory workforce, the supervisors in charge of the men who operated the moulding presses had to resort to less direct methods, such as editing their operatives' time sheets, but the underlying objective was the same.

It could, of course, be argued that the minimisation of waiting is a measure of the supervisors' success in co-ordinating the flows of work (and it was so described in job descriptions proposed to but rejected by the supervisors themselves). However, it should be borne in mind that the records were of the payments made for waiting and that the incentive for supervisors was therefore to minimise these, irrespective of what was happening on the shopfloor. Whatever the intentions of senior management, the practical effect of their use of the 'loss' records was to pressurise supervisors into holding down wage costs rather than devising ways of further reducing down-time in the production process, even supposing that were possible. If, in the terminology of organizational theory, this is 'goal displacement' (cf. Merton, 1968, Ch.8), it is a happy one from the point of view of capital.

The conclusion of this section must be that management's surveillance of the MoFoL supervisors placed far greater stress on the part played by them in the control function of capital than on any technical, administrative or physical assistance which they gave to the productive process. The possibility of the supervisors surviving by demonstrating any technical contribution was in any case undermined by the specialist contributions of the quality control manager and the maintenance fitters. Finally, as regards the question of gaining credit for physically contributing to the production process, it will be recalled that when this was imposed on the moulding press foremen in the form of labouring work, it served only to further degrade their position, both in the eyes of senior management and themselves.

RELATIONSHIPS WITH THE WORKFORCE

Despite the temerity of one foreman who told the works manager that 'us little supervisors have ambitions too, you know', it was clear to everyone in MoFoL that the supervisors were going nowhere. 'They've reached the limit of their personal development' the personnel manager told the Industrial Training Board officer, in explanation of his failure to write staff development programmes. For these supervisors, management surveillance represented a threat to their livelihoods rather than an opportunity to display eligibility for promotion. Superficially this sense of being permanently on trial might be seen as an aspect of proletarianisation, in the sense that the supervisors were aware that management attitudes and actions posed a potential threat to their interests. However, proletarianisation implies an identity of interests with the working class (as locally represented by the MoFoL workforce) as well as a conflict of interests with capital (represented locally by MoFoL's management). It will be argued that the supervisors' relationships with the workforce (both relationships of interest and of attitudes) were, in fact, decisively influenced by the conditions imposed by management on their continued survival.

It is first necessary to consider the possibility that supervisors could secure their position by negotiation and compromise with the workforce; that they could, in other words, play their part in the control function of capital without impinging on the workers' interests, or at least without the workers feeling that they were doing so. Interestingly the literature on industrial organisations, at least since the work of Gouldner (1955) has rather selectively concentrated on instances in which supervisors have coped with management pressure by relaxing the application of certain rules in exchange for co-operation from the workers, rather than by strictly implementing management instructions (see, for example, Katz, 1973). 'Indulgency' patterns certainly existed in MoFoL. For example, one supervisor allowed her workers an unofficial mass fag break in the lavatory (provided HE wasn't watching) which earned her the testimonial 'Maggie's the greatest forelady. She's the only one who does that'. Doubtless the concession was kindly meant, but, as the supervisor herself explained, it also 'prevents 'em going in dribs and drabs'. In any case the implication of a cosy collusion between workers and supervisors to mitigate the worst effects of senior management pressure is quite misleading. When the women in that department started a thin quavering song in order to fill the silence left by a fault in the piped music system, the same forelady quickly stamped out this symptom of incipient riot, possibly fearing that it would be difficult to restore order in time for the next senior management patrol.

In fact, once the focus of attention broadens beyond a selective fascination with those rules and management instructions which are <u>not</u> enforced, it quickly becomes apparent that in MoFoL (and, one suspects, in most workplaces), the characteristic supervisors' response to management surveillance is not 'indulgency' at all. In the case of the invigilation of the automatic presses, we have already seen that the condition of avoiding the threat of a management interrogation was that the foremen had at all costs to keep the machines running. Whilst some of the operatives (being pieceworkers) were as anxious as the foremen to work continuously, others took the view that since they were paid 'waiting time' for stoppages 'it gives us a break like' (although the 'break' might take the form of a spell on the brush if senior managers were around). For this latter group the pressure on the foremen meant that they lost the benefit of those natural pauses in production which even the rational pursuit of profit would have afforded.

This imposition upon the workforce of a cosmetic representation of profit in the making, was in fact the predominant supervisory response to managerial invigilation throughout MoFoL. One of the senior managers, for example, saw himself as engaged in a continuing police action against waste and was famous for picking up rubber bands, for retrieving and confronting operatives with scraps of 'waste' material and for turning out 'unused' lights. Whenever the heat was on, supervisors would insist that hard-pressed pieceworkers should retrieve the rubber bands they hurriedly stripped off the packed uppers and which they would normally have left for the sweepers. (The haul of bands would then be prominently displayed in polythene bags.) Women machinists would be made to snip up any scrap material into tiny unrecognizable fragments. Operatives on nights had to grope their way about darkened workshops if they had occasion to leave the pools of illumination around their normal working positions. In general, the representations of efficiency in the use of resources imposed by the supervisors in their efforts to avoid management censure cost the operatives a good deal of real effort in addition to the petty humiliations involved.

The same was true of the machining room foreladies' definition of discipline as 'getting them all sat down' ('at least it looks as if they're working' as one confided) and of the tendency of certain supervisors to thrust a brush into any temporarily idle pair of hands. In the most glaring instance of the latter, an entire department spent an unpaid half hour clearing up in anticipation of a visit by a major customer - unpaid because, as the forelady pointed out, they were not waiting and therefore not entitled to 'waiting time'. What is clear in all this is that the invigilation of senior management was aimed, with varying degrees of sophistication, at ensuring that the workforce displayed the symptoms, not just of efficiency, but also of profitability (respectively, in the instances cited, that the return on capital investment was being maximised, that waste was being minimised and that as much work as possible was being performed within the working day). However estranged from senior management the supervisors may have felt, they could only keep intact the little sense of security they had by going along with it all. And since it was the workers rather than the supervisors which were under observation, it was from the workforce that supervisors had to extract the designated indications of profitability. For the workforce this involved definite deprivations: the needless (from any point of view) loss of natural breaks in production, the unpaid performance of purely cosmetic work and so on.

The same tendency appears when we consider the supervisors' response to management surveillance through written records. It has already been pointed out that the management practice of monitoring departmental 'losses' and of interrogating any supervisor whose records were out of line in this respect, amounted to a strong pressure on supervisors to minimise the payments made to their workers for transfers or for waiting time. The result was that many workers, particular women, did not receive payments to which they were formally entitled. Again the interests of the supervisors in maintaining their position depended on demonstrating an ability to contribute to profitability by containing wage costs. This, of course, directly conflicted with the material interests of their workers.

It ought to be pointed out that the supervisors' response to the pressures on them could be quite at variance with their own views of the rights and wrongs of the situation. 'I ask you' grumbled one foreman of the quality standards set for an unusually finicky customer 'one millimetre each way. They're <u>slippers</u> for Christ's sake.' Although quality control can, on occasion, be viewed as a contribution to the productive process, this supervisor clearly believed that the standards used for that customer constituted an unnecessary worsening of the terms of the operatives' 'effort bargain' (cf. Behrend, 1957). 'It means the blokes have got to pull the uppers about on the moulds to get 'em right. But they shouldn't have to do that. These men are pieceworkers, they should just have to put 'em on and take 'em off. The trouble is that this firm want hand-made quality at piecework prices.' But, despite his reservations, he still did his best to ensure that the standards were met. In such situations the supervisors' attitudes are scarcely relevant: less sympathetically but motivated ultimately by the same interests, another foreman on the same process growled into the ear of a flustered operative who was having difficulty in meeting the quality standards in question, 'I'm going to get you off this machine. I could train a baboon to do a better job'.

Generally speaking, the relationships between MoFoL's supervisors and workers were well attuned to the basic conflict of interests between them. Whilst at a broad theoretical level few of the workers would have overtly questioned a system of production which depended on extracting a surplus from their own labour, most of them were well aware of which side their supervisors' bread was buttered, and of whose butter it was. A particularly niggardly forelady was described with succinct insight as 'paying you as if it was her own money'. Another, in a more Weberian formulation, 'hates paying them more than she gets herself'. One of the men, reflecting angrily on the way his supervisor had 'whittled away' at his piece-rates over the years, believed that, 'There's a prize every month for the supervisor who saves most on wages. Sid wins it every time, the mean old bastard'. On occasion, it is true, there was some sympathy with the supervisors' predicament, as with the press operatives who explained that their foremen were reluctant to allow waiting time because 'it reflects badly on them, like'. But even this degree of understanding implied no let-up in the guerilla warfare on the issue. Nor did the trade unionists on the shopfloor attach any significance to the recent conversion of their supervisors. There was no contact between the two unions and no sense that any might be desirable.

On the supervisors' side, feelings were the mirror image of the workers' and were equally conditioned by the antagonism of interests. 'It's greed that drives them' explained one foreman of his star crew and the rest of the supervisors in the tea room at the time chimed in with their own anecdotes illustrative of pieceworkers' rapacity – 'Remember that Pole we had here? Five years and never had a piss'. In its perverted form, greed might display a persistent tendency to erupt into dishonesty ('Bloody Sicilians – you can't trust 'em further than you can throw 'em') which provided the perfect rationalisation for the supervisors' own tendency to doctor the operatives' time sheets before handing them on to the wages office. Yet despite their contempt, the supervisors were only too well aware that their own salvation lay in harnessing their workers' greed – a dilemma of dependence and exploitation perfectly captured by the description 'cheating bastards, but they do you a good score'. Always in the background of the relationship of supervisors to their workers was the fear of being shown up, of being exposed to the wrath of senior managers. When one of the pressmen, weary of persistent material faults, declared the job a 'fucking waste of time' and walked out, the foreman who came on the next shift (and was therefore not responsible by any rational standards) took one look at the production figures and let out the desperate and not very sober wail 'Oh my God, HE'll go fucking mad'.

In view of the importance attached by Goldthorpe et al (1969, Ch.4) to the relational aspect of the alleged embourgeoisement of 'affluent' workers, i.e. to the question of their acceptance by established persons of the middle class, it is surprising that the same aspect of the supposed proletarianisation of white collar workers has been largely neglected. Perhaps it is not supposed to matter whether manual workers accept white collar workers. There was, in any event, certainly no tendency in this direction on the shopfloor of MoFoL. Not surprisingly in view of the conflicting pressures on them, the supervisors associated far more with each other than with shopfloor workers or managers (cf. Dunkerley, 1975, pp.82-84) although this tendency was also reinforced by the management practice of providing free coffee for supervisors in a room well away from the shopfloor. And whatever outside social relationships the supervisors may have had with manual workers (which Stewart et al, 1980, interpret as evidence of similar class position) there were those in MoFoL who were not prepared to set aside the antagonism of the workplace: 'I was out drinking the other night when Jimmy (a foreman) came into the other bar. "Come on" he said, "I'll buy you a pint". I lifted up my glass and took a drink from it like this. "What, me?" I said, looking straight at him, "I don't drink" '.

CONCLUSIONS

In the Marxist view, class membership is a question of place in the social relations of production rather than income or other aspects of 'life chances'. Since the work of Lockwood (1958) however, the literature, even when professing a Marxist view, has overwhelmingly concentrated on these latter aspects of the situation of white collar workers in general and of industrial supervisors in particular. Since supervisors and other routine white collar workers are manifestly not doing very well either materially or in terms of prestige, the broad conclusion of this literature is that their situation is, and is usually felt by themselves to be, now indistinguishable from that of manual workers and that they have therefore become 'proletarian'. If, however, the term 'proletarian' is taken at all seriously in the Marxist sense - i.e. that they perform productive labour within the capitalist social relations of production - this conclusion is very misleading. The question of whether or not white collar workers perform productive labour or work within the administrative apparatus for extracting, realising or circulating surplus value, can only be resolved by examining what they do, not how well off or how well respected they are.
    In the less voluminous literature on white collar workers which adopts a more consistently Marxist perspective, the tendency is to restate the old 'man-in-the-middle' thesis. Because some white collar work, including that of industrial supervisors, involves both capital and labour functions it is said to occupy an intermediate class location. Whilst one would not contradict this position at

the theoretical level, the empirical material of this chapter is more consistent with the contrary position of Poulantzas (1978): that any position involving significant capital functions is part of the bourgeois administrative apparatus. What matters for the class position of the supervisors studied here is not so much the proportion of their work which is involved in capital or labour functions but the way in which their interests are linked to the performance of their tasks. This means that the question of the content of supervisors' work needs to be considered in the context of the social relationships within which it is performed. When this is done, it becomes apparent that the senior managers who monitor their performance concentrate heavily on their part in the control function of capital rather than on any contribution they make to the productive process itself. Moreover the case study also indicates that technological developments and the differentiation of white collar work are tending (in the case of MoFoL, by means of 'informal' task redefinitions) to strip the supervisors of their role as technical assistants to the productive process, thus confining their role within the function of capital. Therefore in the sense that their interests can only be defended by demonstrating their usefulness in the function of capital, this is the part of the supervisory task (whatever other tasks may be performed) which counts for the question of class membership. Neither the supervisors' relative impoverishment, nor the fragmentation and de-skilling of their work, nor the fact that they, just as much as the shopfloor workers, are subjected to management control, nor their lack of decision-making power, nor even the fact that some of their work can be considered as part of the productive process - all of which have been claimed to comprise the whole, or part of, the process of proletarianisation - make any difference to the fact that their interests are inextricably linked to the performance of capital functions. As long as this remains the case, these direct supervisors of labour continue to be part of the bourgeois apparatus of control.

This is reflected in the relationships between the supervisors and the workforce. Since the supervisors' interests lie in demonstrating to senior managers their ability to extract surplus value from the workforce, their interests conflict with those they supervise. In the MoFoL case this was fairly clearly exposed by the piecework payment system which supervisors manipulated so as to hold down wage costs and, sometimes, so as to extract unpaid labour from their workers. In the case of MoFoL, shopfloor relationships at the conscious level reflected this antagonism of interests though often in a personalised form. Whereas the workers resented the 'meanness' of their supervisors, the supervisors themselves were suspicious of the workers' honesty (whilst themselves resorting to some dubious methods in their drive to hold down wages) and were contemptuous of their 'greed'. At the same time the supervisors were uneasily aware that they depended on this latter reprehensible quality to achieve the kind of production figures which would satisfy senior management. Proletarianisation in the Marxian usage implies a basic identity of interests with other proletarians. Clearly relationships on the shopfloor of MoFoL were wholly inconsistent with any thought that the supervisors were proletarian in this sense.

Chapter Two

CLASS AND CONTROL AT THE POINT OF PRODUCTION -
FOREMEN 2

Bob Carter

Although foremen have been the object of a large number
of sociological enquiries, few studies have explicitly
attempted to locate foremen within the class structure. The
dominant characterisation of foremen in the literature as
'men in the middle' (Roethlisberger, 1945) or 'marginal men'
(Wray, 1949) could indicate some sort of conception of
foremen as a third force, hence inferring their subsumption
within a middle class. This interpretation is not the only
one, however. Such characterisations are apt to contrast the
present situation of foremen with their much more powerful
and clearly managerial past, and it is only a small step from
emphasising the declining authority of foremen, to advancing
the claim that foremen are being proletarianised and that,
far from being middle class, foremen, who have always come
predominantly from the working class, are increasingly
performing roles and functions commensurate with their social
origins.
This latter view of foremen has been held by writers
from very different traditions. Child and Partridge, for
instance, in the most sustained sociological examination of
foremen published for some time, adopt the neo-Weberian
perspectives first generated by David Lockwood in The
Blackcoated Worker, 1958. While not totally subsuming
foremen into the working class, on several occasions Child
and Partridge come very close to doing so. After an
extensive empirical investigation, for instance, they state:
'judged by their limited authority over others, their work
situation generally and their labour market position, these
supervisors had objectively become members of the same social
class as factory workers' (Child and Partridge, 1983, p.194).
Likewise, Harry Braverman, author of Labor and Monopoly
Capital, arguably the most influential Marxist work of the
1970's, includes foremen in his list of occupations which
have been subjected to both the pressures of the labour
market and 'forms of "rationalisation" characteristic of the
capitalist mode of production' and in which 'the proletarian

form begins to assert itself and to impress itself upon the consciousness of these employees' (Braverman, 1974, p.408).

This chapter takes issue with both perspectives and the implication that there is a simple unilinear development of foremen towards the class position of the proletariat. First, a perspective on class relations is briefly set out, reviewing in the process the inadequacies of existing models.[1] Then, some of the questions raised in class theory are further examined, not in the abstract, but through a case study of foremen's relations with shopfloor workers and trade unionism.

CLASS THEORIES

Varieties of Weberian analyses of social class have dominated British sociology since the 1950s, most commonly emphasising not only different class positions based upon the distinction between ownership and non-ownership of property but also the significance of differences in the market values of skills possessed by people. There are two fairly well-rehearsed criticisms of this approach to class analysis. First, by concentrating on the differences between marketable skills and the gradations of ownership, there arises the problem of whether it is possible to conceptualise class collectivities at all. As Giddens has remarked: 'the range of "goods and capabilities" possessed by individuals is highly variable, and one could push the view to its <u>reductio ad absurdum</u> by supposing that every individual brings a slightly different combination of possessions or skills to the market and hence there are as many "classes" as there are concrete individuals participating in market relationships' (1973, p.78). The second major criticism, advanced by Marxist writers, is that the virtual narrowing of the concept of class to market situation seriously restricts the understanding of social relations in capitalist societies by concentrating on distributional rewards rather than relations within the production process which have generated them. As Crompton and Gubbay have put it: 'We would raise the question as to <u>why</u> skills and resources have assumed this marketable, commodity-like quality. We would argue that these "commodities" have emerged because of the development of capitalist relations of production. Such a mode of production requires both freely transferable property and readily available labour' (1977, p.17).

The considerable influence which, despite its inadequacies, Weberian analysis exercised on British social analysis is testimony to the weakness for many years of credible Marxist alternatives. While it was the case that during the 1960's there was an increased interest in Marxist ideas and scholarship, enquiries from a Marxist perspective into theories of class remained largely absent. This meant in practice that Marxists operated with a two class model of society. Ownership and non-ownership of the means of production provided the criteria for class membership, producing the bourgeoisie and the proletariat respectively. In so far as a middle class was recognised in capitalist society it was largely a remnant of previous modes of production and was destined in accord with Marx and Engels' prognostication in <u>Manifesto of the Communist Party</u> to disappear or at least become of microscopic significance. In short, there was a virtual disappearance from Marxist analyses of the new middle class, a class rooted within the capitalist mode of production and which could neither be assimilated into the bourgeoisie nor the proletariat. Moreover, the disappearance from Marxist analysis of this social grouping occurred despite tendencies which increased its social weight and made the examination of the new middle class more, not less, pertinent. The tendency towards monopoly within the economy, for example, continued apace, a development which meant the growing socialisation of capital and the gradual disappearance of easily identifiable capitalists. The conservative adage of the 1950s that 'we're all middle class now' was therefore double-edged. It was not merely an attempt to ideologically incorporate the working class into the bourgeois society but also an implicit statement that the absolute and individual control of the capitalist had been eroded and that corporate forms held everyone accountable. The fact was, though, that the growing complexity of the organisation of production also obscured the nature and limits of the working class. If, as Marxists claimed, the non-ownership of the means of production was the determining feature of the proletariat there appeared to be much substance to the obverse, but equally conservative, contention that 'we're all working class'.

In practice, Marxists were more than aware of the unconvincing nature of the claim that society was divided into two classes by a single schism. A sign of this recognition was that some of them made considerable concessions towards Weberian analysis, confirming the importance of income levels, working conditions and security as determinants of class (Westergaard and Resler, 1975, p.96). However, it was not until the mid-1970s with the appearance of important works by Braverman (1974) Poulantzas (1975) and Carchedi (1977) that Marxist criticism of Weberian analyses simultaneously provided an alternative to orthodox Marxist class analysis based upon the dichotomy of ownership/non-ownership. This was achieved by refocussing attention on the labour process and, in particular, drawing distinctions between functions of labour and capital within the capitalist production process. It was Carchedi who developed these perspectives most systematically.

Carchedi took as his starting point Marx's view that the capitalist production process comprised two analytically separate processes. The first process Marx termed 'the real labour process' in which the labourer 'creates new use-value by performing useful labour with existing use-values' (Marx, 1976, p.981). But, Marx added, such a definition would hold for any labour process, irrespective of the mode of production or its stage of economic development. It meant nothing specifically for the labour process under the capitalist mode of production. What is unique about this latter mode, according to Marx, is that it is simultaneously a labour process and a surplus-value producing process. In the capitalist mode of production 'the labour process itself is no more than an instrument of the valorisation process, just as the use-value of the product is nothing but a repository of its exchange-value' (Marx, 1976, p.990).

In a pure model of capitalism Marx saw only two polar classes, one, the capitalist class, based on the valorisation process and the other, the proletariat, based upon the labour process. Marx was more than aware, however, that reality is always more complicated than the most subtle of theories and that lines between classes are far from clear and unchanging. The progressive accentuation of the co-operative character of the labour process increasingly meant that commodities were the result of collective and not individual labour - hence Marx's concept of the collective worker. Similarly, Marx was conscious of the increasingly collective nature of the function of capital. These changes in the organisation of the functions of labour and capital do not change their social nature but, nevertheless, do transform the class structure of capitalist societies because the changes allow for the possibility of people carrying out combinations of both opposing social functions. Marx never examined the implications of these social changes but Carchedi, extending Marx's analysis, is able to highlight the role of the new middle class, a class in part comprised of those people carrying out both functions of capital and functions of the collective worker.

In particular, Carchedi stresses the distinction within the production process between, on the one hand, tasks of unity and coordination and, on the other, tasks of surveillance and control. Tasks of unity and coordination would be necessary under any complex system of social production and are, therefore, part of the labour process, part of the function of labour performed by the collective worker. Conversely, the work of surveillance and control is only necessary because of the antagonistic social relations of production and is therefore part of the surplus-value producing process, part of the function of capital. From this perspective Carchedi could summarise the position of members of the new middle class as follows:

1. They have neither the legal nor the real ownership of the means of production.
2. They perform both the global functions of capital and the function of the collective worker.
3. Since they do not have the real ownership of the means of production, the global function of capital is not necessarily the dominant one. This role can also revert to the function of the collective worker.
4. When they perform the function of the collective worker, they are either the exploited or the economically oppressed; when they perform the global function of capital, they are either the exploiters or oppressors. However, since they do not have real ownership of the means of production, when they perform the latter function they are also economically oppressed.
5. Since they are not the real owners, and since therefore the global function of capital is not necessarily dominant, their fundamental role is not necessarily that of exploiters or oppressors.
6. On the basis of points mentioned above, they are partly on the side of capital and partly on the side of labour. This is the contradiction inherent in their position. Moreover, even when they are on the side of capital, they are both exploiters (or oppressors) and oppressed. This is an element of further contradiction inherent in their position (Carchedi, 1977, pp.89-90).

Despite Carchedi's systematic exposition and its advance on orthodox Marxist analyses of class, his work has had limited influence.[2] There has been a tendency merely to note his theory and then either to ignore it or to incorporate only those elements of it which strengthen an opposing position. Frequently, therefore, what emerges is a more sophisticated restatement of the orthodox Marxist model of a society comprising two classes against which Carchedi's theory is ranged.

Peter Meiksins, for instance, in a recent article, acknowledges Carchedi's contribution in emphasising how changes in the organisation of the production process have created the collective worker and made more necessary the labour of conception in the form of new tasks coordinating the increasingly complex organisation of production. But in acknowledging Carchedi's contribution, Meiksins ignores Carchedi's simultaneous emphasis on changes in the surplus-value producing process in which the tasks of the former individual capitalist have been socialised. The explanation for this one-sided reading of Carchedi is that

Meiksins wants to reiterate the synonymity of wage labour and membership of the working class. He is not unaware that numerous employees have authority over others at work and therefore, in Carchedi's terms, carry out the function of capital, but claims that this exercise of authority does not determine class membership. Focussing on the situation of engineers Meiksins states:

> Many observers have pointed to the fact that engineers exercise authority within the production process as a factor contributing a class barrier between them and subordinate employees. It is certainly reasonable to assume that their position in the labor process may affect engineers' consciousness, perhaps encouraging them to think of themselves as superior to or different from other types of employee. Nevertheless, to argue that this is a <u>class</u> barrier is misleading and inaccurate. For to do so is to confuse a group's <u>function in the labor process</u> with the social relations of production. The labor process under capitalism is a complex one, involving large numbers of detail laborers, each of whom has a specialized function to perform. While it is important to consider how a laborer's function may affect his or her consciousness, the question of whether the laborer is totally subordinate (as with the assembly-line worker) or in a position of relative power (as with the engineer) is irrelevant to the question of whether he or she is a wage-laborer (1984, p.193, emphasis in original).

Meiksins wrongly expands wage labour to include all employment relationships. He is thus able to solve the class differences between engineers and labourers by claiming that the authority relationship which the former exercise over the latter, which Carchedi terms the function of capital, comprises merely differentiated tasks within the labour process. On the contrary, however, it is necessary to emphasise that the exercise of control by engineers does not create use-values and is not part of a real labour process and further to reiterate the disinction between, on the one hand, wages paid out of variable capital and, on the other, payments to functionaries of capital, the source of which is surplus-value, even where the source is apparently hidden by the wage or salary form.

In reality, of course, in the case of engineers the two sources of income will be mixed because of the performance of both collective worker functions, in the form of productive labour, and the functions of capital. Once again, in contradistinction to Meiksins, it is necessary to emphasise that these are different social functions and cannot be reduced to a technically differentiated but socially homogeneous labour process. The social relations within the production process show great variations. Meiksins masks these by reducing the concept of social relations to the purely formal legal status of ownership and non-ownership of the means of production at the expense of examining real practical relations.

It is not simply the desire of competing theorists to incorporate aspects of Carchedi's theory into more traditional models of class structure which has limited the impact of his analysis of the new middle class. His failure to integrate questions and problems of consciousness and subjectivity into his analysis has tended to relegate its status to one of taxonomy. Or, as one critic has maintained about the structuralist approach to the new middle class: 'Although developed by writers who are again expressly concerned with the possibilities for a political alliance between the working class and newly emergent white-collar groupings, it conspicuously fails to offer any insight into the form of collective action in which they might typically engage' (Goldthorpe, 1982, p.164). The immediate accuracy of this criticism is not open to doubt, even if the failure of writers to turn their attention to the social action of the new middle class does not represent an inevitable failure of all Marxist attempts to come to grips with the social nature of this class. What the criticism does illustrate, however, is a general failure to examine not just the effect of structure on consciousness but the effect of consciousness on structure. More specifically, by neglecting the dynamics of class struggle Carchedi posits the distinction between the function of capital and the function of labour in such a way as to imply that the two opposing social functions are not only analytically separable but are also empirically separate and identifiable, and that they comprise definite technical tasks. In practice, however, the respective functions are frequently inextricably fused. Moreover, the identification of new middle class position relies heavily on the further distinction between tasks of co-ordination and unity, on the one hand, and those of control and surveillance, on the other: by so framing his analysis, Carchedi's inability to make concrete the distinctions throws doubt on the very existence of a new middle class.

It is contended here that the concept of a new middle class is useful in indicating the distinctive interests of groups of employees within the capitalist mode of production, interests which to different degrees conflict with those of both capital and labour. The following case study conducted in the 1970s is an attempt to counter those theories which regard all 'wage-labour', and foremen in particular, as working class. In doing so the study also takes issue with aspects of Carchedi's theory. In particular it questions the relationship of tasks of surveillance and control and of unity and co-ordination. As already noted, Carchedi's claim that these two functions are mutually exclusive is in practice untenable. No alternative formulation about the relationship can be made, however, in advance of a study of real social relations within the production process - real social relations involving the influence of class struggle. Indeed, on the view taken here, class determination is gauged by the changing balance of class power and confidence at the workplace, which is seen to transform the work of foremen and to an extent their social relations.

This emphasis on the social dynamics of the workplace also allows a recognition of the importance of the organisation of foremen within trade unions, affecting as it does the ability and willingness of foremen to resist the pressures of capital. But, in contrast to writers who see trade unionism as sufficient evidence in itself of the proletarian nature of foremen, the study examines the trade unionism of foremen in relation to their contradictory social functions, believing that while their subordinate position and partial labour functions necessitate some defensive organisation, the supervisory roles of foremen on behalf of capital also affect the nature and form of their trade unionism.

BROWNS: THE COMPANY AND THE FACTORY

As the organisation of capital and labour and the struggle between them are regarded as central in determining the class nature of foremen in any particular situation, it is necessary to sketch the background of Browns, the location of the case study.

Browns was a medium sized engineering factory, part of an East Midlands' company, Browns Ltd,[3] specialising in the manufacture of knitting machines for the hosiery industry. This company was part of a wider engineering group containing other companies making knitting machines and associated products, such as needles and dyeing machinery. This group was owned by a further company, while ultimate ownership lay with one of Britain's largest holding companies with major international assets (see Table 2.1). This chain of ownership was well-known within the factory, as witnessed by frequent mentions by workers of the much publicised private life and finances of the head of the holding company.

The workforce regarded itself primarily as part of the engineering group, which comprised seven factories in the locality. Besides the geographical proximity of these factories there was a frequent exchange of personnel, designs and products. The group consciousness which arose from this interchange was also reinforced by the specialist nature of the industry and the very low labour turn-over in the group.

The close inter-relationships within the group had not, however, produced a strong trade union combine organisation. Feelings towards other factories tended rather to be ones of jealousy and rivalry, not of solidarity. This was particularly the case over the extent of earnings, the development of new machines and the transfer of the production of existing models from one factory to another. These feelings were heightened in the 1970s by growing threats of redundancy.

This is not to suggest that workplace trade unionism was weak. It tended to be strong in all the factories as far as wages and conditions were concerned, making the factories amongst the highest paid in the East Midlands' town in which they were located. But trade union organisation was factory based and issues such as redundancies, work and job transfers, which necessitated a group level policy, were left to be dealt with factory by factory. As a result group management were able to reduce the workforce by half in only four years: it fell from 8,979 in 1972, to 4,479 in 1976. [4]

The willingness of the workforces to deal with problems factory by factory was not replicated by management. There was a high degree of involvement by the holding company's directors in the policies of the knitting-machine group. The increasing redundancies, although in part a response to market conditions, were also an attempt to rationalise the group, the profits of which had grown increasingly marginal to the overall performance of the holding company (see Table 2.2).

Table 2.2: Browns and Holding Company Profits

Year	Browns Ltd Profit after Tax (£)	Smiths Engineering Holding Company Profit after Tax (£)	Net Profit Before Tax
1968	–	3,251,000	18,786,000
1969	–	–	21,461,000
1970	1,766,734	3,853,000	21,917,000
1971	2,054,257	–	27,294,000
1972	2,541,725	7,697,000	32,389,000
1973	972,573	–	45,951,000
1974	999,905	421,000	47,528,000
1975	158,000	1,452,000	35,530,000

Table 2.1: Structure of Ownership 1976

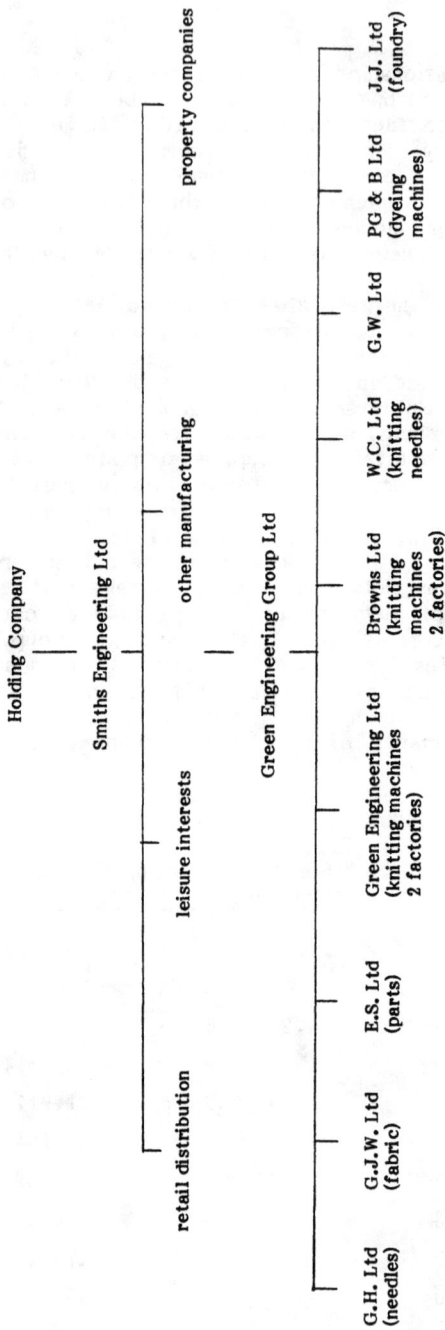

Holding Company

Smiths Engineering Ltd

- retail distribution
- leisure interests
- other manufacturing
- property companies

Green Engineering Group Ltd

- G.H. Ltd (needles)
- G.J.W. Ltd (fabric)
- E.S. Ltd (parts)
- Green Engineering Ltd (knitting machines 2 factories)
- Browns Ltd (knitting machines 2 factories)
- W.C. Ltd (knitting needles)
- G.W. Ltd
- PG & B Ltd (dyeing machines)
- J.J. Ltd (foundry)

The rationalisation programme, however, was not successful. Employment had been lowered but the reduction had little effect on the productivity and profitability of the factories. In short, it had not succeeded in lowering wages or loosening workers' control over working practices. The consequences of this failure, particularly at Browns, which had the strongest trade union organisation, was a stream of new Works Managers and Manufacturing Directors[3] causing changes in all managerial positions above foremen. Increasingly, these appointments were made from outside the industry causing growing divisions between those who knew about knitting machines and those who knew about management. These changes were viewed with some concern by the workforce at Browns. As a shop stewards' press statement in 1977 expressed it:

> Since the boom years the only thing that has changed in the company is management. They have little knowledge or sympathy with the product and constant management changes and insecurity have done nothing for the stability and smooth-running of the factory.

The workforce, as well as being in part the cause of this managerial turn-over, were also in the short-term at least, its beneficiary. Managerial insecurity caused a severe crisis in managerial confidence and authority. Successive holders of posts were never in a position long enough to find solutions to the problem of low productivity and a whole series of work practices continued unnoticed, or at least unaltered, and unabated. In order to maintain or increase production managers had to sanction or increase concessions to the workforce, calculating presumably that such a strategy might retain them their jobs. In order substantially to increase production, however, they would have had to confront the workforce. This was doubly difficult because not only was the workforce willing to defend its job control, but also management was uncertain of its ground and certain managers had vested interests in the failure of others. At Browns, managers most frequently decided that it was better not to take up issues at all than to take them up and lose. As a consequence, no one was prepared to make a decision of any importance and all questions, even the most trivial, were referred upwards. Even the Manufacturing Director's autonomy from the Board of Directors was extremely limited; at one point in time he had not the authority to appoint an extra labourer - it has first to go to the Board. And in the midst of all this the internal structure of management organisation-changes in which could themselves have potentially contributed to productivity (Nichols, 1986) - also remained essentially unchanged. As a positively coordinated organisation Brown's went backwards.

This lack of authority and confidence on the part of managerial personnel and the desire by the Board for tighter control and better results led managers, including the Manufacturing Director himself, to attempt to protect their positions by giving a false picture of the situation in the factory to the Board. One clear example of this illustrates the pressure on managers to increase production. The target figure for the factory was the production of forty machines per month but actual output never reached this figure and was frequently less than half. In order to improve the figures the Works Manager began to invoice the machines before they had even been tested, let alone dispatched from the factory. A proposed visit by the auditor threatened to reveal the discrepancy. In order to cover-up the position, the already invoiced machines were sent to another factory in the group twelve miles away and men were sent daily from Browns to finish them. With such lack of knowledge, rivalries, indecision and inefficiency at management level, it is not surprising that the foremen themselves were less than decisive.

The recruitment of foremen

There were 25 foremen at Browns and in many respects they could be described as not untypical of foremen in manufacturing industry in general. In terms of age, length of service, remuneration, attitudes, training and skills they confirmed profiles of British foremen outlined by the British Institute of Management (1976) and Daly et al (1985). They were recruited from the shopfloor, usually from the same section which they were to supervise. Not one of them was under forty years of age and the majority were in their mid-fifties. In 1977, most of them had been doing a foremen's job for ten years or more.

These foremen supervised 600 well-paid shopfloor workers producing at that date machines costing upwards of £10,000 each. The labour invested in each machine was complex and expensive. Despite the complexity of the labour process, however, the foremen received no systematic training after appointment. They were considered suitable and competent for their posts not as the result of any training in the skills of supervision, but through their knowledge of shopfloor practices and, more particularly, their previous attitudes and actions. They regarded their appointment as foremen as promotion, even though there was little financial incentive in becoming a foreman, the salary [6] generally being only on a par with the shopfloor average. This meant that a considerable number of shopfloor workers earned more than the foreman, the difference amounting in some cases to as much as £30 per week. Shopfloor workers were not, however, in receipt of the various staff perquisites that the foreman received, such as not needing to clock in, extra holidays and a better pension scheme. These perquisites, however, were not of sufficient monetary value to equalise the foremen's salary with the wages of the highest paid shopfloor workers. Nor did the prospects of further promotion compensate for their comparatively low salaries. The positions were not stepping-stones to higher managerial jobs, as the length of service of individual foremen indicates. If the social background and levels of remuneration were sufficient criteria for membership of the working class, therefore, these particular foremen were well-qualified.

A variety of reasons explain why foremen had taken jobs with only marginal benefits. Some of the foremen had been amongst the most deferential to management when shopfloor workers. In the general opinion of the shopfloor workers, they had been singled out by their willingness to cooperate with managerial policies and were known colloquially as 'arse-lickers'. One such foreman worked in the tool room and, a keen horticulturalist, he also looked after the Managing Director's garden. The majority of the foremen could not, however, be so considered, indeed many had displayed a certain independence from management before their appointment. Most of these had been shop stewards, some of them amongst the most militant in the factory. As militant stewards they had undoubtedly been irritants to management and their passage to foremanship had advantages to management in both removing the source of irritation and in confirming ideas that it was difficult to sustain strong trade union organisation because, in the end, everyone, even shop stewards, were only after personal advancement.

The transition from steward to foreman lay not so much in the greed of 'human nature', however, as in the stress inherent in the steward's position. Under pressure from both management and the workers they represented, the stewards – sometimes after a period of years – became demoralised and disillusioned. They were then able to rationalise the transition to foreman by pointing to the apathy or inconsistencies of the membership. As one foreman concluded, 'I'd had enough. They [the section] wouldn't back me up, so I decided they weren't worth fighting for'. This 'breaking point' had been reached by other foremen.

Because of the way that some shop stewards interpreted their role, the transition from steward to foreman was not necessarily a sharp one, at least not in all its aspects. As stewards, many had regarded themselves as having authority over their membership rather than from it. They made the decisions, they sorted out any problems. A militant shop steward in this mould is not one that raises the consciousness of his members, but rather is one who substitutes for members. This type of shop steward was regarded as one who 'shouted his mouth off' and considered his position as superior to that of his members. Regarding the role in such a way, some shop stewards adopted the role of an unofficial foreman. They answered the section's telephone, something that no other shopfloor worker did, and looked for the foreman if he was required. Some also handed out work to the section when the foreman was absent. The authority that such stewards assumed therefore separated them from their members in such a way that there was a much easier transition to foreman that would otherwise have been the case.

The role of the foreman

The foremen had no written job description. With a notable exception that is discussed later their work could be reduced to two major functions: handing out work and acting as progress chasers. Both these tasks might be classified as part of the function of capital. There is no doubt that such tasks can be integral to control. The foremen's <u>actual performance</u> of these tasks, however, showed that the function of capital within them was far from clear. The handing out of work was governed by priorities of work-flow and progress chasing was to ensure that parts needed on the section would arrive on time, and, failing that, that alternative work was available. Failure effectively to co-ordinate and unify the work process brought pressure upon the foreman from higher management, but this pressure was not directly transferable from foreman to the workforce.

The handing out of work was occasionally used as an indirect source of discipline. For the men on piece-work the type of job assigned to them was an important determinant of earnings, some jobs having much better rates of pay than others. At Browns, however, the amount of favouritism in the handing out of work was small, a fact verified by both foremen and shop stewards. Most foremen simply took the job that needed doing to the first available machine. But there were occasions when this random allocation was not followed. It was common for workers to make a specialised tool kit for certain jobs, particularly those which were especially difficult, to which they were then regularly allocated. This was not in itself a source of friction but once a pattern of job allocation was established any changes to it threw up difficulties, which will be discussed below.

Friction did arise when men considered themselves to be consistently receiving work with poor times and, on occasions, some refused to do them. Foremen were usually sensitive to this situation and tried to avoid it, placating anyone objecting to certain jobs by giving them better-rated ones. Paradoxically, this attempt to compensate for poor times by allocating jobs with better ones gave rise, particularly in the case of certain foremen, to a degree of unfairness. The men on the section who complained loudest were given the best jobs because the foremen either would not or could not face constant battles over the issue. It is worth stressing that the discretion exercised by the foreman in handing out work and which could have been a source of power, was either not used, or was usurped, although unevenly, by certain of the men themselves. The tasks of coordination and unity performed by the foremen were designed as part of the function of capital, as a control, but as parts of this control process they had been negated by the men.

The lack of confidence on the part of some foremen over the handing out of work was characteristic of the dealings of most of the foremen over a whole range of issues. Whereas the foremen most commonly described their role as 'supervising the section and being on hand to deal with any eventualities', they actually had little authority to control or discipline the men. In some sections the foremen confined themselves to asking the men if everything was running smoothly and generally chatting and being polite. There were, of course, exceptions. Two or three foremen were regarded as 'bastards' by shopfloor workers and as 'mangement men' by the other foremen.[7]

The weakness of the foremen in relation to their sections was, in large part, caused by their lack of technical knowledge concerning jobs on those sections. With the exception of the test shop, the skill of the men on the section, collectively and often individually, was higher than that of the foreman. As has been noted earlier, the foremen were not selected for their merits as skilled workers, although they obviously knew well individual jobs at which they themselves had worked. This resulted in a number of foremen not knowing how to do particular jobs which they handed out to the men. Many of these jobs needed specialist tools which had been either appropriated privately or made covertly by the workers who normally did these particular jobs. When the occasion arose for a particular job to be done by a new worker, the necessary kit was often not available. When questioned, a foreman might not know whether specialist kit was necessary or, if it was, where it could be located. As a result many men ignored the foreman and directly approached the person who last did the job in order to borrow the necessary kit from him. Another indication of the foremen's lack of knowledge and control of what was happening on their sections was the practice by certain workers of deliberately doing work wrongly. When such work was sent back from the test section to be rectified the worker would then get another job-time to put it right. The worker was, in effect, paid two bonuses for the same piece of work. It was left to the test shop foreman to draw such problems to the attention of the foreman concerned who was usually ignorant as to exactly what should be produced on his section. The removal of the foremen from the production process, therefore, would not have caused any problems from a technical point of view. This is borne out by the arrangements made when individual foremen were on holiday. Their jobs were covered by a foreman from another section with no knowledge of the operations that he was 'supervising'. The foremen, in short, took no part in determining the method of operation because the workforce had a high degree of autonomy.

The second major source of the foremen's lack of authority was the strength and confidence of workers' resistance to the foremen and the concomitant failure of management to support the foremen when such resistance arose. Within the firm there was a history of resolving such conflict by disciplining the foreman or moving him to another section. It is clear that management's stance had undermined the confidence of the foremen and that they consequently retreated from potential conflict situations. This can be illustrated by examining one aspect of the central problem faced by management in the factory, that of the low level of productivity. One of the ways in which this problem manifested itself was in men chatting to each other instead of working. Obviously some talking in the factory was necessary and, indeed, some chatting was probably even desirable in order to maintain morale. However, even the workers on piece-rates worked only abour four hours a day and those workers had an incentive to work, their wages being tied to their production levels. The lieu-rate workers, with no such incentives, certainly did no more than four hours day. The presence of large groups of workers not working but talking together was therefore a serious and visible problem. Foremen who told workers to go back to their machines had in the past been invited to 'fuck-off'. When workers were suspended for such behaviour, the officers of the shop stewards committee took up the case claiming either that correct procedure had not been followed or that the foreman had been belligerent. Such claims were accompanied by the threat of industrial action which was usually enough to have the suspension lifted or, at the minimum, reduced.

When interviews were carried out between 1973-77, no one could remember the last time anyone on the shopfloor had been sacked despite cases of workers' behaviour generally considered sufficiently provocative to warrant dismissal in other firms. Even after management had specifically instructed foremen to keep an eye on particular people who were habitually late for work, no action was taken against the offenders. The foremen had followed instructions. They had warned the people in question and had reported the lack of improvement but higher management semmed unable to take a further step.[8] Serious clocking-in offences, for instance, were common[8] but only resulted in suspensions. Similarly, when a deputy convenor was caught filling the boot of his car with coke from the works supply, he was only suspended for three days despite the feeling of many foremen that he should have been dismissed.

The foremen drew a simplistic conclusion from such events. As one of them remarked, 'We don't count - it's the AUEW that runs this factory. They have done for years'. The foremen had decided, consciously or unconsciously, that there was little point in getting involved in any conflict. They were not convinced that managers were serious when periodically they instructed the foremen to tighten up on discipline, realising that whatever was said there was a tacit agreement not to enforce discipline or to provoke disputes. 'What can you do?', asked one foreman, 'They call you into the office and tell you you've got to tighten up. But you know they don't mean it; they're just going through the motions because one of the chiefs has been down. The threat of a strike and they'd cave in again. There's no way we could do it.'

Unable overtly to discipline the men, the foremen had to approach problems more indirectly. They tried to deal with the problem of men socialising instead of working by asking an individual when his particular piece of work would be finished rather than tackling the group as a whole. This sometimes resulted in the group dispersing back to their machines, but if it did not, then no direct order had been ignored. The lack of outcome did not appear as a fundamental challenge to the foreman's authority and his position was not further undermined. Without the authority and managerial support to deal with the problem of men not working, but nevertheless still expected to cope with the situation, particularly at times when managers were having a campaign to tighten up discipline, the foremen adopted various defensive and collusive strategies. One such practice which grew up in the factory was known as 'the early warning system'. If a particularly important manager decided to inspect the factory, foremen telephoned from one section to the next warning colleagues that, say, the Manufacturing Director was coming. Even then the men were not told to go back to work, they were simply informed of the situation in the hope that the director would instill in them as much fear and trepidation as he did in the foremen. Where there was a reasonably good relationship with the foreman the men tended to busy themselves, to protect their foreman as much as themselves. This was part of the trade-off in return for the foreman not intervening and interfering with the section's customary work practices. Where the relationship was poor and the foreman was regarded as a 'bastard', it provided an opportunity for the men to embarrass the foreman by not moving. In this situation rather than be seen as not being in control, the foreman absented himself from the section before higher management arrived.

For the foremen to have any semblance of control, a web of mutual obligation was needed. The section would tacitly agree not to embarrass the foreman in return for an extreme 'indulgency' pattern.[9] The obligation was, however, personal and localised.

Such a situation gave rise to the following incident. Each morning, at 9.30 a.m., food from the canteen was brought around the factory. It started at a different section each week but the men rarely waited for it to reach their own section, preferring to go the section of its first call and queue for food there. If the trolley was late an embarrassingly long queue formed. The foreman of the section dared not tell the men to disperse, the majority not being from his section. On one occasion, however, the foreman on the milling section was instructed by higher management to disperse the queue and to ensure that only his section purchased from the trolley when it was on his section. His demands that the men from other section should return to them were ignored. It was not until the Works Manager and the Manufacturing Director appeared and stood next to the trolley that the men from other sections began to drift away. This incident inspired both a cartoon and a poem from members of the workforce, the styles of which were influenced by the military background of the manager concerned, verifying that the foreman had no impact whatsoever, and that it needed the Works Manager and Manufacturing Director to supervise the selling of bread rolls. When these highly paid 'supervisors' did not appear on subsequent occasions the situation soon reverted to normal.

A similar situation occurred weekly when wages were paid at 3.00 p.m. on Fridays. After this time, everyone stopped work and collected their wages. On receiving them, work was not resumed, the rest of the afternoon being spent clearing debts between the men on such items as football totes, cigarette bills, transport money and numerous other services (such as the Friday afternoon barber's salon in the toilets) that made the workforce a community. It was important to the shopfloor workers therefore that their pay packets were received well before they left the factory. If the pay was late, as it frequently was, it jeopardised such payments, so the later the pay-out the longer the queue at the pay office, until 4.00 p.m. saw practically all the 600 men in the queue. Faced with such a situation the foremen tended to absent themselves so that, once again, they could not be expected to deal with it.

On one such Friday, however, the Works Manager ordered a foreman to instruct the men back to work. The effect of this embarrassed foreman pleading 'For Christ's sake go back to

Poem: circulated anonymously

Browns Ltd

WILL THE NEW MAN – DAVID RITCHIE
EVER BE JUST QUITE AS BITCHY
AS THE MAN NOW KNOWN AS "HAUPTMAN JOYCE"
WHO, HAVING MADE HIS AWFUL CHOICE
SENT FORTH "OBERLEUTNANT" CAIN
TO HALT THE CANTEEN WAGON-TRAIN

HE SAID SCHWINEHUNDS YOU'LL ALL LOSE YER JOBS
IF YOU STAY 'ERE QUEING UP FOR COBS
AND PICKING ON POOR EDDIE FLYNN
(WHO, MEANWHILE, HAD JUST SNOOK IN!)
AIMED HIS JACKBOOT AT HIS "BOT"
AND EXCLAIMED "DAS WASS GUT BY GOTT"!!

VERY SOON THE QUEUE DISPERSED
THE WORKERS HAVING COME OFF WORSE
THE "HAUPTMAN" SAID "MEIN LIEBER ERN"
YOU SEE ITS NOT TOO LATE TO LEARN
NOW WHEN YOU'VE SORTED OUT THE – FOREMEN
I'LL MAKE YOU "MEIN MARTIN BORMAN"!!

Cartoon: Browns Ltd

work', was less than decisive and the Works Manager was forced to summon the officers of the shop stewards committee to tell them to put an end to the situation. An argument ensued, which resulted in an agreement by management to guarantee the punctual arrival of both the canteen trolley and the wages, thus eliminating the necessity for long periods of queueing.

Another area where the foreman's avoidance of conflict was significant was the shrugging-off of responsibilities connected with the timing of jobs. In the early 1970s, if a piece-rate worker was not satisfied with a job time he had to ask the foreman of the section to call in a ratefixer to re-time the job. Increasingly the foremen were by-passed, as men went straight to the ratefixers, an arrangement with which the foremen were not unhappy. Unfortunately for the foremen this was not necessarily the end of their involvement. Times were normally set with reference to drawings and not from timing work in progress. If, however, no agreement could be reached between the ratefixer and the worker the job had to be timed. When timed the worker normally slowed down in order to confirm his estimation of a 'fair' time and often took longer than he originally asked for. If the ratefixer suspected that the worker had deliberately slowed down, the procedure was to call in the foreman for a decision as to whether this was the case. The ratefixers tended not to do this, preferring to break off the timing altogether or to refuse to accept the final time. Their experience was that foremen usually confirmed that the worker's speed was satisfactory. Foremen made such decisions because they were loath to upset their relationship with their section. Acknowledging their own lack of control, the foremen relied upon the section's goodwill, which in turn depended upon the foreman not interfering with working practices. Consequently, the foremen regarded ratefixers as a source of potential conflict that threatened the peaceful running of the section. In turn, the ratefixers were frustrated by the foremen's defence of what Taylor described as 'systematic soldiering'.[10] They were unable to solve their problems by by-passing the foremen, however, because when they appealed to a higher level of authority such as the Works Manager they usually lost their case on the grounds that they had not followed the correct procedure for settling the problem.

This friction between the foremen and the ratefixers extended to the work-rate of lieu-rate workers, i.e. those on time rates as opposed to piece-work, who had even less reason to work conscientiously. Their work-rate was therefore much more dependent upon effective supervision. Ratefixers who questioned the productivity of lieu-rate workers placed the foremen in a difficult position. If a foreman admitted that workers were slacking and a dispute escalated and came to the attention of the Works Manager, he was at the same time admitting that he had allowed the slacking to take place. The shop stewards were well aware of this predicament and were prepared to exploit it. They let it be known to the foremen that, were such a situation to arise, they would ask the Works Manager what the foreman had been doing while this slacking took place. This led the foremen consistently to make excuses for low productivity, claiming for example that there had been problems with the quality of material or difficulties in obtaining particular parts.

The foremen and trade unionism

All the foremen were members of ASTMS, with two exceptions who retained membership of the AUEW. The ASTMS group was formed in the mid-1960s, although when interviewed no member could remember any specific incidents that led to its formation.[11] Prior to the formation of this group, the foremen had not negotiated an annual salary increase but had automatically received a pay increase on a par with that of the shopfloor. This maintained their differential absolutely, if not relatively, over shopfloor basic wages. This differential, however, was not as great as the bonus earnings of most workers. Moreover, the organisation of the foremen into ASTMS did not reverse this position, despite the fact that the foremen had their own formal salary negotiations. Indeed, the payment system of the factory with an escalating production bonus accelerated the higher earnings of the shopfloor workers. Nor did the ASTMS group manage to increase the prestige and morale of the foremen.

A number of factors contributed to this situation. Some of the foremen complained that their fellow foremen were not prepared to fight the management for improvements, and that whatever had been gained was the result of having gone 'cap in hand' to management rather than through trade union activity. These members looked back with some nostalgia to their days in the AUEW when they were part of a strong trade union: 'We'd have called a shop meeting and made a stand, rather than leaving an individual to argue or plead with management'. Those complained about cited the failure of management to regard them sufficiently highly. These two factors are relevant but any satisfactory explanation must also encompass why these members continued to be deferential to management even when such behaviour demonstrably failed to improve their situation.

It is the contention here that the explanation is to be found in their work roles. Their lack of control over the work process caused, in part, by the absence of technical superiority over the workforce, weakened their performance of the function of capital. But the absence of a strong managerial role, a role which might have commanded greater respect and remuneration from the company, does not suggest, as Carchedi implies, heavy involvement in the function of the collective worker (1977, p.60). The foremen had little confidence in their ability seriously to affect production and this severely weakened their bargaining position as workers and trade unionists. It is true that they performed unifying and coordinating work which increased in importance the more the section was concerned with building complete machines. This work, however, had a negative quality about it. When things were running smoothly no one noticed the foreman's responsibility for this. When problems occurred in coordinating the flow of work the blame was deposited firmly on the foreman. The work could never therefore be the source of much satisfaction or confidence, as it never appeared embodied in the product.

The foremen's weakness in relationship to management made strong trade unionism at one and same time necessary and unlikely. The foremen's lack of confidence strongly permeated their trade unionism making them reluctant to fight for themselves and causing them to vacillate in periods of stress between management and the workforce. They adopted neither the strategy of zealous foremen, nor positions of common identity with the shopfloor union.

Their lack of ability and willingness to cohere as a trade union group can be illustrated by the following episode. In June 1976, shortly after the successful victimisation of the convenor of a factory in the engineering group and an unsuccessful combine-wide strike by the manual worker unions for his reinstatement, the foremen's ASTMS representatives were called into the Works Manager's office and informed that the performance of every foreman was to be assessed and that in due course all foremen would be called in to discuss the results. Subsequently, the milling section foreman was called in, together with his union representative, told that he was considered incapable of carrying out a proposed new disciplinary code, and instructed to return to the shopfloor. It was also stated that there was a possibility of five other such demotions. The ASTMS repesentative formally registered failure to agree and declared that the issue would be fought through the disputes procedure.

The foremen then invited the AUEW officers to an ASTMS meeting to discuss the issue. At that meeting it became clear that the majority of the foremen were unwilling to take any action to defend the foreman in question who was unpopular with his fellow foremen. The AUEW steward from the milling section, reckoning that the foreman's opposition to the demotion would not rise above a verbal protest, asked for, and received from his section, overwhelming agreement to strike if their foreman was removed. This support arose not because of any personal liking for the foreman concerned, but rather because of the background to the demotion which directly affected the interests of the section. Management, in the opinion of the section, wanted 'someone to wield a big stick' over the section, and anyone coming with that brief would mean much more trouble for them. The day after the threat of AUEW action the foremen's representative was called into the works' office and informed that the demotion had been withdrawn.

Having heard of the decision, and having more than a slight interest in the proposals for a new disciplinary code, the AUEW officers met the Works Manager to seek clarification of the situation. They were told that although the proposals to assess the foremen had been withdrawn and no new disciplinary code was to be produced, nevertheless there was still a need for discipline to be tightened in the factory. This tightening of discipline was not to apply to everyone, but was aimed at 'those few who religiously turn up late, leave early and don't work while they are here'.

After management had withdrawn their proposals and revoked the demotion decision, the foremen held a trade union meeting. It was there reported by ASTMS representatives that management were now prepared to back the foremen in any disciplinary action they might take against the shopfloor, a position which, reportedly, made the foremen feel 'much happier'. It would appear that the management tactics were part of an attempt to stiffen the resolve of the foremen to exercise authority over the shopfloor workers rather than a serious attempt to demote a number of them. The behaviour of the foremen altered somewhat after this incident – shopfloor workers recall that the foremen walked around more frequently, uttering phrases such as 'watch it', or 'so and so will be round soon' – but their underlying relationship with the shopfloor remained the same.

The issue had placed the foremen and shopfloor workers on the same side, if only for tactical reasons, and had created a potential for united action. This, however, only lasted as long as the issue lasted. After the event the foremen did not identify themselves any more closely with the shopfloor. Nor were they convinced that management promises of full support made it safe to attack shopfloor practices. They had seen previous managerial attempts to tighten discipline fail and believed that concerted AUEW opposition would also terminate this attempt. They therefore distanced themselves from the new managerial policy, as was apparent in the very language they used when dealing with the shopfloor. They were careful to preface instructions with comments such as 'I've got to tell the section this', 'It's bloody stupid, but I've got to do it', and 'I thought I would let you know'. While the shopfloor organisation remained buoyant and confident and the foremen were compelled to issue instructions, they did so in as indirect a fashion as possible.

This distancing themselves from management by the foremen belies any attempt simply to subsume foremen into management. On the other hand, the opposing view that regards trade unionism as an indicator of foremen belonging to the working class has to be viewed critically. Were this latter position correct, it would be expected that the behaviour of the foremen in a crisis, such as the closure of a factory, would be similar to that of the rest of the workforce. Faced with redundancy, foremen too feel insecure and their consciousness of being wage-labour is at its height. When such an event happened at Browns Ltd in early 1977, however, the foremen while opposed to the closure of the factory nevertheless remained separate and aloof from the resistance to the closure organised by the shopfloor.

The shopfloor union's reaction to the proposed closure, the sacking of the majority of the workforce and the transfer of the remainder to a sister factory, was one of the utmost hostility. This feeling was strengthened by the knowledge, not contradicted by management, that the factory had plenty of orders.[12] What is more, the group Manufacturing Director stated that:

> The demand for . . . the new range of machines has shown a sustained improvement throughout 1976 and there is every expectation that this improvement will continue, particularly in the U.S.A.[13]

The conclusion drawn by the workforce was that their particular factory had been chosen because it had the best trade union organisation in the combine. In addition, management of the engineering group was in the process of introducing a new bonus scheme factory by factory, with losses estimated by trade union officials of up to one third of piece-work rates. At the other Browns' factory, where the new system was closer to being implemented, management had produced the following estimates.[14]

Table 2.3: Estimated Activity Rating of Direct Operative based on B.S.I. Standards, i.e. what percentage increase could be achieved if average man was working at 'good average' on B.S.I. rating.

Section	Existing Work Rate	Average Expected on B.S.I. Rating	Work Rate Percentage Increase Required
Milling	65	90	38½%
Drilling	65	85	31%
Grinding	70	85	21½%
Capstan	65	80	23%

Section	Existing Work Rate	Average Expected on B.S.I. Rating	Work Rate Percentage Increase Required
Vert.Boring	80	90	12½%
Gear Cutting	80	95	19%
Cyl.Finishing	55	80	45½%
Cambox	65	85	31%
Camplate	60	90	50%
Erection	75	90	20%
Mech. Test	70	85	21½%

Management considered that such proposals were not feasible at Browns, because of the strength of trade unionism. At a directors' meeting it was stated that they recognised 'the grave difficulty of persuading the labour force to accept in some 60 cases out of a 190 a drop per week of approximately £25'. They therefore decided to close the factory. They took this course despite serious short-term and long-term dangers to the viability of the engineering group as a whole; it was Browns that pioneered new machines, built experimental models, and produced the most expensive and complicated machines in the group's range. Furthermore, there was no guarantee that the skills lost in the closure could be duplicated at the sister factory that had concentrated on larger batch production of less complex machines.

The fusing of craft pride and trade union principles united the shopfloor and the factory was occupied in an attempt to prevent its closure. Strong support was given by the wives and families of many workers and also the local labour movement which recognised that a key local factory with strong trade union organisation was at serious risk. It is not surprising amid such strong feelings both inside and outside the factory that the foremen joined the occupation. A measure of the distance at which they held themselves apart from the shopfloor, however, was manifested from the outset of the occupation when, although they had a representative on the occupation committee, the foremen did not consider themselves bound by the decisions of that committee.

Their role during the occupation further highlighted their highly ambiguous relationships with the shopfloor and management. The foremen undoubtedly wanted their jobs to be saved. Indeed their anxiety was as high as any on the shopfloor: many foremen were older men and had not worked at the craft for several years and therefore felt that it would be more difficult to them to obtain alternative employment than would be the case for many shopfloor workers. But they were unhappy about the method chosen to fight the closure.

Participation in the occupation threatened the likelihood of job transfer rather than redundancy, yet non-participation left them exposed and threatened their future relationships with their sections should the occupation be successful. The foreman resolved this dilemma by joining the occupation but continuing their role as foremen within it. The foremen met, decided to police the occupation, and worked out a separate rota duty from the shopfloor to ensure that there were always some foremen on the premises to stop stealing and vandalism, and to keep an eye on the 'hot heads'.[15] From the beginning of the occupation they set about gathering up small items of equipment such as calculators and locking up offices. This is not to suggest that they were more successful in disciplining shopfloor workers while on strike than when working. They did not manage to stop numerous items such as typewriters and tools from disappearing, nor did they prevent the minutes of directors' meetings becoming somewhat more widely read than normal. But they effectively distanced themselves from the bulk of the workforce and gave rise, in so doing, to a great deal of tension within the occupation.

Aware of their precarious position within the occupation, the foremen attempted to influence the behaviour of shopfloor workers by requests to the occupation committee, rather than by directly confronting people whom they considered to be acting unreasonably. The AUEW convenor, the most influential on the committee, responded to such requests by saying 'Leave it with me. I'll try and sort it out', although he was hostile to the role of the foremen and, as he confided to me, 'had no intention of sorting anything out'. The friction caused by the foremen led to demands for them to be ejected from the factory. This was resisted by the occupation committee because it was considered that, in the interests of putting maximum pressure on the management and of favourable publicity, the factory should appear as united as possible. Indeed, it was felt that the 'participation' by the foremen in the occupation could be used as a demonstration of how unreasonable were management's proposals to close the factory.

It was mainly for this latter reason that the friction never resulted in any open conflict. This was the case even when the foremen ignored occupation committee decisions. It was decided, for example, not to cover or oil the cylinders on already constructed knitting machines, thus allowing them to go rusty. Such a decision was thought to add to the bargaining strength of the workforce because failure by management to come to a settlement would lead to the wasting of millions of pounds worth of machinery. Nevertheless, the foremen went ahead and oiled and covered them even though in normal circumstances this was not part of their job.

The role of the foremen was confirmed when the occupation ended after a court injunction had been served against various named persons within the occupation. The decision having been made to leave the factory and commence picketing outside the gates, the foremen began to tidy the factory. With the exception of one of the two AUEW foremen, the foremen did not picket the factory because they considered the battle already lost. Furthermore, company property was no longer at risk, so they saw no need for further attendance, particularly on a picket line where the presence of individuals could easily be noted by management observers.[16]

The actions of the foremen at Browns were directly connected to their social roles within the factory. In other words, their behaviour in general, and their trade unionism in particular, were influenced by the fact that they were middle class workers.

CONCLUSION

The position of the foremen in the managerial structure of Browns confirms the historical decline in the authority of foremen noted earlier. Indeed both shopfloor workers and foremen alike painted a picture of almost total ineffectiveness. Aware of this ineffectiveness, management periodically attempted to encourage foremen to take a firmer stand against the shopfloor, but without giving them the means to be successful. The management did not make any serious attempt to alter the foremen's role either by abolishing the existing first-line of supervision, or by restructuring that role into a more managerial one. The reason that the role was not changed is that the existence of a low-level supervisor, who is part manager part worker, has distinct advantages to management. It enables them to test certain plans of action through instructions to foremen and to reverse the plans should strong opposition to them arise. The responsibility for such plans can then be laid at the feet of the foremen and the decisions reversed higher up with no loss of face. The foremen thus become the scapegoats for failed managerial policies. As well as the acknowledged widespread dissatisfaction of foremen being part of a managerial problem therefore, it is part of a managerial solution.

Foremen are not simply passive victims of this process. They may not be able to escape from the situation but they are able to modify it, using the materials available to them. The account of the foremen at Browns shows a number of ways in which the foremen attempted to relieve pressure on themselves in order to escape being caught 'in the middle'. Though clearly intended to carry out control and surveillance, and formally accepting this function, the foremen had all but ceased to perform it. Their effective lack of authority encouraged them, on occasions, to take part in manual labour.   In the hardening shop, for example, the hardeners stopped doing an unskilled part of their job which was then taken over by the labourer in the shop.   This meant that the labourer no longer had time to clean up properly and a danger arose from the cyanide used in the process.   Instead of the foreman re-establishing a proper work structure, however, he attempted to ease the situation by helping the labourer with the unskilled part of the hardener's jobs.   The situation only came to light when the hardeners refused to work, complaining that lack of cleaning had made the job dangerous.   The convenor advised the hardeners to do all of their job in future and leave the labourer to concentrate on cleaning the shop.   If a backlog of work built up as a result then a demand for extra labour could be made.   When the hardeners refused to accept this the Works Manager instructed the labourer to cease doing anything but that which was strictly within his job description.   The foreman also stopped helping the hardeners.[17]

In the absence of any effective authority the foremen could not directly transfer pressure from management to the workforce.   Furthermore,   this   inability   led   to   a re-articulation of management control and direction at a higher   level.   The   foremen   tried   therefore   to   rectify mistakes   and   minimise   delays   that   were   not   directly attributable to them.   When work was behind schedule they attempted to speed it up by working as labourers, collecting materials and parts.   This lack of power also affected their work of unity and coordination, designed as part of the control   function.   This   control   function   was   negated   by shopfloor   opposition   and   lack   of   managerial   support. However, the work of scheduling, progress chasing and handing out jobs remained.   These tasks would be necessary under any system of social production and therefore, if stripped of a control function, are collective worker ones.   But it is not the   technical   nature   of   these   tasks   in   themselves   that determine   their   social   significance,   rather   it   is   the political   and   ideological   relations   that   surround   them. Given   serious   defeats   of   the   workforce   -   or   indeed   a different management-designed organisational structure - the task could once again be transformed into part of the control function.

It   should   not   be   thought,   however,   that   there   is   a simple   inverse   relationship   between   authority   and   the performance of collective worker roles: the decline of the former   does   not   automatically   mean   an   expansion   of   the latter.   For much of the time the foremen performed neither function.   They were neither transmission belts of managerial authority,   nor   were   they   collective   workers.   They   simply chatted to the men on the section or, if it was known that senior   management   were   approaching,   they   might   remove themselves   from   the   section   altogether.   When   problems emerged they either relayed them up the managerial hierarchy or, if of a technical nature, threw them back onto the shopfloor. They were thus highly successful in disengaging themselves from conflict and technical involvement. In so far as they did perform the function of capital it was only indirectly. They acted as relayers of managerial instructions, which they then could not enforce, and they reported to management any emerging problems. Even this latter aspect, it should be stressed, was limited by their collusive strategies with the shopfloor. They could not simply transmit information upwards: they tried to hide from management those problems in which they felt themselves implicated.

The functions of the foremen or, given the absence of clear functions, their social relations inside the factory, strongly influenced their attitudes towards trade unionism. On the one hand they were hostile to strong shopfloor organisation, but, because of their powerlessness to affect it and because of their own weakness in relation to management, they were forced to appeal to the shopfloor for support on critical occasions. Moreover, the foremen only had the confidence to avoid responsibilities in the factory, to perform a non-role much of the time, because the very shopfloor to which they were hostile had established a tradition of job security.

The foremen's role inside the factory also influenced the nature of their trade union activity. Having not been given a definite managerial function with clear authority to perform it, they were distanced from management. At the same time, however, their minimal performance in the labour process meant that withdrawal of their labour was doomed to be ineffective. While they performed work of unity and coordination it never appeared to them to represent concrete labour embodied in a product and thus was not sufficient to give them self respect or confidence in their own industrial muscle. The ambiguous situation of the foremen produced an ambivalence in their attitudes. They were never certain whether to adopt a managerial strategy and identify with ideas to lessen the control and lower the pay and conditions of the shopfloor, or to view their main problem as their own terms and conditions of employment and their weakness vis-à-vis management. As a consequence they held both sets of ideas simultaneously.

So far the analysis has assumed that the role and positions of the foremen were identical, not only for simplicity, but also to lay bare the most important relationships. The role and position of foremen did, of course, vary in practice. These variations, moreover, further confirm many of the points already made. The foreman on the knit-test section at Browns, for instance, was an exception. He was universally acknowledged inside the factory as having more knowledge about knitting machinery than anyone else. That knowledge he used daily, insisting that work was done his way and advising the workers on the section about technical problems. Being at the end of the process of production his role also concerned making sure that parts for testing arrived simultaneously with others that were needed. He was therefore much concerned with the work of unity and coordination. He also dealt with a large number of telephone enquiries from customers, up to seventy-five per day, asking for technical information[18] and requests about the possibility of obtaining spares. All these aspects rooted the foreman in a real work process, and he was respected for his skill by the men on his section.

This foreman carried the tradition of craft pride into his foremanship. He also identified with the men on his section. This, in part, explains his continued membership of the AUEW. More importantly it meant that he was confident because he would not easily be replaced. He had something to bargain with, and consequently was the most militant of the foremen. He argued in the factory with his superiors not only over technical questions but also over his terms and conditions of employment and even proposed bonus schemes for his section. It was he who joined the picket after the occupation. In short, he was in many ways much closer to the situation of the shopfloor workers in his role and in his attitudes.

His identification with trade unionism notwithstanding, he also had a managerial function to carry out. The general evasion of this function by the foremen, and the generally low regard for the quality of management, meant, however, that this was not very prominent in his conception of his role. He did, nevertheless, complain about the ineffectiveness of the management in the area of discipline. He also fully subscribed to the foremen's role in policing the occupation and was proud that his section was the one from which least was stolen and that the completed machines were not damaged. His attitude, therefore, was ambivalent. In conversation he would say 'we' meaning his section, as opposed to 'them', meaning management. But he also maintained that the factory could have been made successful if the two sides, management and shopfloor, had pulled together and viewed himself, and the other foremen, outside both these camps.

At Browns, the foremen's work had certainly been degraded. Not only had they no effective decision-making powers within the function of capital but they were also much concerned with work that could be classified as coordination and unity, thus falling within a collective worker function. Nevertheless, their relations with their employers and with shopfloor workers continued to distinguish them from the shopfloor: they were new middle class workers. This was the case because although their roles within the function of capital had atrophied they were still little rooted within a real work process. It is the case that they performed the work of unity and coordination, but as has been noted this work neither simply filled the roles vacated by their ceasing to perform the function of capital, nor did it give much confidence and satisfaction. Furthermore, in different circumstances the very same work of coordination and unity could be transformed into the work of control and surveillance, thus changing its social character. Whether work such as progress-chasing can be subsumed into either the function of the collective worker or the function of capital depends not upon its technical nature, nor upon definitions or classifications, but upon the relationshps that surround it within a particular work situation. Where a substantial amount of control and confidence resides in the workforce, foremen, and management. generally, have to accommodate themselves to it. The control aspect of unity and coordination can thus be negated. In short, the question as to whether particular tasks have this or that social character depends upon the balance of power in specific situations. Furthermore, not only will the social character of their work change with changes in the balance of workplace power, but foremen will also react to the shifts in power, vacillating between identification with higher management and with shopfloor unionism, depending upon which strategy seems the most viable. Such a perspective places class struggle at the heart of the analysis, thereby connecting what takes place at factory level to the outcome of struggles between classes at a societal level. This link between events inside factories and outside is crucial in determining the wider political and ideological stances taken by middle class factory labour.

Of course, the linkages between class struggle at the point of production and class struggle in society generally do not operate in one direction only, and class struggle generally is more than the sum of its parts as it bears back on particular points of production. But it is hoped that even this specific, and obviously limited case study of one tiny segment of middle class labour, at one particular point in time, does serve to underline the limitations of attempts to classify middle class employees' relations by theoretical fiat. Neither Poulantzas' contention that foremen stand in ideological and political domination of the workforce because of their monopoly of knowledge of the technical processes and the subordination of their roles to the exigencies of capital, nor Carchedi's stipulation that tasks fall into the discrete functions of either capital or labour are borne out.

It is not necessary to argue that the significance of the situation at Browns rests upon it being typical or proto-typical - in fact this is clearly not the case today.

The situation was one where the function of capital performed by foremen was minimal because of a combination of factors – the payment system, trade union strength and managerial weakness. This had two particular consequences. It caused a re-articulation of managerial authority at a higher level and, in part, increased the collective worker function performed by foremen, albeit unofficially. The study shows, however, that even where the function of capital is performed only minimally, foremen continued to display a separate and distinct consciousness from that of the shopfloor. This should be even more the case elsewhere where the devaluation of foremen within the management function is not so great and workers' organisation is not so strong. In consequence, their attraction to the workers' pole will be less likely.

NOTES

1. A fuller treatment of approaches to class theory and the position of the new middle class within them is given in Carter (1985).

2. Of theorists emphasising the crucial importance of non-working class employees, it is Poulantzas (1975) whose influence has been most widespread. Ironically, Poulantzas gives theoretical 'Marxist' backing to the commonsense, everyday equation of white collar with middle class.

3. 'Browns Ltd' is a pseudonym. The name of the original company has not been used for two reasons. Firstly, some of the information was taken from confidential documents discovered by workers during an occupation to save the factory from closure. More importantly, many people talked to me during the period of the study, some of whom were anxious not to be identified in any work that resulted from the research.

4. These figures are taken from Company Reports. Much of the following section is taken from reports by Labour Research commissioned by the shop stewards committee and internal company documents.

5. Directors' minutes listed forty-six senior members of staff leaving the employment of Green Engineering Group between 1972 and 1976, four of these departures were from Browns. In addition, there were transfers, promotions and demotions.

6. Their salaries and terms of employment, in fact, varied. Some foremen were monthly paid staff, receiving slightly higher salaries than other foremen. The rest were weekly paid staff who, unlike the monthly paid staff, received overtime payments which normally more than made up for their lower salaries.

7. The knit-test foreman was particularly hostile towards these 'management men'.

8. It was not uncommon for some workers to clock-in at 7.30 a.m. on a Saturday, immediately leave the factory and only return to clock-out at 12.30 p.m.

9. For the classic discussion of indulgency patterns, see Alvin W. Gouldner (1954, pp.45-56).

10. According to F. W. Taylor there were two forms of soldiering. The first type springs from 'the natural instinct and tendency of men to take it easy, which may be called natural soldiering'. This contrasts with the second type which stems from 'more intricate second thought and reasoning, which may be called systematic soldiering' (Taylor, 1947, p.19).

11. Records of the group's formation are missing from the Divisional Office, having been destroyed in a flood.

12. The delivery time for machines was nine months. Minutes of the directors' meeting (27 January 1977) stated that there were over £7.5 million of machines on order in December 1976, compared with £8.1 million a year earlier.

13. Private letters discovered by the shop stewards during the occupation.

14. Minutes of directors' meeting 27 January, 1977. For a criticism of the arbitrary nature of work and time study see Cliff (1970) and Grant (1983).

15. This term was adopted by the foremen to describe those workers thought likely to damage machinery inside the factory. At one stage this possibility was very real: as the occupation began there was a strong feeling amongst some of the workers that even if the occupation failed and they lost their jobs, they would make sure that if they could not operate 'their' machines again - machines which they had operated for, in some cases, twenty to thirty years - nobody else would.

16. The AUEW foreman (foreman of the knit-test section) was asked very pointedly by the Works Manager why he was there.

17. The situation was eventually resolved by promoting the labourer to a semi-skilled hardener and recruiting a new labourer. The solution was made more difficult by the fact that the Manufacturing Director had first to get permission from his Board to recruit the additional labourer.

18. The stores were notorious for not having spare parts. The knit-test foreman was frequently able to locate the needed parts, an unofficial but important role. This role also ensured contact with managers of other firms, which ensured him a job as an independent engineer after he left Browns.

Chapter Three

CLASS RELATIONS, DIVERSITY AND LOCATION - TECHNICAL
WORKERS

Chris Smith

INTRODUCTION

This chapter offers an insight into the work and social
relations of a variety of technical workers and is drawn from
research conducted in the late 1970s at a British Aerospace,
Aircraft Group factory in Bristol.[1] Its main concern is to
explore the importance of the craft association between most
middle range technical and skilled manual workers. It
examines the threats to this craft tradition posed by the
growth of indirect, college-based training for higher
technical occupations, technological change and the growing
trend towards separating design from production via a spacial
division of labour (Massey, 1984; Child, 1984; Smith, 1984).
It is argued that as the post-war period experienced a
significant increase in all technical occupations, with most
of these concentrated in large engineering establishments,
there has occurred a formalisation in the hierarchy of
technical work, a major attack on conditions of technical
workers, and a polarisation in relations within and between
technical occupations.

The views expressed by the following three workers
contain many of the elements that make up the structural
complexity of technical workers' work and class experience.

> Do I regard myself as middle class or working class? It
> depends on what you mean by middle class, what is middle
> class? Is it high working class, a bit above the
> average worker. Or is middle class someone who owns a
> factory or owns a business? I don't know! (Vic Sage,
> Electrical Planning Engineer, British Aerospace,
> Filton)

> I think (class position) will vary from plant to plant
> and a lot has to do with peoples' experience and what
> sort of policies they have pursued. I don't think there
> is anything inevitable about their class position.

TASS's attitude, as defined by people like Jim Mortimer,[2] in evidence we submitted to the Donovan Commission (was) that TASS members were basically the higher manual workers, the skilled men who were creamed off into the drawing offices and technical departments, but had nevertheless started on the shop floor, served an apprenticeship, (had) fathers' (who) were working class people and lived in working class surroundings. We were the higher levels of the working class. And I think there was a lot in that. Obviously the situation in a firm like Parsons is changing because the high level of technology (means) a lot of people come in from university . . . The social composition is changing to that degree, although a lot of the graduates will have fathers who come from a working class tradition. (Terry Rogers, Draughtsman and TASS activist, C. A. Parsons, Newcastle-upon-Tyne)

I think there are residual attitudes within technical staff. For instance, some of the people I know have been managers in the past, and they've had to re-think their whole attitude towards life - being workers rather than managers. Its been forced on them, it didn't arise as an abstract thing. It meant in their day to day working their wages were being held back, (they didn't correspond) to their skills, knowledge and experience, therefore they want more money. The same as craftsmen do, exactly the same as the Leyland toolroom dispute. (Bob Murdock, Designer and TASS activist, C. A. Parsons, Newcastle-upon-Tyne)[3]

These quotations direct attention to the ambiguity of class position, the craft links with skilled manual workers and the growing diversity and differentation within technical work as graduates move into the design offices and production engineering areas. The coexistence of groups with different training backgrounds, although perhaps common class origins, is further complicated by the transformation of small ex-owners, managers and those who have been the self employed into 'workers'. I encountered pockets of individuals in most departments who were ex-owners or managers of sub-contract drawing offices, now working within non-supervisory functions. The rundown in work following the ending of Concorde left Filton with an abundance of managers and supervisors who were often faced with the prospect of either going 'back on the board' or taking redundancy. This is not a feature peculiar to Filton or aerospace and indicates the function of the technical areas as a 'dustbin' for managements' downwardly mobile and conversely the significance of technical areas as a starting point for managerial careers (something noted by historians of technical occupations see

Read (1980); Melling (1982). Hetrogeneity characterised the technical offices I investigated, but there was also a core of established employees that were neither moving up, out or down, but standing still in career terms.

What does occupational diversity and complexity at the level of the technical department within the firm have to do with the class position of technical workers? It may complicate class identity and consciousness, but does it effect the determination of class position? I think it does and as work is the major site of class struggle and action it is necessary to relate the structure of class at this level to wider determinations. The debate about the 'new middle class' is generally pitched at a high level of abstraction where contextual, historical or national variations in the class structure and balance of class forces, are suppressed in favour of more general statement on who fitted in where. Despite a more rigorous and complex analysis of class structure in the advanced capitalist economies, this lack of engagement with historical class structure, actually produced rather crude and simplistic differentiations between productive/unproductive, dominant/subordinate and mental/manual fractions; and polarisations within wage labour towards either manual labour (the working class) or towards the bourgeoisie.

Although for the most part the actual workplace has been absent from class analysis at this level, there have nevertheless been powerful assumptions built into new middle class theories about relations of production within the workplace. These concern (i) the pattern of authority; (ii) the issue of autonomy; (iii) the relationship between new middle class labour and manual workers; and (iv) the existence of a rigid mental/manual split between the two classes. These assumptions, even though they are not usually historically or empirically analysed, are the key to the apparent coherence of much new middle class writing. It is assumed that authority will be present in certain functions, technical labour for example, when in fact the structure of authority relations will vary from country to country, and from one industrial sector to another. It is assumed that certain jobs are universally autonomous. Autonomy, according to Wright (1978), Johnson (1982) and other structural Marxists, is a crucial ingredient of new middle class jobs. But again, the limits of this job autonomy will vary by occupation, industry and country, as will its meaning. A further assumption concerns the degree of control exercised by new middle class workers over the technical division of labour or other workers' labour power. For new working class theorists the enlarged appetite for "control" created by new process industries and bestowed upon the technical and manual workers in those industries, promoted a new militancy. Unlike wage militancy – mere economism – the 'new working class' was supposed to be primarily concerned with extending and maintaining 'control' <u>over</u> production with capital's opposition to 'encroaching control' providing the dynamic to generate a higher form of class struggle than in early periods. For new middle class theorists control invariably means control <u>of</u> manual workers through access to authority, monopolisation of engineering knowledge or place within mental labour. Again these assumptions are contentious, especially in relation to technical labour in Britain where the character of the craft tradition places a premium on <u>cooperation</u> across the collar divide. Finally, the notion of mental labour or the belief that the conceptualisation of work is restricted to certain white collar occupations, is based on the belief that production 'knowledge' is housed in a single store, rather than a series of formal and informal stores in which there is a differential access to the formal information process. Braverman's (1974) analysis of intermediate occupations emphasises their power in the formal division of labour and flow of information, but underplays the interplay between different groups of workers and the significance of the informal system. It is part of my purpose in this chapter to examine empirically these sets of assumptions as they apply to technical workers in British engineering.

My approach to the class position of British technical workers emphasises the enormous importance of the craft tradition for cementing a strong bond between manual and qualified white collar workers. I reject the idea of technical workers belonging to a "new middle class". Through their status as wage labourers, producers of surplus value, craft and historical links with the wider labour movement, they have actively participated in the British working class.

Having said this however, it is clear from the comments that opened this section that concentrating on functional work relations does not reveal the full picture of the social environment occupied by technical workers. The technical department, more so than the shopfloor is the starting point for certain managerial careers and the respository of those who have come back into wage labour from self-employment or petty ownership positions. It therefore contains historical 'traces' of different class ideologies and aspirations for future managerial positions (Gramsci 1957, p.59). Poulantzas (1978, p.326) grasped something of this ambiguity when he said technicians 'retain their sense of being "those in charge" '. I however see this ambiguity as flowing out of the character of the technical department rather than simply the social interaction between rank and file technical and manual workers. To Poulantzas, Carchedi and other structural Marxists these contextual details are irrelevant to the objective determination of class based on imputed functional relations. While I acknowledge the centrality of class determination and utilise functional analyses of occupations, I also stress the importance of craft in locating the 'form of association' between white collar and manual workers. Within non-manual waged labour there are two 'forms of association', what I call the qualitative and the quantitative. Technical workers generally, unlike foremen and ratefixers have a qualitative form of association with manual workers in that they are not geared into monitoring and pacing those workers, and relate to them via the skill, ability and craft they bring to their work. They are linked through the quality of the product. What I call quasi-technical workers by contrast are engaged in the direct exploitation of productive labour, and have a quantitative form of association with manual workers.

The nature and product of an industry affects the structural location of technical workers in many ways. For example, in the aerospace industry there has always existed a highly 'qualified' white collar and manual labour force. In certain sectors, e.g. guided weapons and electronic computers, technical staff out-number manual workers. In others e.g. food, drink and tobacco, construction and textiles, technical staff are a tiny fraction of the overall workforce and in such situations they are more likely to be incorporated into management or supervisory functions and possess an elitist attitude towards manual workers. If they are a minority, it will be less important for manual workers to establish joint trade union associations for regular or one-off industrial activity. Technical staff will be under less pressure from manual workers as the latter will feel strong enough to act on their own and the former may not have cause to resort to collective struggle when career opportunities are more open. In companies where technical staff are more engaged with process engineering, producing a simple product, they may well constitute more of a production control function. Where technical workers are not unionised, where they form an elite or fraction of the workforce located within a quantitative or monitoring position, their relations with managers and other workers will be qualititatively different than where they form a sizeable bloc of waged labour.

Notwithstanding these qualifications it is important to point out that most technical staff are located in large manufacturing units. TASS membership reflects this concentration. In 1973 53 per cent of the 114,000 members were located in 46 companies. By 1982, there were 60 per cent in under 60 companies. In the South West, of the just under 10,000 members over 50 per cent worked in just three corporations - Rolls Royce, BAe, and Westland Helicopters. 65 per cent were found in ten companies and the remaining 35 per cent were spread across 150 small and medium sized companies. The technical workers I discuss in this chapter are illustrative of those within a large technologically orientated sector and a company with a paternalist background and recent professional, bureaucratic structure. I also draw off information from interviews with those from other large companies – Lucas Aerospace, Rolls Royce and C. A. Parsons – all of which tend to support the broad characteristics described here.

THE GENESIS OF BRITISH TECHNICAL OCCUPATIONS

The early development of technical occupations in Britain is under-researched, but it is apparent that change was uneven and incremental rather than universal and systemic. Technical education began to grow from the mid-1880's, and the creation of the new science-based industries in electrical and gas supply increasingly meant that apprenticeships, on-the-job training or the education of a few individual managers could no longer produce the knowledge base needed for production in those industries (More 1980, pp.200-203). Manual workers gained training in these industries, but it was technical staff who were the main beneficiaries, although only a minority of employers insisted on their technical staff attending colleges and only a minority of these sat exams. The apprenticeship system remained the dominant and universal mode of training.

During the period 1880-1920 rate fixing, progress chasing, inspection and planning engineering all appeared as distinct functions and tasks. Estimators, calculators and time control clerks also appeared and can trace their origins back to duties previously performed by foremen. It was only within the large firms that distinct occupations were practised, estimating, for example, was frequently combined with planning, rate fixing and other commercial functions in all but the big companies. Within production engineering, the foreman and not the craftsmen lost out with the development of the above occupations (Melling, 1983). Some tasks that had embodied a direct or political command function became 'purely technical'. However, quasi-technical jobs like production control and rate fixing retain attachments to shopfloor supervision, whereas established technical function like, estimating, draughting and design relate to manual work with more autonomy from managerial control structures.

Draughtsmen, who were the archetypal British 'technical worker' have a longer history of independence from foremen and craftsmen going back in engineering to the 1850s (Mortimer 1960; Booker 1963; Read, 1980). In construction their links with art, architecture and architects make the use of the term 'draughtsmen' difficult to sustain without considerable qualification to the actual meaning of the occupational category in engineering sectors (Bowley 1966). According to Read, the term 'draughtsmen' in shipbuilding originated with the practice of preparing a 'draught plan' from wooden models of ships hulls prepared by patternmakers and draughtsmen for use in contract tendering. In other words the occupation initially arose for the purposes of securing orders from clients not as a managerial control practice in relation to the manual labour process. The desire to see the end from the beginning, the increasing complexity 'of modern vessels' and the need for a quicker and larger return on fixed capital all stimulated the later expansion of indirect labour (Read, 1980, p.83). This economic logic while first applied to draughtsmen, remains a central dynamic behind the development of other technical occupations. Both the scale of production and technical complexity of products and production tend to accompany or follow this pattern. Incentive schemes, new machinery and more timed work increased control over manual workers, while the transfer of certain planning, processing and progressing operations helped expand and change the nature of the drawing office.

Draughting did not develop homogeneously, as standardisation of practices and the desire to cheapen overheads created an internal differentiation within the drawing office between design draughtsmen, detail draughtsmen and copyists or tracers - the latter rapidly becoming an exclusively female occupation. This formal separation of design and production - drawing office and workshop - first occurred in railway workshops and shipyards and then spread to other engineering sectors, primarily for the economic reason of cheapening production costs, but also for aim of increased managerial control over the production process as a whole. It was only in the larger firms that draughtsmen were separated in a department away from the shopfloor, whereas in Germany draughtsmen 'enjoyed privileges which elevated them above the worker (and) worked in drafting rooms that were separated from the workshop' (Kocka 1980, p.117).

Those writers who interpret these developments as signifying the subordination of manual workers to technical, scientific or generic 'mental' labour, ignore the continued interaction between craftsmen, draughtsmen and the newer technical occupations. Read notes that the shipwright performed operations that were a 'crucial check on the accuracy of (draughtsmen's) plans' (1980, p.83). I later highlight the continuity of this cooperation.

Along a different axis, writers, like Poulantzas and Gorz (1977) have also viewed these changes as representing the political subordination of craftsmen to office workers. They assume that technical staff directly control the production process or product of manual workers. I argue that technical workers create drawings, instructions, plans or programmes which are controlled by management, who act as the agents of capital in the production process. The symbolic nature of this division of labour produces dominant and subordinate places and polarisatons between 'works' and 'office' labour, but these conditions coexist with cooperative tendencies based on craft, engineering knowledge, daily interaction and the sharing of many of the universal conditions of waged labour under capitalism. Without examining both features there is a danger of inventing class-based fractions, divisions and oppositions within wage labour and ignoring cooperative or common elements. While the historical balance of forces between classes and the condition of the labour market influences the likely pattern of dominance between these two tendencies, differentiation within technical labour, which I will now discuss, also determines the general form of association between technical workers, manual workers and management.

HOMOGENEITY AND HETEROGENEITY WITHIN TECHNICAL WORK AND ITS SIGNIFICANCE

In the 1960's DATA, the predecessor of TASS recruited from within design and production engineering with ASSET and ASw recruiting scientists and laboratory technicians in research and development. Today differences between design and research and development are less obvious and recruitment between ASTMS and TASS more aggressive and competitive. TASS retains its core membership within its previous stronghold, where typical technical occupations consisted of draughtsmen, designers, tracers, planning engineers, calculators, estimators and 'other technicans however designated whose function is related to design' (DATA, 1963, p.50). In the 1960's these general categories could be subdivided to include perhaps fifty or sixty titles. When, a decade later, TASS issued a list of 'typical posts' held by the membership the number was 468 - 400 of which were of technical nature, the remaining 68 titles consisting of clerical administrative and supervisory positions.

The phenomenal growth in titles reflects the increased complexity of the division of labour within technical work. At Filton, for instance, there are around 100 technical job titles on the company's books which TASS has consolidated into 26 bargaining categories. Similarly, at C. A. Parsons, a power engineering company with a similar density of technical staff to BAe, there are approximately 26 occupations for which TASS has negotiating rights (CIR, 1973, pp.18-26). Draughtsmen remain the largest technical occupation, alongside designers, planning engineers and 'other engineers' of various designations. All large engineering companies have estimators, technical illustrators, authors, metallurgists, computer programmers, NC programmers, systems analysts, and increasingly CAD (Computer Aided Design) draughtsmen and designers.

Technical occupations have developed and divided because of specialisation and technological change. Behind these forces is the concern to cheapen the costs of indirect labour, intensify that labour and increase the speed with which design appears as production. Occupational differentiation represents the major source of diversity within the technical sphere. At Filton, departmental sectionalism founded on this specialisation was quite common, especially between established groups and the newer occupations based on computers. Often the hostilities were based on craft sectarianism, e.g. between designers or draughtsmen towards quasi-technical groups like cost controllers. The transformation of TASS in the 1970s from an exclusive technical craft union, to a more open engineering white collar union reinforced this sectarianism. In addition to this source of division the command structure and the ranking of occupations along an abstract-practical technical continuum created division and differentiation. Further sources of diversity stem from the place occupied by technical workers in the cycle of production, i.e. whether they are located in development, design, planning, production, distribution or financial/commerical areas. Location frequently determines the pattern of interaction between technical groups and the relationship with manual workers and management.

Before describing in more detail the forms of association between different technical groups and manual workers, I will pinpoint the general elements within the work situation of most middle range technical workers. Firstly, the craft character of many technical jobs requires a practical knowledge of machinery and production processes in addition to more 'theoretical' skills. As draughtsmen and planning engineers are preparing the guides, maps and plans for manual workers, some direct experience of manual operations is crucial for established and new technical jobs. The high value attached to craft competence ensured that the shopfloor remained a central source for recruitment into technical areas. This also acted against any stark polarisations between skilled manual and technical workers.

Alongside craft skills, technical workers, despite departmental variations in the style of management, exercise a high degree of individual autonomy on the job. In certain instances it was both impractical and unnecessary for management directly to control their work. Motivation was maintained by self-supervision, a pride in the job, and time deadlines on processes and 'whole jobs' that individuals knew better than either office management or section supervisors. However, despite constantly being told that it was impossible to pin down technical work to definite time limits, a new 'time consciousness' was entering those areas that were moving into contract work for other aerospace companies. In addition the intervention of capital equipment and computers with methods for monitoring output and scheduling the sequencing of tasks had increased the possibility of timing work. 'Working to the clock' is characteristic of contract drawing offices, and its appearance at Filton reflects the international division of labour in the industry as British air-frame manufacturers became sub-contractors to American and European companies. It also demonstrated the increasing use of technical control by management in these areas.

Related to job autonomy was the 'freedom of movement' enjoyed by technical workers who were not screwed down to a particular place or task. The manual workers I interviewed resented this condition above all others, although their perceptions of an unlimited freedom of movement for all technical workers was more fact than fiction. Most needed managerial permission to leave the office, liaison was increasingly by telephone and the computerisation of links between design and production meant many intermediate technical workers sat at VDUs (Visual Display Units) for long periods, paid fewer visits to other workers and relied on information from a computer-terminal more than the technical library or colleagues in other departments.

Autonomy and relative freedom of information exchange and movement are important components of the generally high degree of job satisfaction amongst technical workers. Such autonomy was not a permanent feature however. In those areas where computerisation was assisting the transformaton of the pace, pattern and organisation of work, workers spoke of the mental stress, boredom and frustration of performing progressively fragmented sets of tasks.

A final point about the work situation of technical workers, and one emphasized by Weberian writers, is that, like clerks, draughtsmen, planning engineers and designers work in offices that are clean, quiet and unadulterated by the smell, noise or architecture of a machine shop or toolroom. In the technical offices I studied there were no uniforms, graded overalls or other facets of a shopfloor environment. Staff wore collar and tie, jackets and trousers, with only the occasional pair of jeans or sweatshirt on a generally younger technician. All these characteristics reinforce the space for individuality afforded by the office, which distinguishes, in an immediate and very striking way, 'staff' from 'works' employees. But, there are also differences between clerical and technical offices. The drawing board, VDU, computer terminals, pieces of automatic drawing equipment and increasingly CAD room, occupy space in technical offices. At Filton, rows upon rows of drawing boards stood in the open planned Engineering

Design Organisation and this produced a strong image of men and machines together, unlike the situation in the clerical departments which were smaller, and where people seemed to dominate compact pieces of equipment like telephones and the occasional VDU. The encroachment of computer equipment may be standardising the appearance of the two offices but CAD equiment is tending to transform sections of the drawing office into a 'laboratory', while in clerical areas this may not be the case (Baldry and Connolly, 1984).

These features of the work situation of middle range technical workers are not inherently stable. In order to get beyond these impressions and generalisations, I will now document more specifically the main forms of association between technical workers and others as they existed at Filton before outlining some of the threats and challenges to these social relations.

The Work and Social Relation of Some Technical Occupations

Marginal Technical Jobs   By marginal or quasi-technical jobs I mean those that are not recognised by established technical groups, management or manual workers as performing technical work.   To be included in their number at Filton were production controllers, progress chasers and ratefixers. Those in these groups were required to liase with shopfloor management and groups of technical workers, but by training, social identity and the content of their work they did not perform strictly technical functions.   I focus here on production controllers.

Production controllers were located within the technical offices adjacent to the machine shop, alongside jig and tool draughtsmen, planning engineers and NC part programmers. The office was divided between those engaged in long term forecasting of work, and others involved with daily, weekly or monthly planning and scheduling of work for the machine shop.   It was organised by APEX the major clerical union on site, but amongst those I interviewed, especially in the forecasting section, there was a widespread belief that they were carrying out technical duties and should be regraded into a technical area by the company.

Production controllers used to be referred to as 'progress chasers' but within Filton the latter function was performed by a group called 'pointsmen' who were based on the shop floor and logged the progress of work through the machine shop. Production controllers were part of the process of 'scientifically' or systematically organising shopfloor loading and forecasting. The function appeared with the reorganisation of engineering prior to the First World War. Those employed on it were performing operations previously the preserve of foremen and there continued to be a definite degree of conflict between the two groups, a battle between 'custom and practice', 'common sense' and the methodical, bureaucratic procedures of shop loading. Production controllers were dependent upon the authority of foremen to legimate their work, so the relationship was not straightforward. Computerisation threatened to eliminate a lot of work in production control, dividing and transferring tasks between planners, shop supervision and shopfloor operatives. Competition from these areas, the lack of an established identity and productive status meant that production controllers were increasingly emphasising the technical 'skills', which accompanied the greater use of computers, and simultaneously their role in improving shopfloor productivity. Of these two, the latter dominated their thinking, which meant a different perspective and relationship to manual workers than that encountered in established technical areas.

Unlike the direct relations between draughtsmen and toolmakers discussed later, those in the PCU (Production Control Unit) had a semi-supervisory hold over the operators. The operator was not obliged directly to do as required by the controller, but he knew the latter could always get the foreman to lend authority to his decision. There was no sense of craft equality because the relationship was not concerned with technical, craft difficulties in producing the job, but the pacing and scheduling of the work. One production controller I interviewed, Richard Grass had no technical knowledge of machining, was a chemistry graduate and uninterested in technical problems related to the job. His primary concern was with production. The relations between technical and manual workers in other areas demanded the technical worker negotiated his own position, and although this often meant adopting managerial skills in 'dealing with the shop floor', the absence of authority was not considered an obstacle or difficulty. For the PCU, however, this was not the case. Richard Grass:

> Its a very awkward job, production control or project control because you very rarely have direct authority over anybody but you've got to get people to do things that you want them to do. How you do that varies depending on the individual you're dealing with. Sometimes you jump up and down at them, and sometimes you ask nicely, and sometimes you go and find the boss . . . Because I've got freedom of movement and I see so many people, I can almost invariably find someone to put the pressure on if I need to. People put pressure on me too occasionally as well.

The real gulf between these quasi-technical jobs and technical occupations proper is demonstrated by this quotation. All the advantages Richard Grass has over the manual workers - freedom of movement, alliances with management, meeting a larger number of people - are used <u>against</u> the manual worker. The assorted control strategies for <u>dealing with</u> the operator are designed to ensure the continuation of production.

The normal routines, planning schedules and longer term forecasts were 'upset by a dispute on the shopfloor'. Disputes however were part of the 'contingency planning' of those in the PCU. Richard Grass compared the problems created by disputes in a machine shop with other types of production:

> If your shop's on strike you don't get any production but if one small section of the shop went on strike you might find that the rest could work. It doesn't give you such a problem as, say, on an assembly line. With an assembly line you get a lot of boredom so they tend to strike anyway, it's an awkward problem. In process engineering your greatest trouble is trying to schedule your type of runs because you may not be able to follow one process with another without a major clean down.

The others in the PCU were equally against strikes because of the way it increased their work load. Their identity with management appeared to be common sense. Manual unions were seen as 'too powerful' by constantly interfering with managerial authority. The case of sub-contract bans illustrates this. As far as the production controllers were concerned, the faster the work flowed through the shop floor the better. If there was a bottleneck at any juncture, then the work should be sent off the shop floor to ease the flow of work. They believed that the greater the volume of work through the shop, the more competitive the machine shop became and the more orders it could secure. A subcontract ban not only increased their own work load considerably, it also represented a challenge to this rationale for expanding production, an afront to the logic of continuous production. Fred Hoyle, a controller in his early fifties, told me:

> Their idea [i.e. the manual unions] is that they want to see work on this shop, and <u>we</u> tell them, there's work on this shop but <u>we</u> say if they increase their production flow through the shop, there's a greater chance that they will get more work back into the shop than what they would gain by being dogmatic and stopping sub-contract and getting behind on the programme. Customers are not going to repeat orders as far as I can see.

Here we can see the conflicting ideologies that clearly

reflect a management and trade union divide. Trade union principles and industrial tactics, informed by the experience of three waves of redundancies following the ending of Concorde production, are transformed into 'dogma'; the rationality of labour is really 'irrational' and attempts to maintain work at Filton are only 'ways of losing customers'. Richard Grass summed up the different logics with the standard bourgeois addage:

> Management are thinking long term and the workers are thinking short term, that's where the real stumbling block comes.

The inherent tendency towards over-production within capitalist production always means severe crisis for unfettered production. The ideology of production engineering did not recognise the dominant corporate rationally within industry, that of finance capital, where profitability, market share, return on capital, shape economic judgement (Spybey, 1984). Neither did it comprehend the importance of national political values for shaping the aerospace sector in particular.

The PCU was strategically placed to pass on information to staff and shop floor unions about future workloads. While the majority were unionised by APEX, there was a general belief that the union was ineffectual and their wages, job status and conditions could not be changed. An air of apathy and powerlessness pervaded the office. Instead of this information enhancing their trade union consciousness, it only backed up their prejudices against the 'short sighted acton by shop floor unions'. This was a prejudice their place in production predisposed them towards. They were concerned with quantifying the work of the shop floor machinists, while other technical workers were interested only in the quality of the product produced and the degree of craftsmanship machinists brought to the job. Those in the PCU had no direct authority over manual workers but there were definite aspirations in that direction and their identity as workers was bound up with a strong association with shop floor supervision.

By embracing the ideology of production, production controllers, like ratefixers, were clearly trying to establish their place in the control of labour to compensate for their marginality, lack of skill and real authority over manual workers. I will now demonstrate, how different was the social identity, work relations and perceptions of those groups in established technical positions.

Established Technical Occupations

My treatment of occupations under this category, draughtsmen, planning

engineers, and programmers - is concerned with the social
identity and social relations within which these jobs exist.
Unlike marginal positions these jobs require a technical
training, are universally regarded as technical, not clerical
or supervisory, and involve the conceptualisation, in various
forms, of the future production of physical commodities.
Technical workers do not directly produce the object, they
design it, draw it, and plan its production and distribution
requirements. Their involvement with 'conceptualisation',
the issuing of instructions and information of other workers,
their physical separation from the manual workers'
environment and product, have been read by structural
Marxists as signifying a class gulf between these two
categories of labour. Here I want to show that such a
reading is too simplistic as it reduces the complexity and
variety in the 'forms of association' between the two groups
to a single relationship of domination and subordination,
which is then considered in social class terms. Poulantzas's
economic, political and ideological levels all possess the
weight of class determination, i.e. while technical workers
are workers via their production of surplus value (economic)
and non-supervisory location (political), at the ideological
level their involvement in conceptualisation, makes them, for
Poulantzas, a fraction of the new middle class. On the view
taken here, by constrast, it is held that whereas production
controllers perform a <u>quantitative</u>, monitoring and ultimately
managerial role, established middle range technical workers
have a <u>qualitative</u> craft form of association with manual
workers which makes them act in a cooperative way towards
manual workers. They are not concerned with monitoring the
intensity of manual labour, they do not control that labour,
but are rather chiefly concerned with the craft aim of
ensuring the quality of the finished product. The pace and
efficiency of production are secondary to the quality of
work. There is also a craft link through a common
apprenticeship and/or transfer from the tool room or machine
shop into the drawing office.

A young draughtsman, who had been at Filton since 1970,
confirmed how the identity of technical staff had this strong
craft image:

> I still think really you're a craftsman . . . One hears
> of 'technician' but I more or less ignore that fact ...
> if people ask me what my job is I say a draughtsman.
> People can readily identify you as a draughtsmen. I
> believe it is a craft, yes . . . I did two years in the
> machine shop which was just going round from machine to
> machine learning the various things about the machines
> and learning what various turning operations do and what
> they produce.

This craft background and concern for quality persisted against a background of more timed, contract work across all the technical areas at Filton, as this draughtsman revealed:

> I take pride in my work, we all do out here, we don't want it to come back with a scrapped job. I don't worry about time because I always put the job first. Sod the time, that job has got to be right when it leaves my board.

While this qualititative form of association brings the two groups together, the content and type of instructions flowing from the office onto the shop floor also shapes the attitudes of technical staff. At Filton draughtsmen and others felt they had to provide the shopfloor with more detailed information and basic instructions than was previously considered necessary. This was universally interpreted as signifying the demise of the old style skilled machinists or toolmaker.

In a sense, draughtsmen acted as the craft memory for manual work, and this affected their evaluation of existing manual workers. To test the claims of draughtsmen, I examined drawings from the 1950's and found that they tended to be larger and the standard instructions were 'machine where necessary' not, as in later drawings, 'machine where shown'. The large number of small, detail drawings of the later period, appeared to confirm the draughtmen's judgement that foreman and skilled workers today had less initiative and control over their work relative to early period. But this is only one interpretation. The designer, who took me through the drawings argued that the internationalisation of airframe production had standardised design and drawing methods, therefore leading to more detail drawing with a greater amount of instructions. In addition, the increased interchangabily of parts had spread the need for common drawing methods and the greater concern for safety had created the need for detailed and reliable records. Many draughtsmen acknowledged these changes and the revolutionary impact of Concorde on the organisation of both technical and manual work corrected any tendency to denigrate modern craftsmen out of hand. But perhaps an inevitable feature of the division of labour between the two groups was for draughtsmen to be very aware of changes in the work of toolmakers or machinists, and to see these changes primarily through their own work environment, rather than in relation to wider, technical and international changes in the division of labour.

The relationship and attitudes between planning engineers and machine shop operators were similar to those described for draughtsmen. As in the drawing office, there had been an increasing volume of instructions passed on to the operators and while the planners did not actually say shop floor operators had lost their skills, they considered that most of the skilled craftsmen had left the machine shop. Peter Win, a senior planner, told me a now familiar tale:

> Go back quite a few years and the type of operator you had on the shop floor then, you could very briefly instruct as to what he's got to do and he would look at the drawing and produce the job with less written instructions. But the type of operator that's coming along now, you've got to spell it out a lot more than in the past . . . As far as I'm concerned an operator should remove the burrs off every component he produces, but unless you write it down, they don't do it and then it takes more time in the long run.

All but one planner had worked on the shop floor, and the average age in the office was about fifty. So it was not surprising that this concern with declining skills should be emphasized. Young planners who had entered the office from the shop floor or from another company were unable to make these comparisons. Paul Hart had only been in the office six months and had previously worked as a setter in a medium sized engineering plant at Bath. Having recent experience of the shop floor he was aware of the way staff view manual workers. To him it was the irresponsible machinists who 'let the side down' and fostered or encouraged feelings of animosity by reducing the sense of craft that should, in his view, bind the skilled machinist and technical worker:

> I would say that the majority of people in this office consider shop floor workers on average pretty thick – for staying on the shop floor. When I was on the shop floor you were looked down upon to a certain degree, because we were the people who actually got our hands dirty and produced the final goods . . . It's the people that are idiots that let the others down. Obviously there are a lot of very good machinists, but its the ones that aren't so good that let the side down.

The number of indentured operators had declined and with the expansion in NC machinists the apprenticed man was in a minority. Peter Win again:

> Over the last ten years the best part of the operators on the shop floor have gradually moved on. Some of them have come off the shop floor and gone into staff jobs, others have left, redundancies and that, and you've just lost the best operators. Plus we've less apprentices coming in and those that do come in are not content to stay on the shop floor and want to move into the

technical side. So the skilled craftsman on the shopfloor is gradually diminishing, fading out. You're ending up with, not exactly semi-skilled, but not the same skill that there used to be.

Unlike the PCU the planners did not use the authority of shop supervision to enforce their instructions. The main point of contact with the shop floor was, nevertheless, through the foreman and it was foremen and not other planning engineers or technical staff, that the planners used as reference group on wage bargaining. Peter Win drew a direct parallel between their relationship with manual workers and the position of foremen:

> The foreman is in charge of the men on the machine shop . . . We are on the same sort of level where we are instructing an operator to do something and we're telling him, almost, in a sense, how to do it. Now we're on vitually the same level as the foreman, but we haven't got the same supervisor's badge. You know, we can't go out and tell an operator he's 'got to do this'. You've got to do that through the foreman, although we do tell him on paper this is the way he should do it. You could say we're on par with the foreman.

The act of instructing operators confers on the planner a symbolic authority, although as Peter Win says, they have no direct power to tell operators what to do. The gap between the generation of the instruction and the making of the product, between planning and production proper, allows both planners and operators to assert the importance of their labour to the process of production. Although the older planners bemoaned the loss of craft skill and pride on the shop floor, there is always a disjuncture between what is written on a planner's schedule and what is eventually produced. The mental/manual divide was real enough to Peter Win and the productive/unproductive divide shaped the operator's assessment of the contribution of the planner to production.

I interviewed three NC operators, and they were unanimous in claiming their work not only to be productive but more responsible. Andy Grey, an operator who had worked at BAe. for seven years:

> You're more responsible. If I make a miscalculation on paper that can be altered or it can be seen to be wrong easily enough. But if I make a miscalculation on the job then the job's scrapped. And you might be on the last cut of a massive job and you put the wrong cutter in. In the final analysis you're responsible.

Peter Win agreed with this operators assessment of their own work, but was also clear on the strains that the operator does not see.

> If you make a mistake, you've got a rubber you can correct it, if an operator makes a mistake then its too late. But in trying to make sure that you write it down correctly, because you're telling someone, it becomes more mental work than practical work and this in itself is quite hard . . . I don't actually produce something at the end of the day, but I put down enough instructions to produce the spark . . . It may seem very nice to sit down most the day, but when you get a man that comes in off the shop floor and becomes a planning engineer he realises just how wrong his first impressions were.

The changes in the machine shop had been witnessed by most of the planners. They were consequently acutely aware of the decline in the number of time-served conventional operators and the rise in the number of semi-skilled NC operators. To these planners there had been a loss in craftsmanship and they now had to give instructions that would have been an insult to the earlier generation of machinists. This sense of lost craft was very real and, as with the draughtsmen, this reflects their interpretation of change through the own working practices. It is a feature of the qualitative form of association between an established technical occupation, where change has been minor, and a manual occupation where change had been significant. But, as I will later show, planning engineers, themselves were also the subject of change.

Braverman's treatment of NC is a useful starting point for examining programming because it represents an interpretation of the objective socialisation of the division of labour my research would seek to qualify. For Braverman, NC machine tools represented Taylorism in action as skilled machinists - jig borers, fitters, turners etc - were deprived of the conceptual part of their labour which was objectified in a new category of labour located in a technical office removed from the shop floor and within management's sphere of interest. The formerly skilled positions, which embodied in an organic form the conceptual and operational elements of machinery are deskilled and craft unity, pride, identity and control are replaced by dissassociation and the subordination of manual functions to bureaucratic, hierarchical control relations established between operations and programmers. At a universal level this general process produces a new class of 'intermediate employees' located along a continuum with working class or capitalist polarisations at each extreme. NC part programmers and planners, as part of this new class are located in working class polarisation but are nevertheless not working class themselves.

The introduction of NC machine tools was designed to increase managerial control over the machine shop (Noble 1978). While recognising the very real movement of craft skill off the shopfloor, I want to show here that there persists a strong relationship between part programmers and operators. This not only parallels relations between draughtsmen and craftsmen, but is surprising given the polarisation one would expect from Braverman's analysis. Jones (1983) rejecting Braverman's theoretical project and questioning his empirical sources, supports a contingency analysis where the impact of NC on skill relations will be influenced by the product market, labour market, organisational structure and trade union policy within an enterprise. Essentialist arguments about capitalism possessing a built-in 'tendency to deskill because of laws of capitalist exploitation and accumulation' are strongly rejected by Jones (1983, p.198). I support Jones's evidence on the composite nature of NC part programmers' skills, as my study noted the importance of metal cutting experience and knowledge, and the lack of a rigid division between the two areas, but I support Noble's explanation of the capitalist logic behind the development of NC. My main purpose in this section is to examine part programmers' perceptions of manual workers.

Part programming especially in the aerospace industry was considered to be a highly technical job by management, manual workers and other technical groups. The department at Filton, unlike other middle range technical areas had more people with engineering qualifications and only a quarter had been recruited off the shop floor. It was common in estimating, planning and many draughting departments for over half of the office to have entered via a skilled shopfloor position. The original department established in the mid 1960's consisted of a graduate, a jig and tool draughtsman and machine shop planning engineer. Draughtsmen and planners, together with engineering graduates, fed the expansion of NC part-programmers before formal training for the occupation. Management at BAe still preferred to recruit people from other technical departments rather than go outside and this meant taking NC setter–operators off the shop floor. The departmental manager claimed that the ideal programmer should possess ten years machine shop experience, five years planning, two years in jig and tool draughting, and be about 25 years old. Practical machining experience and a knowledge of technical departments closely allied to the machine shop continued to be emphasized as a central element of the job. Those who had transferred from the shop floor spent six months each in planning and jig and tool – 'learning the system' – and then twelve months obtaining basic programming skills. Compared with shop floor entrants in other technical departments the length of training was considerably greater.

The programmers had frequent interaction with foremen and NC operators, especially on tape 'try outs' before production proper. All the programmers got satisfaction from going out onto the shop floor and seeing a machined wing section they had written the programme for. Apart from the real need to check the job for future improvements, there was also a desire to see the results of their 'abstract' labour, which may have taken several months, realised in a material form. This engagement with a product was summed up by a programmer who said "we're the next thing to cutting the material, you can't get closer than that". Whereas designers I interviewed boasted of not being wrapped up in the mechanics of drawing, programmers like draughtsmen, did not build conceptual barriers between themselves and operators but emphasized the importance of 'mental' and 'manual' aspects of both functions. John Greeson, a senior programmer told me:

> John:
> I don't see why you should look down on anyone who works with their hands.
> Chris:
> Do you think the label 'mental labour' fits your work?
> John:
> No I don't. At a very naive level it might fit. But you've got to have the whole broad level of engineering experience. To bring the whole set of skills and knowledge together.

The formal flow of information, from programmer to operator, disguises the operators' involvement in checking programmes and plans before production and in manually operating machines when a tape breaks. However, programmers had 'open access' to the shop floor and usually the final say in the running of a programme. While programmers and operators I interviewed agreed that each side generally accepted the others' advice, one programmer remembered an incident when he as an NC operator had scrapped a job after he failed to convince a programmer of the incorrect sequencing of his programme. The operator had his judgement backed up by other operators who agreed with his assessment of the incorrect planning sequence, but all this failed to challenge the authority of the programmer.

The hostility around the machine shop was between conventional foremen and operators and NC programmers and operators, i.e. on craft and authority divisions, rather than ones structured between manual and office based workers. In the words of the manager of the programming department, conventional foremen felt threatened by NC 'because its a technology they can't understand and control'. Because the operator is following tape instructions, 'as soon as he's in the hands of the tape, he's in the hands of programmer'. Conventional machinists were scathing about the lack of apprenticeship training and apparent simplicity of NC work relative to conventional machining. As one ex-machinist remarked:

> Conventional men think NC is all laid down in black and white [where] you just [have] to follow the instructions laid down and press a button and away you go.

The company policy of recruiting non-engineering workers when NC expanded in the 1960s and 1970s reinforced the animosity between the two groups. Within this debate programmers sided with operators, partly to defend the general interests of NC, but also out of a working experience that demonstrated the variety of NC operations, programming methods and operator performance, against the alleged uniformity and simplicity imposed upon it by those within conventional skill categories.

A NC programmer, who had also worked as an operator, took up the defence of the operator:

> They're looked down on a lot by the conventional operators . . . I've had a lot of arguments with them in that respect. They say, 'you've just got to press a button'. Obviously, its not as easy as that. You can go out there and just press a button and probably turn out a job. But the quality of the work is low. This is where the skill comes into it and separates a good operator from a bad one.

While defending the unrecognised skills of the 'good' NC operator, he also related the ability to use these skills to the different stages of production. When he entered the NC programming department, he brought with him a judgement on the good and bad operators, based on his experience, and tended to allocate workloads accordingly.

> When I first came in here most of the jobs were still in a try-out stage and there were maybe six operators out there who were doing these jobs. [On try-outs] you iron out all the faults with the operator and once the job's going, when most of the Concorde and Boeing jobs got going, you just give them to anybody. Then it becomes pretty boring [for the operator], pretty routine. They're stuck down there doing crossword puzzles against the machine. Not really my scene.

To the conventional operators and foremen, NC was 'all the same'. But for the programmers and operators I interviewed, hetrogeneity was important. For the former there was a strong differentiation between operators based on accumulated experience.

Objectively, NC had produced a new layer of operators and technical workers. While this replicated the existing pattern in the division of labour and information flow from office to shop floor, the lines of differentation were not structured in this way. The programmers not only defended operators against those engaged with traditional technology they also argued that their skills had improved and not declined over the years. The novelty of the positions meant there was no golden age of craftsmanship for technical workers to romanticise and filter their perceptions of the shop floor. Formally, the operators were totally dependent on the quality of the 'tape', but its development through try-outs and the operators' ability to anticipate problems by analysing planning schedules, acted as a crucial check on the skills of the programmer. There were no demarcation disputes between operator and programmer on the editing of tapes chiefly because of the absence of CNC machines.[4] The widely acknowledged complexity of programming, the lengthy training and its relative newness conferred status and identity on the programmer, without at the same time this group of technical workers belittling the work of the manual operators. The craft division was greater in some respects than that between conventional operator and draughtsmen or planner, but movement into the office was still possible, and the form of association was not quantitative but qualitative to the degree that programmers ranked operators by their relative ability rather than the quantity of products produced.

This section has examined some of the working relations between technical workers and manual workers. My conclusions do not support the idea that technical staff are part of an oppressive and dominant category - or class - of 'mental labour', which sits on the backs of manual workers. Technical workers did not directly supervise or control manual workers but their labour prepared the instructions, tapes, drawing or processes to enable manual workers to produce commodities. Those quasi-technical workers in production control functions had a distinct involvement with the labour and productivity of manual workers. They monitored the performance of the shop floor and disputes on the shop floor increased their work load. There was a tendency in these areas to adopt management's perspective on shop floor productivity and in a conscious way some workers in the PCU aided management by disguising 'blacked' work and shifting it to sections unaffected by a particular dispute. No other technical workers had this political and quantitative relationship to manual workers' labour. Within this structure these groups may seek to pass on information to shopfloor unions on long term trends in the company. Such information, as Wainwright and Elliot (1982) argue, was useful at Lucas Aerospace as an early warning to the shop stewards combine on management's redundancy strategy within different branches of the corporation. At Filton this was not the case.

Established and new technical groups had to work out their own 'day to day' engagement with manual workers. In direct engagements between operator and technician, the latter drew off a common fund of experience that emphasized a shared class origin or training experience or mutual engineering knowledge based on the craft tradition. The polarisation between 'workers' and 'staff' was chiefly to do with 'conditions' of work. It also reflected the objective division of labour that separates and excludes manual workers or those at the operational level, from understanding the work of office staff. While the dominant tendency within class theory and ocupational analysis has been to emphasize the gulf between 'office' and 'works', the craft differentiation within both areas complicates divisions and undermines any clear cut white collar - manual worker model of polarisation. But this craft tradition has been under threat for two decades and it is this threat that I will examine in the conclusion to this chapter.

THREATS TO THE CRAFT TRADITION

There are several threats to the craft tradition: changes in training, with the demise of apprenticeships and the growth of graduate engineers; technological change; and the growing tendency spatially to separate design and production functions via disaggregation and subcontracting. The decline in apprenticeships within both manual and technical areas at Filton was a frequent topic of concern for workers and management. In 1982 there were 150 technical and manual apprentices on site, an increase from 1978, but still down on early periods. Nationally the recruitment of first year craft and technician trainees into engineering has been in decline since a peak of under 30,000 in 1967. There has been a steep decline since 1977, with annual first year take-ups dipping below 10,000 in 1983 (EITB, 1984).

All technical departments I investigated except those in the Engineering Design Organisation and NC Part Programming contained over 50 per cent of individuals who had started work as craftsmen and then transferred across into the office, some taking additional qualifications and others learning on the job. Some individuals also transferred after two years from a craft to a technician apprenticeship. Both routes were major avenues of training in Britain for all grades of technical workers until the 1960s, when indirect training through universities and polytechnics introduced a ceiling between middle range and professional or graduate engineers. Albu (1980) documents the slow growth in full-time university educated engineers who only became the dominant group within the Engineering institutions in the middle 1960's. As late as 1939, nearly 70 per cent of entrants into the dominant Institute of Mechnical Engineers were non-graduates - the reverse of the position in Germany, France and the USA (Albu, 1980, pp.80-82). According to Cooley, the growth of indirect training of engineers in the 1960s accompanied the decline of 'the traditional 7-year apprenticeship for designers', which in addition to creating a graduate divisions within design, did not actually keep pace with the demand for technical labour[5]. Qualified professional engineers are the expanding section within technical and scientific labour, whereas draughtsmen have been in decline since the early 1960s and 'other technicians' have grown, but not as fast as graduate engineers. The latter represented 30.2 per cent of scientific and technical labour in engineering and related industries in 1979, while draughtmen constituted 23.4 per cent, 'other technicians' 40.0 per cent and scientists, metallurgists and other technologists 6.4 per cent.[6]

At Filton in 1981 there were approximately 200 qualified engineers, out of a total of 900 technical staff. At C. A. Parsons in 1979 there were 222 qualified engineers in TASS out of a technical membership of 789, and significantly only 41 out of that 222 total did not possess a degree or higher qualification. Qualified engineers constituted 28 per cent of the technical labour, those with other qualfications (HND, OND, City and Guilds etc) repesented 51 per cent of the total and the unqualified 21 per cent. (The significance of these changes at the trade union or organisational level are examined in chapter six.)

In terms of relations within the technical area the creation of graduate engineers formalised the hierarchy in technical work by generating educational barriers and reducing craft and common forms of association between the two groups. This generated an exclusive ideology that combined professional elitism with craft sectarianism, practices that possess a similar form but receive different expressions. An interview with two avionics designers, both from manual working class backgrounds and both with engineering degrees, illustrates the basis of this separation:

John:
Some draughtsmen see themselves in a design role and they call themselves Design Draughtsmen.

Bill:
I found that at the weekend school [organised by TASS on
new technology] I'm not normally elitist but I did get a
bit worried when a lot of the people there were getting
up and saying they were designers and they were not.
They were draughtsmen.   There's a world of a difference
in the two terms.   O.K. it didn't worry me that much,
but they seemed to think of themselves as designers and
why? I don't think of myself as a draughtsman.
Chris:
Do you do any drawing yourselves?
Bill:
We don't do any drawing at all.
John:
We draw pretty pictures on scraps of paper.
Bill:
Yea! Very loose sketches [laughter].

The craft basis of their separation from draughtsmen is
revealed here.   They believe that designers work within an
indeterminate,   creative,   flexible   setting   (hence   'pretty
pictures',   and   'loose   sketches'   on   'scraps   of   paper').   By
contrast,   according   to   the   designers,   draughtsmen   are   more
concerned   with   regimented   detail   which   is   relatively
inflexible   and   uncreative.   This   technical   elitism   or   craft
sectarianism   is   common   to   all   craft   hierarchies,   but   the
difference   is   that   the   movement   into   craft   positions   has   been
fractured   by   a   "graduate   barrier"   and   this   has   been   used   as   a
source of exclusion in organisational terms.
    In addition to changes in training the development of NC
and CAD threatened changes, not only to craft links, but to
the existence of many technical jobs.   At Filton there was an
awareness,   amongst   planners,   estimators,   draughtsmen,
production   controllers,   rate   fixers   and   part-programmers   that
microelectronics   would   radically   change   or   eliminate   their
work   (a   technology-consciousness   that   was   surprising   because
Filton,   despite   the   dynamic   nature   of   aerospace,   was   behind
other   airframe   manufacturers,   especially   regarding   CAD).   But
alongside   the   expectation   of   change   was   the   belief   that   the
individuals   within   a   particular   function   would   adapt,   because
experience   had   taught   them   to   expect   any   change   to   be
incremental   rather   than   radical   or   systemic.   The   NC   part
programming   department   had   gradually   expanded,   changed   and
developed   in   line   with   technical   change,   as   this   programmer
explains:

They've   just   brought   out   another   weird   and   wonderful
terminal   which   involves   two   things: you   can   do   your   tape
on   the   terminal   and   you   can   also   make   your   tape   locally.
And   there's   sheets   and   sheets   of   instructions   and   all
that is new, it's all got to be learnt.

101

Against a strategy of adaptation, technical change had also eliminated occupations - e.g. because of new inks, plastic film and reprographics, tracing is now virtually dead; the occupation of technical calculator did not exist at Filton because of the development of electronic calculators. In electrical planning, planners alternated between manual and computer terminal work; in estimating most work was with books, telephone and technical manuals, although there was a VDU terminal in a separate room, and work on it was expected to increase. In drawing areas there was evidence of automatic drawing equipment in one department but this was underutilised and referred to rather contemptuously as the 'white elephant'. State of the art CAD was not in widespread evidence, but its introduction was being negotiated during my research. I interviewed managers involved in this process and designers and draughtsmen operating experimental systems. For both managers and some designers interactive designing via a computer terminal offered the prospect of greater autonomy premised on the elimination on draughtsmen, planners and other intermediate human links between design and production:

> With the old system you had a design engineer produce a diagram, and when that diagram was finished it was issued to planning and production engineering departments . . . Now with the new system these intermediate stages will be eliminated largely because of the computer. Once the design engineer inputs the original scheme onto the computer he will have automatically created a data base which will provide him with all the answers he wants.

In addition to transforming many of the old craft based occupational bridges between the manual and technical areas, CAD also threatened to undermine the working conditions of technical staff and change the spatial division of labour. Cooley (1972, 1976, 1980) and others have criticised the view held by the above designer that CAD is a liberating force and at Filton a draughtsmen working on NC and automatic drawing equipment acknowledged the drawbacks to specialisation:

> If you produce a drawing there are routine and mediocre parts, which have to be done anyway, so there's a quiet time where the stress is minimal. Now, being specialists, you find that the mental stress is there practically the whole working day.

Rader (1982, p.173) examining the organisation of CAD facilities within the firm, encountered two main managerial practices; one where all design staff worked CAD and the other where specialist CAD functions existed. For the individual designer or more likely draughtsmen, specialisation may isolate him from other technical workers and the shop floor. Baldry and Connolly (1984), in one of the few studies on the impact of CAD to interview technical workers as well as managers, found in all the seven Scottish based engineering companies they studied specialisation to be the pronounced pattern of working. This was against TASS policy which states that CAD training should be open to all draughtsmen. They found that whether by intention or default, particular individuals monopolised CAD facilities. They contrasted these specialists, located within small, dark capital intensive computer rooms, often working shifts and on a product that did not bare the individual identity of a single draughtsmen, with the 'social cohesiveness' of the drawing office, its well lit open layout, solidaristic values, daytime hours and the autonomous working on a drawing that is the responsibility of one individual. The fragmentation of drawing threatens to reduce the interest and identity draughtsmen have with the finished product and with shopfloor workers engaged on particular products. This potential for loss of contact via the product with individual operators altered the common medium between the two groups. Conversley the autonomy of working on single jobs has its own pressures and Baldry and Connolly ignore the fact that management can readily locate responsibility for mistakes where individuals sign their own drawing, plan or programme.

Shiftworking represents the single biggest change in the working conditions of technical workers. Successfully resisted by TASS in the first phase of CAD in the early 1970s, by the late 1970s and 1980s a slack labour market and weaker union policy on CAD put shiftworking firmly on the agenda (see Baldry and Connolly; Incomes Data Services, 1982; Wrench and Stanley, 1984). At Filton, early attempts to introduce shift systems had been resisted, but experience from Rolls Royce and other companies indicated that the company would be obliged to increase the utilisation of high technology through lengthening the working day.

The appearance of small, capital intensive units within or outside labour intensive low capital technical departments was evident at Filton in the NC geometry group, NC part programming and avionics design. This was not undermining the autonomy of the technical staff in a straightforward way. Computer terminals did make monitoring more of an option but there had been resistance, the electrical planners, for example, had blocked the use of a supervisory mode of their VDU's. What was more apparent was the reduction in contact between technical staff and the creation of specialist barriers between technical and manual workers. Contact via direct physical communication and through a shared body of craft knowledge were both in decline, which laid technical workers open to the elitism and exclusiveness inherent within a division of labour and information flow formally structured from the office to the shop floor. In the electrical planning department computerisation had reduced but not eliminated the necessity of planners sharing practical electrical knowledge or theoretical knowledge. One planner had moved into the office from a clerical job and lacked any electrical craft training. Interestingly, he was more convinced than other planners that they were instructing electricians to such a detailed degree that the 'skills' of the electricians had disappeared: '<u>Idiots</u> could do it'. In other words, he lacked the craft knowledge to appreciate the electricians' work and the inevitable gap that exists between the issuing of planning schedules and the actual performance of operations. To this planner there was no gap, no transformation problem, it was simply a case of electricians copying the instructions generated within the planning office. And within this world, the planner was dominant, the electrician a subordinate 'idiot'. So, although the craft link, as we have seen, does not create a straightforward unity between technical and manual workers, its removal will have the result of fracturing the association and respect that a shared practical background and regular interaction can foster.

At Filton there was an opportunity for contact between technical staff and manual workers because the two groups were together on one site. Developments in new technology and managerial philosophies may mean such a situation is increasingly rare, as design and production are spatially separated or disaggregated. The American production cycle for micro electronics demonstrates the possibilities of globally dividing 'design' and production functions within an international division of labour. External contracting can also be an important means of management gaining greater indirect control over labour productivity. Sweated trades, petty commodity production and home working have increased considerably during the current economic crisis and have been funded by large manufacturing companies in textiles, clothing, electronic components, leather goods and engineering, which sub-contract work around the globe to cheapen the costs of production. The growth of cottage industries, or the putting-out system has been used to significant effect in, for example, Italy by such giants as Fiat (Sabel, 1982; Murray 1983; Amin 1983). The cheapening of high capital equipment in design and improved information technology may make subcontracting functions increasingly attractive to management operating within very competitive markets. A 1984 CBI survey of 838 firms which accounted for 4 million employees found the trends towards greater subcontracting most pronounced in the largest firms (CBI, 1984, p.9). Design and R & D are all prone to this pattern of breaking up integrated operations via external contracting. In low technology sectors technical and engineering functions are increasingly 'bought in', for example at Cadbury Ltd, Bourneville the 90 draughtsmen who were employed in the early 1970s were down to only twelve in the early 1980s. The increase in subcontracting may take the form of buying in expertise from small or medium sized companies or consultant engineers or engineering entrepreneurs, ie the transfer of senior technical staff from being wage labour within a large corporation to being self-employed or a petty proprietor or a fee-based consultant of a specialist engineering firm.

Huws (1984) in a study of 78 white collar homeworkers found that 95 per cent were female, 80 per cent computer specialists, and the majority mothers who opted for homework because of its flexibility faced with the difficulties of finding childcare. That new technology makes this option possible does not mean that male workers, who are the overwhelming majority in technical areas will necessarily want to work at home, although when I interviewed Mike Cooley on this subject he thought the attractions of increased independence may tempt many engineers into opting for homeworking. At BAe and NEI Parsons subcontracting was widely used. In aerospace it has always been common, but it did not look like eliminating technical workers from the Filton site where they remained concentrated on a large scale. In other sectors disaggregation could increase and produce a new spatial barrier between technical workers and others.

CONCLUSION

The post war growth of technical labour within engineering, constituting a quarter of a million people in 1979, has resulted in an increased union density, as technical workers are socialised into the collective conditions of waged labour within large bureaucratic corporations like BAe. This expansion was achieved through continued use of the apprenticeship system which maintained the craft links and traditions between technical and manual workers and prevented exclusive elitist third force politics gaining ground within British engineering. Developments within the technical division of labour up until the 1960s chiefly entailed incrementally grafting new occupations onto an existing set of social institutions, pattern of training and craft association. However, the rise of college-trained engineers in the 1960s and 1970s altered this pattern by formalising the existing hierarchy and, more importantly, creating the means of exclusion not given by the old seven year apprenticeship system for engineers. Engineers have been open to appeals to their professional autonomy by unions like UKAPE, now defunct, and the EMA. They have also been recruited through emphasis on the craft autonomy by general unions like TASS. Where they remain concentrated in large numbers alongside other technical groups then their experience of wage labour allows a potential for the promotion of solidarity and unity against senior management – who are typically drawn from financial and administrative backgrounds (Armstrong, 1984; Smith, 1985). Education, training and the increasing absence of social interaction with other groups creates barriers, but ones which are not class based. What is more significant, is the growth of self employment amongst engineers and their location within entrepreneurial functions in consultancies or small, specialised firms within electronic computers and other infant engineering sectors. Disaggregation as a new managerial strategy in more established areas of engineering may mean the progressive break up of concentrations of lower and higher technical grades and if TASS policy has been overwhelmingly geared towards the large concentrations within corporations then unionisation will be affected by these changes. Small scale patterns of employment, self-employment and the lack of rigid differentiation between engineering and finance functions, has maintained a petty bourgeois position amongst engineers within construction, relative to the engineering industry (Smith, 1985). Any movement towards this pattern within general engineering would create class-based forms of differentiation.

NOTES

1.   For a full discussion see Smith (1982, 1986)
2.   Jim Mortimer, ex-General Secretary of the Labour Party was a researcher and editor for DATA between 1948-1968.
3.   On the Leyland toolroom dispute see Scullion (1981).
4.   At Rolls Royce, Bristol there had been major problems of jurisdiction and demarcation between the AUEW Engineering Section and TASS.
5.   From an interview with Mike Cooley (Rader and Wingert 1981).
6.   In 1979 Technical and Scientific labour constituted 262,230 or 27 per cent of total white collar employment in engineering and related industries. Professional engineers stood at 79,530; scientists etc. 16,750; draughtsmen 61,430; and other technicians 104,520 of the total.

PART TWO

THE POLITICS OF WHITE COLLAR

TRADE UNIONISM

Chapter Four

WORK SUPERVISORS AND TRADE UNIONISM

Peter Armstrong

INTRODUCTION

During fieldwork carried out for the study reported in chapter 1, the writer was struck by an incident involving two middle management members of ASTMS. Briefly, a security guard at 'Lancashire Electrical Fittings' had been dismissed for working at a part-time job whilst absent on a sick note. At a well attended meeting on the issue the on-site ASTMS representative decided to contest the dismissal on procedural grounds. As the outcome of the meeting became clearer, one of the managers remarked to the writer: 'Hey. This is bloody serious. If they get away with this, you won't be able to discipline anyone anymore'. A few days later they both resigned from the union.

At a more public level, in 1983, the delegates at the annual conference of the Post Office Engineering Union voted to exclude their managerial members in protest against a plan by British Telecom management to sack members who refused to cross picket lines during the union's campaign against privatisation (Guardian, 9 November, 1983).

Such incidents raise an important question which has been very much neglected in the voluminous literature on white collar unions: that of the nature of the trade unionism of those who are paid, at least in part, to control the labour of others. It will be argued in this chapter that such questions cannot be answered without reference to the place, in the Marxist sense, of supervision in the social relations of production. Only in this way is it possible to make sense of supervisory trade unionism as an articulation of the relationship between supervisors, managers and workforce. Formulations which see white collar unionism simply as a response to the degradation of a once-privileged section of the workforce are as inadequate in this respect as those which see it as the passive benificiary of 'enlightened' employer and government policies. The chapter begins with a review of this literature, then proceeds by showing how the early theoretical framework of Crompton (1976) can be reformulated so as to make sense of the antagonisms between supervisory trade unionists, management and workforce. After presenting some findings from the literature in support of this thesis, the chapter then presents the results of a small-scale survey on the nature of the 'demands' which supervisors are likely to make on white collar trade unions.

No great claims are made for this survey: the intention is simply to place certain issues on the agenda for future debate. The sample is small (48 first and second line supervisors) and biased (they were attending a part-time Certificate in Industrial Management course at their local Polytechnic). On the other hand, the supervisors <u>were</u> allowed to express their views unhampered by the imposition of survey categories (they were simply asked, prior to any teaching, to write an essay entitled 'What white collar unions should be doing for the industrial supervisor'). The essays were completed in class time without consultation between the supervisors, thus ensuring an unusually high response rate of 100% . Despite the limitations of the survey, the results suggest a conception of trade unionism amongst supervisors which is considerably different from what might be expected from the current literature.

FACTORS BEHIND WHITE COLLAR UNIONISATION AND THE 'CHARACTER' OF WHITE COLLAR UNIONS

For Lockwood (1958) the major factor behind the growth of clerical unionisation was the bureaucratisation of the workplace which, in destroying the former particularism of the employment relationship, created a setting in which the collective representation of clerical workers' interests became the only alternative. Also important was the blockage of internal promotion channels due to the 'graduate barrier' (cf. Roberts, Loveridge and Gennard, 1972, p.299), which created conditions in which collective action aimed at improving conditions at lower organisational levels was a more realistic strategy than individualistic competition. Finally, as clerical workers grew in number, so their social background and work situation came to include direct contact with manual workers and their trade unions, thus overcoming some of their former inhibitions against unionisation.

Whilst pointing out that the unionisation of clerks entailed their 'coming to terms with' the wider class character of the movement, Lockwood was at pains to stress that there was no necessary association between unionisation and the development of class consciousness. Instead, the 'character' of white collar unions (in the sense of their degree of identification with the labour movement as a whole) could vary, depending partly on the social consciousness of their membership, which, in turn, depended on certain features of their work situation and background (Lockwood, 1958, p.137 and pp.195-198).

For engineering technicians, Prandy (1965, p.175 <u>et seq</u>) found that it was loss of authority in the workplace and features of the work situation which emphasised that fact (such as low pay and strict supervision) which lay behind the development of a 'class' view of the employment relationship and its expression in the form of unionisation. Though the process highlighted by Prandy is consistent with Lockwood's emphasis on bureaucratisation, the apparent assumption of a direct relationship between class consciousness and unionisation seemed to be in flat contradiction to Lockwood's views on the matter, and it certainly attracted the later criticism of Bain, Coates and Ellis (1973, especially p.154). However a closer reading of this early work reveals that Prandy was actually using the term 'class view' in the highly restrictive sense of an oppositional view of only the immediate employment relationship, explicitly stating that it could co-exist with a 'status' view of society in general (Prandy, 1965, p.186). Later, Prandy and his co-workers introduced the term 'enterprise unionateness' to distinguish this parochial consciousness of conflicting interests from the wider 'society unionateness' (Prandy, Stewart and Blackburn, 1974).

In Loveridge's view, the effect of the developments outlined by Prandy could be subjected to a kind of 'cultural lag'. White collar workers could continue to believe that their jobs were important and their positions privileged for some time after they had ceased to be so. Unionisation or militant action could then result from a sudden 'clarification' of the real situation, for example, if senior management were to substitute or de-skill their work (Loveridge, 1982).

In his study of the unionisation of bank clerks, Blackburn (1967, especially pp.266-272) formalised (and arguably modified) Lockwood's concept of union character by introducing a seven-factor index of 'unionateness' which was essentially a measure of the similarity or otherwise of white collar unions to their typical blue-collar counterparts. It was Blackburn's interpretation of his evidence that any given 'situation' (by which he meant the characteristics of the employees, the employers and the historical and institutional background) allowed for a certain degree of 'unionisation'. Given this, the extent of recruitment ('completeness') and the 'unionateness' of the recruiting organisation were, he claimed, inversely related according to the formula:

$$\text{unionisation} = \text{unionateness} \times \text{completeness}$$

Thus Blackburn's work, although propounding no particular view of white collar union character as such, implied that the 'situation' (as defined) would place some restricton on the character of organisations which could successfully recruit. It is also worth observing, at this stage, that both Lockwood and Blackburn's conceptions of union character were one-dimensional: a question of greater or lesser identification with the labour movement in the first case, and of greater or lesser 'unionateness' in the second. Blackburn's own problems in applying his scale to organisations such as the BMA, which he found high on some indices of 'unionateness' and zero on others (1967, p.261n), should serve as a caution against reifying such concepts, for example in the form of assumptions that any differences between white collar and manual unions can only be ones of degree.

In later works Prandy, Stewart and Blackburn (1974) extended the concept of unionateness in two ways. Firstly they applied it to the policy preferences of individuals as well as to the actual policies of organisations. Secondly, as already pointed out, they separated the original seven factor index into items concerned with the immediate employment situation ('enterprise unionateness') from those measuring identification with the wider labour movement ('society unionateness'). In some degree such a concept allows for qualitative as well as quantitative differences in character. White collar and manual workers could, for example, differ in their relative preference for enterprise and society unionateness, though these are possibilities that have not yet been explored. Even if they were, the conceptual framework certainly lacks the flexibility to deal with the issues with which this chapter is concerned.

Recently, these same authors have attempted to restate the connection between trade unionism and social stratification in a manner which sidesteps the issues of the intentions of union members and even the policies of individual unions (Prandy, Stewart and Blackburn, 1983). Having demonstrated that the effect of trade unionism at the aggregate level is to diminish wage differentials, they argue that the practical result of individuals joining trade unions and taking part in their affairs is to contribute to this process. Irrespective of the subjective intentions of individuals and union leaders therefore, these authors argue that trade unionism is class action insofar as it contributes towards the substitution of egalitarianism for market criteria of distribution. Whatever the ultimate merits of such an approach, one obvious drawback is that the questions which it avoids are important and interesting.

Writing in 1970, Bain specifically took issue with much of the earlier work on white collar unions, claiming that there were no significant relationships between aggregate white collar union growth and bureaucratisation, blocked promotion or proximity to manual workers (Lockwood) nor union 'image' and recruiting policies (Blackburn). Instead he proposed that white collar union growth could parsimoniously and adequately be explained by employment concentration, the recognition policies of employers and government action to encourage recognition (Bain, 1970, pp.183-184). Bain's work, with its implication that white collar unions were largely the passive beneficiaries of enlightened government and employer policies was heavily criticised by Adams. In particular Adams (1975) pointed out that government policies favouring recognition also coincided with economic conditions favouring trade unionism and that, even so, the willingness of unions to apply pressure was a crucial factor. Further, he argued that Bain tended to explain union growth as a consequence of employer recognition whilst failing to explain how unions could ever have grown in the first place, to the point where recognition was on the agenda. Thirdly (which by no means exhausts Adams' criticisms), he pointed out that Bain's variable of employment concentration was, in fact, an (unsatisfactory) attempt to operationalise the degree of bureaucratisation of the workplace (Adams, 1977). If this was indeed the case it was generous of Adams to refrain from pointing out that Bain had not only claimed that employment concentration was a factor in white collar unionisation but also that bureaucratisation was not.

In a later work, Bain, Coates and Ellis repeated their earlier findings and also put to the question Prandy's evidence on the role of loss of authority in white collar unionisation. More generally they claimed to have established that there is no link, at least at the aggregate level, between questions of social stratification and union growth or policies (1983, p.37 et seq, pp.154-155).

These are large claims and one of them in particular appears to be founded on very shaky ground. It is one thing to quote occasions on which white collar unions and even professional associations have resorted to collective action. It is quite another to claim on such a basis that this indicates a broad similarity of character between these and manual workers' unions (Bain et al, 1983, pp.60-77). As has been pointed out by Prandy, Stewart and Blackburn (1983, p.4, pp.11-12), this assertion ultimately depends on a reduction of the concept of character to a question of whether or not organisations are concerned with job regulation. And since manual workers' unions, white collar unions and professional associations are all concerned with job regulation, they naturally look very similar in the light of this now very fuzzy concept of character. In any case, Bain's assertion that union growth is influenced by government and employer policies but not by questions of social stratification necessarily depends upon a conceptualisation of the latter

113

which is so narrow that it actually manages to exclude the relationship between capital and labour.

In fact, as has been chronicled by Price (1983), the later work of Bain and his colleagues has, at least by implication, retreated from some of the austerities of his earlier position. In their econometric studies of union growth, Elsheikh and Bain (1980) found that white collar unionisation was, after all, responsive to price movements. This was explained as a response by potential members to the 'threat' represented by rising prices and the 'credit' which trade unions could claim for gaining wage rises to offset them. Surprisingly this mass imputation of motive so far remains unchecked at the empirical level. Nor have the obvious implications for a re-consideration of the relevance of social stratification been explored.

The debate on the connection between social stratification and white collar unionism took a new turn with the work of Crompton (1976). Following Carchedi (1977) and Wright (1979a), she argued that the crucial determinant of the social class of an occupation was not the income or style of life which went with it but its economic function in the capitalist mode of production. Unambiguously proletarian occupations performed the function of producing surplus value whereas occupations which formed part of the 'global function of capital' performed the functions of extracting surplus value from the proletariat, of realising it in the market place or of distributing it between capitals. Most white collar work consisted of a mixture of the two functions and could therefore become proletarianised in the sense of losing capital functions whilst gaining functions concerned with the necessary organisational component of producing surplus value. Moreover, with the developing division of labour <u>within</u> the functions of capital, white collar work could also become proletarianised in the sense of losing decision making power and being confined to the routine execution of the control function of capital. Though this latter component of Crompton's concept of proletarianisation recalls Lockwood's identification of bureaucratisation as a factor in white collar unionisation and Prandy's view that loss of authority is a decisive influence, it is important to stress that it is the loss of those functions peculiar to the capitalist imperative of extracting surplus value which is at issue, not the loss of control in general. Having identified two aspects of proletarianisation, Crompton went on to argue that white collar unionisation is most likely when it occurs in both senses ('double proletarianisation') and attempted to demonstrate the thesis in the case of insurance clerks (Crompton, 1979).

Crompton's approach was criticised by Banks (1978) on the grounds that her Marxist conceptual framework was inappropriate to contemporary societies. More or less the

114

opposite criticism was made by Roslender (1981) whose objections flowed from Crompton's failure to use the term 'proletarianisation' as Marx and Engels had used it before her. The observations of Heritage (1980) were more substantial: firstly he demonstrated that Crompton's evidence on the alleged linkage between 'double proletarianisation' and the unionisation of insurance clerks was actually very scanty. Secondly he identified the source of the trouble as Crompton's assumption of an <u>unmediated</u> link between 'double proletarianisation' and union growth. Important mediating factors, he suggested, might be the contextual influences identified by Bain, competition from staff associations and the fact that the impact of 'double proletarianisation' had fallen disproportionately on the female section of the workforce. In fact Crompton's latest research (Crompton and Jones, 1984) amply recognises this latter aspect of the problem, though without exploring its implications for her earlier theoretical perspective. Heritage's other criticisms were well fashioned but they do not invalidate Crompton's basic approach. Instead, they lead to the more refined hypothesis of a link between 'double proletarianisation' and the <u>predisposition</u> to join unions rather than union growth as such.

More recently Prandy, Stewart and Blackburn (1983) have objected to Crompton's attempts to establish links between unionisation and proletarianisation on quite different grounds. Their main argument is that the concept of proletarianisation can only have meaning within capitalist social relations of production and that these are fundamentally defined by the existence of markets in labour and products. Since the latter do not always exist in the state sector, the major part of white collar unionism cannot be related to proletarianisation. This not very substantial objection seems to stem from the assumption that the existence of capitalism depends ultimately on the determination of the reproduction costs of labour power by a market in wage goods – a view which, unconventionally to say the least, effectively defines welfarism as revolutionary. Nor is it consistent with Prandy, Stewart and Blackburn's concern throughout their own work to establish that trade union action <u>is</u> class action in that it serves to challenge the operation of market principles of distribution – since their argument against Crompton is that these do not operate anyway over a large sector of the economy.

Though Crompton's basic approach emerges relatively unscathed from these criticisms, it nevertheless stands in need of further refinement before it can usefully be applied to the question of white collar union character. Indeed it may be the lack of development in this respect which has led Crompton virtually to abandon her earlier theory in her latest study of white collar workers, in which the question of the economic <u>function</u> of white collar work, as opposed to its fragmentation and deskilling, remains practically unexplored (Crompton and Jones, 1984). The problem lies within the concept of 'double proletarianisation' itself. Whilst the first aspect of this - the replacement of capital by labour functions - is clearly fundamental to proletarianisation, it is doubtful whether the second aspect - the loss of decision making power <u>within</u> the capital function - is an aspect of proletarianisation at all. Indeed Crompton has argued elsewhere that, in the case of foremen, the economic function of an occupation is not changed by the manner of its execution (Crompton and Gubbay, 1977, p.190). Thus the transmission of management orders appropriate to the function of capital is as much a part of the capital function as is their initiation. Indeed, as the present writer has attempted to demonstrate in chapter 1, a loss of decision-making power by foremen may lead to a sense of antagonism towards senior management which has nothing at all to do with proletarianisation on any definition. In other words a loss of decision-making power within the function of capital gives rise to conflicts of interest and antagonisms <u>within</u> the global function of capital, not to proletarianisation (cf Poulantzas, 1978, pp.314-327).

If this is accepted - and it is only fair to add that writers as authoritative as Braverman (1974, p.30, <u>et seq</u>) and Johnson (1977) would disagree - some of the difficulties associated with Crompton's position disappear. Instead of needing to assume an association between proletarianisation and unionisation (which is, in any case, disputed by the great majority of authors in the field), one can now re-state Crompton's hypothesis in the form that unionisation may be a response (1) to proletarianisation in the sense of the replacement of capital by labour functions, (2) to a loss of autonomy <u>within</u> the functions of capital. The importance of this modification is that process (1) creates, in the white collar workforce, interests substantially in common with those of the rest of the proletariat. Process (2) however creates conflicts of interest <u>between</u> the different groups which vie for the privilege of carrying out the control functions of capital, a process described, in the case of the professions, by Johnson (1971). In other words, what is at stake in the second process, at least for those whose function is to extract (rather than to distribute or realise) surplus value, is the authority to make decisions which run <u>counter</u> to the long-run interests of the proletariat. To the extent that these considerations can be shown to contribute towards white collar unionisation therefore, they create the potential for action against shopfloor unions as well as against other sections of the management structure. Thus Carter (1979) found that the trade unionism of lower management members of ASTMS left unmodified the hostility of these employees towards the 'obstruction' representated by shopfloor unions. The possibility exists therefore that the character of the unionisation of certain sections of the white collar workforce is different from that of manual workers in ways which are not allowed for in unilinear concepts of 'unionateness', 'proletarianisation' or in blanket assertions that all collective organisations are essentially similar. The crucial questions are: (1) Has a loss of autonomy within the control function of capital played a role in white collar unionisation? (2) If it has, are there any signs within these unions of demand associated with a restoration of that control function?

On the first point, it is possible to be fairly confident. If anything is firmly established by the literature reviewed earlier, it is that bureaucratisation has played a substantial role in white collar unionisation. Whilst some of this process may have involved the replacement of capital functions by the extra work of co-ordination necessary in an increasingly complex division of labour (ignoring for the moment, the argument that this is, in itself, a device for controlling labour), many writers, such as Edwards (1980), Goldman and Van Houten (1979) and Johnson (1977), would agree that much supervisory work is still concerned with the more routine aspect of controlling labour in the interests of capital. In the terms used here, there are good grounds for believing that a loss of autonomy within the control function of capital - as well as any proletarianisation of function which has occurred - has played a substantial role in white collar unionisation.

The second question - that of the nature of the demands on white collar unions made by the membership - is the one to which this chapter is addressed. However there is also a literature bearing on the point which gives some ground for re-examining Bain, Coates and Ellis' (1973) view (which is probably the 'industrial relations' orthodoxy) that the goals and methods of white collar unions are essentially similar to those of their manual counterparts. Whilst this may be broadly true at the aggregate level, it does not preclude the possibility of more local divergences of aims and methods, still less of differences in the 'demands' made on their unions by white collar and manual union members, especially in view of the same authors' observation that union character is not simply a reflection of the predispositions of the membership (1973, p.159).

In Weir's view (1976), the industrial relations literature tends to treat managers either as surrogate employers or as white collar workers and this results in a neglect of their interests as managerial employees. Thus management unionisation is approached as if it necessarily concerned only the interests of mangers as <u>workers</u>, with a consequent neglect of the possibility of collective representation of their occupational interests as managers. In his survey of 1400 managers in a large British Company, Weir found that there was a general demand for a greater say in policy making, though there was disagreement within the sample over whether formal consultation through union channels was an appropriate means of achieving this. Although only 14% of Weir's sample were union members at the time of the survey, roughly half were potential members in the sense that they said they would join a union were the company to recognise one. According to Maurice's study of <u>cadres</u> in the French aircraft industry (Reynaud, 1983), increased participation in management decision-making was actually the most important motivation behind the collective organisation of this group of employees. These findings were closely paralleled in Hartman's survey of West German managers (1974), the vast majority of whom wanted a greater say in decision-making and about half of whom saw collective representation on the supervisory and executive boards of their companies within the West German system of industrial democracy as an appropriate means of achieving this. According to Carter (1979) this view of industrial democracy as a route by which lower management may seek increased influence within the global function of capital, is also that of the National Executive of ASTMS. Such a 'demand for control' has also been observed amongst managers in local government by Nicholson, Ursell and Blyton (1980) though these authors oddly interpreted it as a sign of 'union radicalism'.

There is further evidence of a 'demand of control' in the more impressionistic writings of 'management academics'. Distinguishing 'level 1' goals (employment conditions) from 'level 2' goals (career prospects, autonomy, work satisfaction and the like) for managers, it is Frost's opinion (1980) that, although professional associations might be more appropriate for pursuing 'level 2' goals in isolation, the overall interests of managers might best be served by organisations geared to the pursuit of both types of goal - a conclusion reached earlier by Weir (1976). Farnham too (1977) advocates some form of collective representation for management so as to influence 'major policy decisions affecting their interests' and sees the BIM as developing a role in this respect.

There is some evidence, then, that at least a proportion of managers are seeking, and that their spokesmen and mentors are advocating, some collective means of obtaining for themselves a greater share in decision making within the function of capital. For some, these demands might be made, not on trade unions as such but on staff associations or professional associations though it is worth recalling in this connection that, on Blackburn's terminology either of these alternatives would also constitute unionisation of a

kind.
It is also worth making the point that although the demand for access to control within the capital function may be collective in form, the form of access demanded may be individual. For example, evidence will be presented shortly that there appears to be, amongst industrial supervisors, a collective demand for increased promotion opportunities and indeed Crompton and Jones (1984, p.207) found, and appear to have been puzzled by, a positive correlation between interest in promotion and unionisation amongst female clerical workers. Such demands are often defined out of existence by the commonplace distinction between individual and collective strategies. More aware of the possibilities, at least, Prandy, Stewart and Blackburn (1982) explicitly, and quite arbitrarily excluded from their discussion those forms of collective action aimed at strengthening the market position of individuals. This must gratuitously distort their characterisation of white collar unions.
If control is a demand made on capital, there is also evidence from the literature that it is a demand made against labour, particularly by those in the front line. On the basis of case studies in five factories, Bowey (1983) concluded that the unionisation of supervisors was, in part, a response to being by-passed by manual workers' shop stewards. Child and Partridge (1982), in case studies of two firms, concluded that the challenge of shopfloor unions to supervisors' control was a factor behind unionisation in both cases. Unionisation as an expression of the desire of managers to counteract the power of the managed was also apparent in Blyton, Nicholson and Ursell's (1981) study of a NALGO branch, in which the authors suggest that this partly accounts for the tendency of NALGO shop stewards to be drawn from the more senior positions in the management structure. Crompton and Jones too found higher levels of union membership at higher levels of promotion amongst clerks, though they offer little in the way of explanation (1984, p.206).
Again, there is more impressionistic evidence to the same effect. The European Association for Personnel Management (1979) believes that, in the context of European worker participation schemes, managerial unionism is seen as a means of balancing the power of workers. Such commentators as Farnham (1977) and Marchington (1982) have made essentially the same point in a British context, the latter explictly mentioning the need for backing on disciplinary matters as a motive for unionisation.
The idea that those white collar workers who are engaged in the direct control of labour have a specific interest in countering the power of manual worker unions is also consistent with the well established preference of managers and supervisors for unions separate from those of manual

workers, though of course it is not established that it is a 'demand for control' which <u>causes</u> this preference (see, for example, Child and Partridge, 1982; Weir, 1976; Hartman, 1974). Indeed Jenkins and Sherman (1979, p.44) have, not entirely disinterestedly, advocated separate unions for white collar workers on different grounds, namely that the dominance of the manual partner in joint organisations tends to squeeze differentials. As a consequence (they claim), separate white collar unions (such as their own ASTMS), have grown faster than the white collar sections of manual unions.

The question of differentials as an issue in white collar unionisation threatens to become a minefield, not least because there are those who appear to believe that the work of Bain, or even that of Lockwood has once and for all demonstrated its irrelevance (see, for example, Heritage 1980, pp.286-287). This is not so: what has been demonstrated is that variations in the <u>rate</u> at which differentials are squeezed do not correlate with the growth of white collar unions and that variations in the <u>extent</u> of the squeeze do not explain the pattern of unionisation (Bain, 1970, p.71). Quite how these conclusions need to be modified in view of the later admission of the effects of inflation into Bain's model of white collar union growth (Price, 1983, especially pp.153-156), is not yet clear. Even so, given that the erosion of white collar differentials has been virtually universal, it is still perfectly possible that it will be found to have operated as a background factor whenever actual cases of white collar unionisation are studied, as is argued in the work of Child and Partridge (1982, pp.174, 177-178).

Of course a concern to maintain differentials is by no means peculiar to white collar unions. However the conclusion of Roberts, Cook, Clark and Semeonoff (1977, pp.125-128), that white collar unionisation signifies a determination to stay ahead of the proletariat rather than solidarity with it, indicates a more broadly based antagonism and a more fundamental divergence of interests than the occupational factionalism observed amongst craft unions. What is lacking in this connection is data on the <u>meaning</u> which white collar workers attach to their differentials. Whilst for Jenkins and Sherman (1979, p.83), they are justified by 'self-investment' in education and training, for Wright (1979c) they also represent an economic 'return to control' in which case the concern of white collar workers over the narrowing of their differentials represents more than the normal factionalism of trade unions and more, even, than the anguish of disappointed 'self investors': it relates intimately to the devaluation of their role within the control function of capital. Although Stewart, Prandy and Blackburn (1980, p.266 <u>et seq</u>) have rightly criticised Wright's attempt to operationalise and test the concept of the 'return to control', the concept itself is not thereby invalidated and there is other evidence in its favour, for example, the 45% salary advantage gained by professional engineers who move into general management (Berthoud and Smith, 1980, p.8). If Wright is correct, then, the attempts of Weir (1976) and Frost (1980) to separate, in the case of managers and supervisors, the issue of employment conditions on the one hand and that of autonomy and participation on the other are not soundly based, since the former partly depends on the latter. The writer suspects that it is the linkage of these issues which is encapsulated in supervisors' frequent complaints that their responsibilities are not adequately rewarded on the one hand and that they lack the decision-making power adequately to discharge them on the other (see, for example, Hill, 1973, and Child, Pearce and King, 1980, pp.363-399), since the former complaint makes little sense if the latter is true. In the absence of firm evidence, however, all that can safely be claimed is that the differentials issue, as it is pursued by white collar unions is consistent with their loss of influence within the control function of capital as well as with proletarianisation (defined here as the replacement of capital by labour functions).

In summary, then, there are four strands of evidence consistent with the view that white collar unionisation contains, as a potential issue, the restoration of the lost influence and autonomy of supervisors within the control function of capital. These are (i) that actual or potential managerial trade unionists are concerned to pursue this issue, via collective means, (ii) that for supervisors, unionisation may be a question of collective mobilisation against the power of shopfloor unions, (iii) that the demand for unionisation amongst managers and supervisors is essentially a demand for separate representation, (iv) that the economic concerns behind white collar unionisation are a concern to restore a differential in relation to manual workers as a whole and that this may be seen as the just reward for discharging the control functions of capital as well as for knowledge or specialised skills.

This being said, it is worth repeating the remark of Bain et al (1973, p.159) to the effect that there may, for a variety of reasons, be a gulf between the policies of white collar unions and the concerns of their membership. In Carter's view (1979), this stems, in part, from the fact that union negotiators, due to the nature of their activities, are selectively attuned to the conflictual aspects of the relationship between their members and senior managements. However, the finding of Nicholson et al (1980) that the views of NALGO shop stewards were more similar to those of manual workers' shop stewards than to those of their own membership suggests that this gulf may also exist within the workplace.

121

At higher levels the kind of constraints which operate have been illustrated in Kelly's (1980, pp.138-140) 'modified cash nexus' interpretation of the bargaining behaviour of Civil Servants. Whilst the discontents of these employees were primarily with reduced discretion and job satisfaction, bargaining in practice has been concerned with negotiating monetary compensation rather than with rectifying the dissatisfactions themselves. Kelly's explanation was that only pay and other employment conditions are regarded as legitimate areas for institutionalised conflict and bargaining. What Kelly seems to be saying is that although unions themselves may not be purely economistic, economism, as it were, is imposed upon them by one of the core presuppositions of capitalist society.

Whilst interesting, this is overstated, if only because the 'cash nexus' argument can apply only to the proletariat proper and not to those who participate in the control function of capital. The Swiss white collar associations studied by Hopflinger (1981) operate in a capitalist context which nevertheless allows for representation both of 'employee' and 'professional' interests, a combination which, it will be recalled, has been advocated in a British context by several writers. The members of these associations are, Hopflinger reports, keen to avail themselves of the professional training which they provide (thus demonstrating that there can be a <u>collective</u> means of securing a structure in which individuals can advance to positions of corporate power, a fact which the frequent discussion of the 'alternatives' of individual as against collective action for managers serves only to obscure). What Hopflinger's study demonstrates is that a collective representation of sectional interests within capitalist control structures can indeed exist and that when it does there is a real demand for it.

SUPERVISORS' DEMANDS ON WHITE COLLAR UNIONS - SURVEY DATA

Sample and Methods
The survey data were obtained from 48 first and second line supervisors who were attending a part-time Certificate in Industrial Management course at a Polytechnic. The supervisors were asked to write a short essay in response to the single open-ended question, 'What should white collar unions be doing for the industrial supervisor?' At the time when the question was put, none of the supervisors had previously met the writer, nor had they received any teaching on industrial relations at the Polytechnic. The essays were completed in class time and without consultation between the supervisors.

No question is perfect, and although the one used

suggests no particular function which white collar unions should perform, it could nevertheless be argued to 'lead' inasmuch as it suggests that they should perform <u>some</u> function. In the words of one of the two supervisors who pointed this out before proceeding with their essays:

> This question presupposes that the supervisor needs a union to get something for him that he cannot obtain for himself.

Additionally, a further three of the respondents found space within the question as posed, to make it clear that they were not at all attracted to the idea of trade unionism:

> To me unions, whether it be white collar or not, has given this country a bad name, in the fact that it cannot meet contracts because of trivial strikes; i.e. who shuts off a valve at the end of a shift? Costing a company and the country millions.

Not surprisingly, these three anti-union replies produced no positive views on what policies white collar unions should pursue, though they have, of course, been included in the overall count of replies.

The main method of analysing the essays consisted of coding them according to whether or not they mentioned the issues listed in the headings of Table 4.1. Essentially these headings were derived from the discussion in the introduction of this chapter, with the addition (after an initial cursory glance at the essays), of a coding according to whether or not they mentioned task-related education or training.

At first glance, the open ended nature of the question would lead one to expect that a count of the number of mentions of an issue would, if anything, lead to an under-estimate of its salience, if only because the writers of the essays might not trouble to mention what they take to be obvious. For example two of the essays mention the function of unions in 'representing' their members without explicitly stating any respect in which they might do so. Naturally the coding of the essays includes no guesses as to what such 'representation' might mean.

Against this, it could be argued that the method of posing the question 'leads' in that, having mentioned the obvious issues (say, wages and other employment conditions), the supervisors, feeling a certain pressure to fill out their essays, began looking for issues of peripheral importance (say, control and other task-related issues). If this was indeed the case, it would be expected that task related issues would be mentioned later in the essays than employment conditions. However, within the 45 'usable' replies which mentioned either issue, a count showed that employment conditions were mentioned first on 29 occasions whereas task-related issues were mentioned first in 16 cases. The latter, at one third of the sample is a substantial minority and whilst no one would doubt the generally greater salience of employment conditions, the result indicates that task related issues are far from an afterthought.

Given the small size and self-selected nature of the sample, it is almost bound to be untypical and background details will not therefore be presented. The findings are only of interest because they deviate markedly from the conventional view of white collar unions and even then they must be regarded as tentative.

Results and Discussion

Employment Conditions   The results from the coding of the essays are shown in Table 4.1.   Unsurprisingly the most frequently mentioned issue (by 70% of the sample) was that of wages.   On the other hand, given the rate at which redundancies are currently being declared, it is perhaps surprising that employment security was mentioned by only one quarter of the sample.   On past experience with this course something like 3 to 4 of the supervisors could expect to lose their jobs during the year and it is, of course, the 'commonsense' view that insecurity is a motive behind white collar unionisation.

Of those mentioning wages, just over half explicitly referred to the restoration of differentials over the shopfloor.   In fact a fair number of the supervisors made a case for considering themselves worse treated than manual workers. For example:

> I work a 37½ hour week which may be argued is not a lot but I am on call for the rest of the week and if I am called out I receive no extra pay. I think this system, that has for a long time become regarded as a staff 'privilege', should be rectified.

Some of the supervisors, in an interesting reversal of the logic of an economic 'return to control' argued, in justification of differentials, that by generating respect, they actually served to enhance the ability of supervisors to control labour:

> This differential is important because, providing the supervisor proves his competence to his subordinates the greater the differential, the greater the respect a supervisor can command hence his job should be easier than if there was only a low differential.

Table 4.1: Results from Coding of White Collar Union Essays

TOTAL REPLIES = 48   UNION MEMBERS = 23 (48% of total)

Employment Conditions

Mentions of employment security	= 12	(25% of sample)
Mentions of wage issues	= 34	(71% of sample)
Mentions of differentials	= 18	(38% of sample, 53% of mentions of wages)
Mentions of responsibility for subordinates in wages context	= 14	(40% of mentions of wages)
Mentions of responsibility for subordinates in differential context	= 11	(60% of mentions of differentials)

The Control of Labour

Mentions of some form of assistance with controlling subordinates	= 27	(56% of sample)
Mentions of training or advice related to control of subordinates	= 11	(41% of mentions of control)
Mentions of other forms of assistance with controlling subordinates	= 17	(63% of mentions of control)
Mentions of assistance in counteracting shopfloor union power	= 12	(44% of mentions of control)
Mentions of assistance in gaining greater control from management	= 10	(37% of mentions of control)

Education, Training and Advice

Mentions of task relevant training or advice	= 22	(46% of sample)
Unions should provide this	= 15	(68% of mentions of training or advice)
Unions should inflence managements to provide this	= 6	(27% of mentions of training or advice)
Training or advice related to control of subordinates	= 11	(50% of mentions of training or advice)
Training or advice related to career advancement	= 6	(27% of mentions of training or advice)

Few of the supervisors left the mention of wage issues without offering some form of justification, either for an increase as such or for the restoration of a differential over the shopfloor. These varied from vague references to 'a proper rate for the job' to quite detailed references to experience, qualifications and the variety of tasks that supervisors are expected to perform. In view of the earlier argument that wages may be linked to control issues via an economic 'return to control', arguments using the control of labour as a justification are of particular interest. Of course the control of labour is a somewhat broader concept than the control function of capital, since some aspects of the direction of labour are arguably a necessary part of the productive process. On this point, the content of the essays offers no help since the supervisors can scarcely be expected to draw a distinction between control for capital and control for production. Nevertheless references to the direction of labour are most unlikely to exclude at least the transmission of those aspects of control aimed at the extraction of surplus value. Moreover when supervisors speak, as many did, of their 'responsibilities', the implication is one, not only of co-ordination, but of delivering the labour force (as it were) to capital in the persons of senior management.

Of those mentioning wage issues, 40% offered their part in the control of labour as a justification whilst, amongst the smaller number mentioning differentials, the proportion was 60%. Though the numbers are small and too much importance should not be attached to the exact proportions, the results are notable, given that they depend on spontaneous mentions of quite detailed points within a broadly conceived topic. The following is typical:

> Many supervisors do not receive a satisfactory remuneration. This is made even more acute when the point is made that first line supervision is the most important in terms of man management.

Control Issues 55% of the sample believed that white collar unions should offer supervisors some form of assistance with controlling their subordinates. Though less than the proportion mentioning wage issues, this is a considerably greater proportion than those mentioning the 'commonsense' issues of differentials (40%) and employment security (25%). Within the limits of the survey, then, this is a considerable vindication of the argument developed earlier; that not only is the loss of position within the control function of capital a motive behind white collar unionisation but the restoration of that position of control exists within white collar unions as a potential issue. The following is a typical explicit mention of the control issue:

The second answer, whilst not as obvious, is, I think, more important and that is to fight for the supervisors' status. By supervisors' status, I mean the authority and power that a supervisor needs to ensure that the job gets done in the most efficient way.

The power and authority that a supervisor has should extend, if necessary, to the ultimate of being able to dismiss a subordinate, should that person exhibit persistant and unreasonable refusal to conform to the supervisor's aims.

Whilst most of the mentions of the control of labour were similarly unequivocal, three borderline cases were coded in the same way, of which the following is the 'weakest':

The other side of the union should be to help its members in their jobs, for example to give professional people updated professional advice on technology and management techniques.

After some deliberation, this was included as a mention of control on the grounds that 'management techniques' would probably include some aspect of controlling labour.
As the preceding quotation indicates, a frequently mentioned form of assistance in the control of subordinates was training and advice, particularly on the supposed constraints on supervisors represented by labour legislation. Of those mentioning control issues, 40% referred to assistance of this type (as against the 60% who mentioned other forms of assistance). It should be stressed that it is not education and advice in general which is at issue here, but only that which is clearly directed at the problems of controlling labour. Again the preceding quotation illustrates the minimum standard of explicitness on this issue which was used in the coding. The following is more typical:

The supervisor is constantly in touch with varying Human Opinions and therefore training could be given in the various aspects of Human Behaviour. Being in constant touch with others makes him more of a Man Manager than just making alterations to the system employed.

Ironing out problems could become an everyday task so training in the Behaviour of Humans would give the supervisor an idea of why people act the way they do.

Of those who thought that white collar unions should pursue control issues on the behalf of supervisors, 40% specified that the problem, as they saw it was one of counteracting the power of shopfloor unions. This is a fairly 'raw' version of the viewpoint:

> Secondly [the white collar union] should help its members to become powerful enough to hold their own in any free–for–all fight with the manual workers' union.

More typical is:

> White collar unions need to give the Industrial Supervisor help in gaining better social conditions when dealing with personnel who can be so well insulated by the unions, that his effectiveness is impaired to a level.

There were also 'educational' versions as in the following reference to dealing with shop stewards:

> It is my personal viewpoint that the white collar union should aid the industrial supervisor by encouraging the employers to ensure that a standard of management exists which will enhance industry in general by, e.g. further education, training managers in particular fields such as employee relations, the ability to deal with shop stewards, employee motivation, etc.

However, references to confronting or otherwise dealing with organised labour were only part of the theme of enhancing control. Of almost equal concern (mentioned by 37% of those who mentioned control issues) was union assistance in gaining from management a greater share in the decision-making process:

> Also the supervisor should have more say in how the firm is run, meaning they are more in contact with the shopfloor than what management is. They see and hear what goes on at this level. Come in contact with the people from shopfloor, and know how the people cope with problems they face at this level.
>
> The union could also . . .

Although manipulatory or confrontation tactics were sometimes thought appropriate in enhancing control at the expense of organised labour, other supervisors clearly thought in terms of an ambassadorial role for white collar unions, more particularly, though not exclusively, when the question of gaining backing and autonomy from senior management was on the agenda:

128

The union should promote the status and explain the role of its members such as Industrial Supervisors so that other people can better understand why the supervisor acts or reacts in a certain way . . .

The white collar union should recognise the importance of the industrial supervisor and encourage senior management to do so by improving pay and status. They should encourage other unions to see the industrial supervisor as an intermediary and not simply as a hatchet man for the company, even if he is one at times.

Education, Training and Advice   It may already have become apparent that the supervisors' essays frequently mentioned task-related education, training and advice as services which should be provided by white collar unions.

Apart from Spoor's study of NALGO (1967), there is little in the British literature on white collar unions which would lead one to anticipate this. However, the issue of opportunities for further education and training is one pursued through their unions by cadres in the French aircraft industry (Reynaud, 1983). European managerial unions generally tend to provide career-related educational services and one might conclude that a demand for such services may well exist in this country too. Note that it is task-related training and information which is in question, not information on the supervisors' rights as employees and the like.

These services were spontaneously mentioned by 45% of the sample: fewer than those who mentioned wage issues (70%) but more than referred to the 'obvious' issues of differentials (40%) and employment security (25%). Examples have already been quoted but the following is a further illustration:

The union should try and encourage firms to make sure that supervisors are well trained in both the technical and man-management aspects of the position.

This is untypical however, in that a majority (70%) of those who mentioned task-related advice or training, thought that white collar unions should provide it themselves as opposed to the 27% who thought that unions should try to obtain it for their members from management:

Therefore to conclude, I would say that the White Collar Unions should be helping the Industrial Supervisor by educating him in an impartial method. This resulting in an improved personal performance and improved company performance.

Thus for a majority of those who mentioned task-related training or advice, what might be regarded as the more typical trade union tactic of demanding training from management took second place to the 'management union' approach of providing it themselves. Though two of the supervisors who mentioned union provision of vocational training were NALGO members (which union has provided such training for many years - Spoor, 1967, pp.397-436), a subtraction of these replies is insufficient to affect the overall trend of this particular result.

As mentioned earlier, there are, for supervisors, connections between the issues of control of the workforce and task-related training. Thus half of those who mentioned advice or training as desirable issues for white collar unions to pursue, gave sufficient detail in their replies to make it clear that they had in mind information related to their present task of controlling subordinates. Besides earlier quotations which refer to training in 'man-management', 'employee relations' and the like, the following is typical of the references to employment legislation in this context:

> In most industries the supervisors have developed from the shopfloor and in this way they have been ignored by the white collar unions. In today's technological environment it is becoming essential for the supervisor to be properly trained in management skills because of increased legislation.

As one of the supervisors pointed out, training can be related to future as well as to present tasks, which raises the issue of access to positions of greater influence and autonomy via individual promotion rather than collective action:

> Supervisory positions also tend to be the bottom rung of the managerial ladder and if the union ensured that the company supplied the best possible training for the supervisor then if he proved to be capable he should be able to progress up the management ladder and achieve his rightful position within the company.

Although only a minority mentioned this aspect of training (about a quarter of those who mentioned advice or training at all), it perfectly illustrates a point made earlier: that there can be a solution to the problems of lack of influence and autonomy within the control function of capital based on a <u>collective</u> attempt to secure a structure in which <u>individuals</u> can progress to positions of power.

CONCLUSIONS FROM THE SURVEY

Given the limitations of the sample, it is probably unncessary to stress that any conclusions must be very tentative indeed. Nevertheless the results indicate that a restoration of position within the control function of capital is an important motivation for the supervisory members, or potential members, of white collar unions. As well as implying a demand that white collar unions should assist in counteracting the power of the shopfloor, this also entails a desire that they should somehow influence management in the direction of enhancing and backing up the supervisory function.

There also appears to be a demand amongst supervisors that their unions should, on the model of European managerial unionism, provide task-related education, training or professional advice. Whilst the major demand is that this should relate directly to the function of controlling labour, there is a subsidiary wish that the educational services to be provided should enhance the prospective control of supervisors by opening up career channels to higher and therefore more influential positions.

For supervisors, even wage issues are permeated by the question of control since, for them, a major justification of their economic position (or rather, the one they would like to occupy), is the control they exercise (or would like to exercise) over the labour of manual workers. For supervisors, then, trade unionism although it concerns employment conditions just as it does for shopfloor workers, also involves the entirely different issue of control over the shopfloor. There is therefore, as the literature abundantly asserts, no question of a facile identification of the unionisation of white collar workers with proletarianisation. At the same time, the question is not, as it sometimes asserted, irrelevant, since the implication of this study is that there are demands within white collar unions which imply interests directly <u>counter</u> to those of the shopfloor.

However, it needs to be remembered that supervisors are a minority amongst white collar workers and that there are likely to be differences between the demands of white collar union membership and policies actually pursued by the leadership. In this connection, it is worth recalling that the managers, whose disaffection with their branch of ASTMS sparked off this study, actually left their union. The demands indicated by this research may therefore exist in the form of a tension <u>within</u> the ranks of white collar unions as well as in the form of overt local or national policies.

Chapter Five

TRADE UNIONISM AND THE NEW MIDDLE CLASS: THE CASE OF
ASTMS

Bob Carter

The 1970s saw several attempts by Marxists to
re-theorise the class location of employees who, while
clearly not owning the means of production, performed roles
on behalf of capital within the production process
(Braverman, 1974; Poulantzas, 1975; Carchedi, 1977; Wright,
1978). With this advance in Marxist class theory came the
promise of an enriched understanding of 'white collar' trade
union behaviour. In particular, no longer would the lack of
militancy of white collar trade unions have to be explained
in terms of the 'false consciousness' of their members or by
abandoning a Marxist framework altogether and adopting a
neo-Weberian one which considered variations in, amongst
other things, the work situation as a determining factor
(Lockwood, 1958). The promise of a more sophisticated
analysis of the nature of trade unions organising the new
middle class has not, however, been fulfilled.

Not only was concern for the organisational forms of new
middle class trade unionism ignored by the original
contributors to the new perspectives, but where similar
frameworks have been adopted there is still a tendency to see
trade unions as unambiguous representations of the function
of labour. Rosemary Crompton, for instance, recognises the
ambiguous class situation of many white collar employees and
claims it is both rational and understandable that some of
them 'see their interests as being best fulfilled by
co-operation with management (or the capitalist function) -
for example, in staff associations - and others in the same
occupation see their collective interests as being served by
identification with the labour function - in trade unions'
(1976, p.442). But, by radically dichotomising the nature of
staff associations and trade unions Crompton implies a
homogeneity of social purpose to trade unions which in
practice does not exist. Moreover, as Bob Price has noted of
Crompton's argument, if the distinction between TUC unions
and internal staff associations is the only measure of
heterogeneity in collective representation and the ambiguity

132

of class situation we seem to be faced with few conceptual problems. In 1978, less than five per cent of white collar unionists were in staff associations, suggesting that 'British white-collar workers are in little doubt as to where they stand in the class structure' (Price, 1983, p.170).

To maintain that many white collar employees are middle class while simultaneously insisting that trade unionism necessarily constitutes a proletarian form is a mistake. To be consistent, it is possible to say either that variations in policies between unions comprising managers and those of manual workers merely reflect the heterogeneous nature of labour or that the variations reflect not just sectionalism or economism but stem from the qualitatively different social functions within the workplace. Within this latter view it is perfectly feasible to have demands emanating from trade unions which seek to enhance control over the labour of others, demands which belie the proletarian nature of <u>all</u> trade unionism. But the policies of trade unions cannot be simply attributed to their class composition (even where, exceptionally, this is pure). Rather they are a product of complex interactions. The demands of members are managed and transformed by unions, or more particularly union activists and bureaucracies which face pressures other than from the membership, both organisational and from other institutions. The following study of ASTMS, a union much given to organising the new middle class, seeks to take this proviso into account when exploring how this particular union is influenced by the social roles of its membership.

ASTMS

The membership of ASTMS is extremely heterogeneous, perhaps more so than any other British trade union. Its members, 390,000 in 1985, span a variety of industries, bargaining structures and traditions. The Association refuses to release any breakdown of its membership but a survey carried out by its research department in 1975 estimated that of its membership of, at the time, 325,000, 150,000 were in the engineering industry, up to 50,000 in insurance, 17,000 in banking and 20,000 in the National Health Service. In addition, ASTMS had substantial numbers in the chemical industry, in publishing, and amongst university technicians and commercial travellers. It is likely that since that date the relative weight of the different section will have changed somewhat, with members in engineering declining because of the recession and an increase in banking and finance, aided by the merger with ASTMS of various staff associations.

The heterogeneity of the membership derives not only from it being drawn from a wide variety of sectors of employment but also from the inclusion of people who hold positions of widely differing authority within those sectors. In 1978, ASTMS had 75,000 members from Britain's 20 largest manufacturing companies, over one sixth of its total. This meant at GEC, for example, that the union was able to claim bargaining rights that 'go clean across the board, and embrace professional engineers, managers, scientists, technicians, supervisors and clerical workers' (ASTMS Journal Nov/Dec, 1978). Without details revealing its members' grades and roles at work, however, it is not possible to generalise about the extent to which the membership of the union is middle class. The union certainly has in membership testers, clerks and technicians who undertake neither supervisory work nor any wider managerial functions and therefore do not fall within the definition of middle class. Nevertheless, it would appear that many, if not the majority, of ASTMS members carry out some managerial functions. The argument which follows attempts to support the contention that the leadership of the Association is more than conscious of the social relations of its membership and has devised an organisation and strategy specifically to appeal to sections of the new middle class. On the view developed here, when its General Secretary, Clive Jenkins, lists his hobby in Who's Who as 'organising the middle classes' there is a serious truth behind his jocularity.

Strategy and Growth

ASTMS was formed in 1968 by the merger of the Association of Supervisory Staffs, Executives and Technicians (ASSET) and the Association of Scientific Workers (AScW). While ostensibly a merger of equals, in practice, what emerged was a take-over of AScW by ASSET. ASSET was not only much larger, having 53,000 members compared with the 22,000 of AScW, but it was also a much more dynamic organisation. Between 1964 and 1968 ASSET had expanded by 17,000 members, or 47 per cent, compared with a growth rate of only three per cent per annum of AScW. It was the tradition of ASSET rather than that of AScW which held sway in ASTMS. The overall aims, strategy and tactics adopted were modelled on those of ASSET. The new association possessed an identical structure to that of ASSET as well as a similar leadership style and, after a brief period of joint leadership from the two general secretaries of the former organisations, the same General Secretary, Clive Jenkins.

The growth of ASSET was in no small measure due to a consciously worked out and openly debated strategy. After a heated debate at the 1958 Annual Conference an executive policy paper was adopted which abandoned random recruitment in favour of concentration on major companies. The paper was based on an analysis of the movements in industry towards monopoly, oligopoly, take-over and rationalisation, and argued that it would only be possible to build up financial strengths and membership rapidly and efficiently by organising the big employers (Jenkins, 1965, p.57). It was maintained that only the implantation of the union within major companies would give the union influence on national salary and employment policies. Responsibility for recruitment in key companies was given to full-time officers and, as membership built up, the officers retained overall responsibility even where companies had plants outside the divisional structure of the union. This strategy for growth, and the union structure which evolved to carry it through, represented a radical break from the exclusively regional orientation of many unions.

Another transformation of the Association was also in process although this time not consciously adopted. The union was moving towards open recruitment, but to do so had to overcome important obstacles. The Association had, for instance, always been at pains to distinguish itself from the industrial and general unionism which surrounded it. According to the union, 'as industry becomes more automated, the technician, trained in a particular discipline or specialisation feels he has more in common with a technician with a similar background and training employed in a quite different industry than he has with other differently employed and trained employees in his own company or "industry" ' (ASSET, 1967, p.2267). ASSET therefore gave as the rationale for its existence the need for a specialist union for technicians and supervisors, but, at the same time, this restricted its willingness and ability to recruit other categories of employee.

Alongside this orientation, however, a competing model of future growth was developing. The union was beginning to see the possibilities of transforming itself into a general union based upon the new middle class. In order to achieve this, however, it needed to concentrate not on particular categories of staff but all categories. This shift of emphasis coexisted for some time with the continued belief in the necessity for a specialist union. The Association's evidence to the Donovan Commission in 1966, for instance, contained a section entitled, 'The Case for a Specialist Union', but also went some way towards advocating a more widely based union, arguing that:

> One of the motivations impelling the sort of people we organise to join a union is the feeling that they have been falling behind in the struggle for better salaries and conditions. At one time, 'staff status' carried with it all kinds of benefits: apart from higher pay, there were substantial differentials in holidays, sick pay schemes, superannuation and so on (ASSET, 1967,

pp.2247-8).

By shifting the focus from specialist staff to a more broadly defined 'sort of people' and by introducing the concepts of 'staff status' and differentials, the potential membership was enormously widened. Reflecting a concern among supervisors and technicians over loss of status and erosion of differentials, the union became aware that many people outside its traditional areas were also highly responsive to this view. While the union still claimed that 'a foreman or technician in engineering has more in common with a foreman or technician in chemicals or transportation than he has with manual workers with whom he is associated in engineering' (ASSET, 1967, p.2268), it was not referring to identification through common skills or occupational title, but rather a common belief in their superiority over manual workers. And once the leadership of the union became clear on this, it could break with the limiting legacy of the union's past.

ASSET had discovered the formula which was eventually to transform it into a general union organising both new middle and working class members. Such transitions are rarely smooth, however, and the Association's roots in supervisory and technician grades were still apparent in 1968. In that year, the British Iron and Steel Management Association (BISMA) voiced an interest in amalgamation. It was an independent staff association in the steel industry organising, in competition with ASTMS, both middle and senior management, administrative staff, and qualified scientists and engineers. ASTMS refused to consider it because it did not regard clerical and administrative staff as eligible for membership. Such a decision would have been unthinkable just a few years later.

The main limitation to the expansion of ASSET was not its lingering attachment to the idea of a specialist union but a practical one - ASSET was simply too small to be a major pole of attraction to the unorganised middle class. The importance of the merger with AScW was not that it diversified the membership, although it did this to a small degree, so much as the confirmation of the momentum of ASSET. It confirmed one of the main characteristics of ASTMS - its ability to merge with and swallow up other organisations. Since 1968, a string of mergers, particularly with staff associations, has taken place.

Mergers with staff associations having little or no trade union tradition, and especially associations of managerial employees such as the Kodak Senior Staffs Association and the Courtaulds Group One Staff Association threatened to lower further the trade union perspectives of the Association. In 1976, for instance, the Association merged with the United Commercial Travellers Association (UCTA), most of whose 18,000 members were employed as sales representatives, although approximately 2,000 of them were manufacturers' agents. There was obviously some logic in ASTMS taking into membership those UCTA members employed in large companies where ASTMS already represented supervisory and technical staff. But UCTA also had substantial assets and a large and modern head office and land at Knutsford, Cheshire, which offered ASTMS much needed space to expand its office facilities in the north-west of England. Whatever the attraction of the merger, however, it certainly was not the functioning of UCTA as a trade union which made the organisation attractive or compatible, since UCTA mainly provided legal services to individual members rather than collective bargaining expertise and assistance. There was considerable justification for the fears of certain officials and lay members of ASTMS that the integration of former UCTA members would take some considerable time. At the UCTA Section Conference in 1978, for instance, the executive report came under considerable criticism from members who objected to the adoption of quite elementary trade union positions such as not affiliating to Chambers of Commerce because they were employers' organisation. ASTMS Assistant General Secretary, Muriel Turner, visited the Conference and commented that she 'would like to see more discussion and more thinking about collective bargaining and moving towards organising salesmen into bargaining units and negotiating agreements with managements' (Selling Today, June 1978). Further evidence that the UCTA section was not operating as a real trade union is revealed in the section's newspaper Selling Today, which has on occasion shown a preoccupation with anything but trade union activity: topics advertised for branch discussions have included guest speakers from radio stations, 'Selling at Trades Fairs' and 'The Growing of Sweet Peas'! (Selling Today, June 1978).

While dramatic gains in membership were made early on the period during which such mergers were numerous is now past. Despite the fact that since 1979 the recession has placed increased strains on the resources of small, independent associations, ASTMS has not managed to continue with its rapid expansion through mergers. This is in part because other unions have recognised ASTMS's success in attracting middle class associations and have made similar appeals, sometimes making even more concessions to their consciousness by changing their organisational forms. AUEW-TASS, for example, established quite separate managerial branches and a National Managerial Staffs Committee. It also now produces a special quarterly magazine for managerial members, combined with an aggressive recruitment policy aimed at managerial staffs. GMWU-MATSA appointed a senior officer to devote time specifically to initiate mergers with non-TUC bodies dealing with professional staffs. The EETPU and the EMA have also been active and successful in securing mergers with managerial associations. It was the success of these other organisations which, in 1982, prompted ASTMS to set up the National Professional and Management Staffs Council in order further to attract managerial and professional employees.

The recession had also dented the general appeal of trade unionism. In a different economic climate, the Association had much success in recruiting by keeping itself in the public eye, both through extensive and imaginative advertising and the frequent public appearances of the General Secretary on radio and television. The Association's image has been closely tied to the ebullient and acerbic Clive Jenkins and no distinction can be made, as one Divisional Council requested, between his professional union activities and his role as 'a light entertainer' (No.4 Divisional Council Minutes, September 1977). Critical of both employers and governments and avowedly left-wing on many issues, Jenkins has nevertheless managed to portray himself as a champion of the middle class. While managers and supervisors may have strongly disagreed with his politics, they also welcomed his appearance of aggression and militancy, projecting on to him the ability to deliver them from their sense of decline and frustration.

The Appeal of the ASTMS
While now experiencing with other organisations the general difficulties faced by trade unionism during the recession there is little doubt, in view of its once successful recruitment, that for a time the union had great appeal for large numbers of middle class employees. The growth between 1968 and 1978, for instance, was over 500 per cent, suggesting that its propaganda found a sympathetic response. A major feature in this propaganda was its appeal to those employees who considered themselves by-passed by management and overtaken by manual workers. There was a brief period in the mid 1960s when ASSET's analysis of its growth appeared to rest on the belief that it was a result of middle class employees being proletarianised. Such an analysis was consistent with recruitment targeted on major companies where concentration and rationalisation of middle class labour was proceeding most quickly and where, as a consequence, traditional autonomy was being eroded. Such developments generated the possibility of a radical movement of white collar workers:

Just as the highly skilled manual engineer group formed the aristocracy of labour and was the most militant vanguard element of the trade union movement in the nineteenth century, it seems that technicians are scheduling themselves the same role in the last part of the twentieth century (Jenkins, 1965, p.60).

The argument was advanced that as a white collar employee joined a union and acted against his employer 'the class and political barriers which separated him [sic] from other employees are being dissolved' (Jenkins, 1965, p.70). But for all the talk of the formation of a radical movement of white collar workers no programme was ever indicated. Demands for higher status and the restoration of a differentials were made, but these hardly constitute the programme of a radical movement which is about to lead the whole class.

The belief that the growth of the union signified important social changes was no doubt sincerely held but the contention of the Association that it represented a new and more dynamic force than the traditional unionism of manual workers also served a more narrow purpose - it bolstered the superiority of the Association and distanced it from other sections of the labour movement, a stance of no small importance to a union trying to extend unionisation further up the social hierarchy. Some such rhetoric still lives on but what it more important is that the perspective of organising an increasingly proletarian white-collar movement has been entirely abandoned in favour or organising white collar workers as middle class workers. The Association is now fully committed to organising around those aspects which are specific to middle class work situations, in order to maintain those aspects (and with them class relations at the workplace).

One aspect of the Association's adaptation to the now recognised conservative aspirations of much of its potential membership is the way in which the importance of membership activity is minimised. ASTMS has marketed itself as a professional service:

> If you feel unwell you visit a doctor; if you have a toothache you visit a dentist; if you are involved in litigation you visit a solictor; if collective bargaining needs to be done, workers approach a trade union. We live in the age of the professional and in the case of trade unions this applies not only to the negotiators, but also to their research, legal and educational staffs (Jenkins and Sherman, 1977, p.2).

The transition from an individual to a collective perspective, which was seen earlier as of great significance, and as the harbinger of a new radical social and political movement, is now totally absent. Passivity, not action, is the keynote. Trade union membership is marketed like an insurance policy which may be needed one day if there is a threat of redundancy or even periodically for wage claims, but which has little day to day relevance:

The insurance industry recently advertised by using the slogan, 'get the strength of the insurance companies around you'. In this modern capitalist world it would be remiss of the white-collar worker not to take that advice in industrial terms and join a trade union (Jenkins and Sherman, 1979, p.11).

It has been suggested elsewhere that one of the explanations for the success of ASTMS is that when attempting to recruit senior grades the campaign frequently has had the not altogether unintentional affect of increasing the membership of lower grades (Roberts et al., 1972, p.116). Certainly there is some evidence for this view from the union itself. One of the Assistant General Secretaries is on record as saying:

Managers are an important opinion-forming section of the industrial and commerical community. A union which organises the managers effectively will have less difficulty organising the rest of the staff (ASTMS Journal, July/August, 1981).

Whether the tactic of associating with prestigious groups has been used consciously or not, there can be little doubt that the union's distancing from manual workers has been deliberate. The assertion that its members and potential members are superior and more worthy than manual workers has been a central component of recruitment strategy. Potential members have been flattered by evaluations claiming that: 'The new white-collar trade union member tends to exhibit the traditional traits of this special grouping. He or she is articulate, gets information from newspapers rather than television, and is personally ambitious for his or her children' (Jenkins and Sherman, 1979, p.9). The same sentiments insidiously informed an issue of Finance News, ASTMS's paper for its insurance, shipping, banking and commercial membership. Sandwiched between two photographs, the top one of terraced housing and the one below of semi-detached housing, was the caption, 'Few insurance workers would want to start married life in the type of house shown above. To live in a street like the one below is a natural aspiration for white-collar staff' (Finance News, Spring 1977).

There have been objections within the union to such an orientation. At one meeting it was suggested that the union placed too much emphasis on the differences between its membership and shopfloor workers and that more effort should be made to stress the common problems which face both groups. Such arguments have made little impact and on this occasion Jenkins replied that the union recruited by telling prospective members that they were handsome and sun-tanned and that the union would make them more handsome and more sun-tanned. To a cry of 'bullshit' Jenkins responded: 'This may be bullshit, brother, but it's the best bullshit you'll ever hear!'

The emphasis on the superior worth of white collar workers has sometimes brought the Association close to denying the justice of other workers' claims. This tension is apparent in ASTMS recruiting literature:

> The skills and expertise that scientists and engineers have acquired painfully over many years are not being rewarded by renumeration, security of employment or promotional prospects. The professional, whether a man or a woman, whether a scientist, engineer or computer specialist, has seen other less skilled, less qualified groups of workers catch up with and indeed surpass his or her salary, whilst at the same time enjoying more secure employment. This is not to say that others do not deserve their wages and salaries; what it does say is that the time is approaching when skill, qualifications and responsibility will also have to be adequately rewarded (Professional Scientists, undated).

The necessity for the disclaimer clearly demonstrates the Association's awareness of what might be taken to be implicit in the way it presents its case. It also indicates the parameters within which the union works. The hostility towards other sections of workers is raw material which the Association has to convert into hostility towards employers. Failure to do so would threaten ASTMS's relationships with the wider trade union movement. The Association's formal policies clearly emphasise the organisation of its members as wage-labour. But if it does not frame demands which aim to strengthen members' roles as agents of capital, neither as indicated below, does it seek to challenge them.

The structure of the union
The basic unit of organisation of ASTMS, like ASSET before it, is the workplace-based group. There were approximately 10,000 such groups in 1979. Each of these groups elect officers, the most important of whom is the group secretary, whose role, in addition to handling negotiations, is to maintain co-ordination and communication between the group and the Divisional Officer, and between the group and the branch to which it is attached. Members either form groups or are allocated to them on the basis of work performed or their grades of work. It is not uncommon therefore to have several groups and sub-groups at one workplace. If the collective membership of a group at a workplace is over 250

then the group can apply to the Divisional Council to become a closed branch. Where the membership of the groups at a workplace is insufficient to form a branch, groups are attached to a branch on a geographical or industrial basis.

The concentration on work-based groups is a distinctive feature of the structure of ASTMS and has the consequence of reflecting and reinforcing the narrow and instrumental commitment of many middle class employees to trade unionism. This narrow and instrumental commitment is not of course unique to middle class employees, but few unions have created a structure which accommodates it so fully. Potentially, the group structure encourages a high degree of membership involvement, allowing distinct and separate problems to be discussed in detail. At the same time, however, it can foster parochialism and become, instead of a lower unit of organisation than the branch, a substitute for it.

The group structure tends to isolate members from members in other workplaces and also from members within the same workplace. Not only is there little pressure from the union to build up strong workplace organisation but the diversity of opinions and the autonomy of groups are paraded as a positive virtue. If people are hesitant about joining the union because they might have to abide by wider collective decisions and show solidarity with fellow members, the union assures them that these fears are groundless. After a meeting with the Institute of Mechanical Engineers, for instance, the Association reported:

> The union made it quite clear that its structure provided a great deal of autonomy to the varying groups of members and that special provision were made for professionally qualified members. Confirmation was also made that different groups within the same firm could adopt different policies if they so wished (ASTMS Journal, March/April, 1978).

The ASTMS structure tries to accommodate with as little friction as possible differing ideas and varying levels of trade union activity and commitment, levels themselves conditioned by members' positions in production relations. Within the same workplace, therefore, militant test engineers could be engaged in industrial action while production engineers or foremen went about their work undisturbed. There is no compulsion whatsoever to support other groups as has been made clear by the results of a number of attempted disciplinary actions. In 1974, the Investigating Committee, a sub-committee of the National Executive Council, heard an appeal from the branch at Dowty Rotal Ltd., for the expulsion of a number of members in the junior management grade who had failed to participate in a dispute. The Committee's decision was that it was not policy automatically to call out executive staff in a dispute involving other grades. Furthermore, in defence of the staff concerned, it was stated that they had been recruited into the union on precisely this basis. In the particular instance in question, it was decided that the junior management staff were to be informed that they had acted incorrectly in not joining the dispute because the decision to withdraw labour had been taken by the group of which they were part. A similar situation was to be avoided in the future by the branch establishing a separate grade for the executives, rather than by forcing them to accept group discipline (<u>NEC Minutes,</u> January 1974). In a similar case the Committee decided that there were no grounds for proceeding against someone since 'it was against union policy to insist that managerial staff should be bound by decisions to participate in disputes called by members not in their bargaining unit; or that they should be bound by decisions taken by committees of members in subordinate grades' (<u>NEC Minutes,</u> November 1975).

ASTMS's policy and structure seek to remove higher grades from the scene of disputes. This is possible only where higher grade members have no direct managerial command over members in subordinate grades, who are participating in official disputes. Disciplinary actions against managers who have tried to undermine disputes are rare, however, either because few members expect managers to do otherwise or because it is recognised within the union that disciplinary attempts will almost certainly fail. For instance, when members of the Swansea University branch of ASTMS, sought the expulsion of a professor who had told a meeting of staff in his department that they should not take part in officially sanctioned union action, the Investigating Committee decided that expulsion was not appropriate because the professor felt that he was performing the managerial function for which he had been contracted (<u>NEC Minutes,</u> January 1974). The conclusion is clear: where all or part of the function of ASTMS members is to resist or undermine trade union organisation, including that of ASTMS itself, then this function is respected by the union and not regarded as subject to union control. This is presumably why the union could contemplate the recruitment of personnel officers (Jenkins, 1973, p.35).

<u>Differentials</u>
Much of the Association's success in recruiting sections of the new middle class can be attributed to the way in which its propaganda 'appeals unashamedly to the values of the well-paid, ambitious, young professionals' (<u>Financial Times,</u> 15 May 1984). In particular, the union has emphasised the necessity and justice of pay differentials for skill and responsibility. In doing so it finds itself echoing a deeply

conservative position, one which is shared by many implacable enemies of trade unionism. The future prosperity of Britain, so the Association's argument runs, is tied up with the establishment of 'correct' differentials. Change 'differential' to 'incentive' and the following report in the Association's, <u>Journal,</u> could have been part of a Conservative Party election manifesto:

> Differentials, contrary to much current propaganda, are not a device born of greed by those working elsewhere than on the shopfloor. They are a necessary reward for people who have acquired skills, who accept responsibilities and who put up with the stresses without which modern industry could not operate. Low or non-existent differentials devalue the very qualities which are essential to the development of wealth-production and thus higher living standards for all (<u>ASTMS Journal,</u> March/April, 1977).

The same idea was expressed somewhat differently in a book written jointly by Clive Jenkins and Barrie Sherman, the Association's Director of Research:

> We live in a capitalist society in Britain. Profit is made and its ethic widely accepted. An employee who has a skill or responsibility will want to be paid for carrying it and the training-cum-experience which probably needed some considerable self-investment. Equal pay for all could, theoretically, mean that there would be no return on this investment and equally that would mean a diminution in the number of people acquiring skills or prepared to accept responsibility when something goes wrong (Jenkins and Sherman, 1979, p.83).

In this view the dangers to skilled workers comes not from employers' attacks through rationalisation and the devaluation of their labour, so much as misguided equality-mongering. There is little in this policy of the union, therefore, to enhance its reputation for being left-wing. A correspondent to the <u>Journal</u> was much closer to the truth in pointing out approvingly that 'the union fight for skill and responsibility differentials is more akin to Conservative than to Socalist philosophy' (<u>ASTMS Journal,</u> March/April, 1977).

Conscious of suspicion and hostility from manual unions, the union has become sensitive to claims that its policy on differentials is reactionary and has sought to prove that in reality all wage earners benefit. The union claims merely to be acting as a model of good trade union practice believing that 'this helps to lift the whole concept of adequate pay at all levels, and is therefore an aid to all trade unionism' (ASTMS Journal, March/April, 1977).

Attempts to preserve differentials are, of course, not absent from relations between manual workers and it is true that differentials encourage claims for parity from lower paid workers, thus generalising increases. There is little evidence, however, that ASTMS policy has this effect. Shopfloor workers generally do not compare their wages with the salaries of supervisors and managers. As one study commented, 'the choice of pay comparisons is typically unambitious and powerfully shaped by custom: major inequalities which form an established part of the incomes hierarchy are rarely a focus of attention' (Hyman and Brough, 1975, p.61).

The comparison of salaries to wages, therefore, has largely been one way. ASTMS has attempted to set up a stable relationship between salary and wage levels that involves a fixed formula for settling salary claims after shopfloor claims have been settled. The relationship has clearly been one of 'wage-push' and, not as the union claims, one of 'salary-pull'. This situation has had advantages for the Association and has been welcomed by the membership as indicated by the following statement by an Assistant General Secretary in 1967:

> At Babcock and Wilcox we organised an agreement for supervisory grades. This meant that we were able to go to the Company and make a plan on behalf of one particular grade at a time, and traditionally we used the argument of differentials for manual workers. The Company realised that this was a very cumbersome way of handling the matter. We wanted to make an agreement whereby we established a reasonable relationship between the wages of the supervisory and technical staff as against the earnings of manual workers in the factory. Having done this, we than devised a system whereby the average earnings of the manual workers were fixed over certain periods - in this case six monthly periods - and correspondingly adjustments were made on the basic rates of supervisory and technical staffs . . . It has worked very well indeed, we think, and we will certainly be willing to go into further agreements with the Company. It has saved internal argument and it has saved a lot of time for the Company officials and ourselves, and has allowed the Company some stability in matters concerning their staff workers. This has been a very good type of agreement in our opinion, and we certainly would be willing to look at this type of agreement again (ASSET, 1967, p.2283).

The above agreement was not unique. In 1974 the union signed an agreement at Massey Ferguson's Manchester plants which established a 25 per cent differential for production foremen above their highest paid group of subordinates (ASTMS Journal, November/December 1978). At Leyland Bus and Truck Division management and union accepted the 1977 McCarthy Report on foremen's wages which noted a tradition of a six per cent differential over the highest paid toolroom worker and recommended that this should be raised to ten per cent (NEC Minutes, November 1977). What is formally enshrined in these agreements has been informally accepted in thousands of other workplaces. There seems some justification, therefore, for the feelings of shopfloor workers that they go into bargaining carrying some ASTMS members on their backs because the eventual outcome will automatically benefit members of ASTMS without their engagement in struggle.

Incomes Policies

The main threat to procedures like those above has come not so much from employer hostility as from a series of government imposed incomes policies. Not surprisingly ASTMS has been amongst the unions most opposed to incomes policies and some of its credibility as a left-wing union is based upon this opposition. Under closer examination, there is little to sustain this reputation. The central argument of ASTMS against incomes policies has been not so much that they are designed to increase the level of surplus value but that incomes policies disrupt the differentials enjoyed by its membership:

> Both within society as a whole and within individual companies, indeed departments, there is a delicate framework of relativities and differentials. These have evolved (and continue to do so) over time and represent the truest picture of what employees are worth in the labour market-place . . . Incomes policies deliberately set out to provide rules and norms and invariably distort and sometimes fragment these established relations (ASTMS Journal, July/August, 1976).

As a vehicle for opposing the results of these policies, however, its effectiveness is open to doubt. The Association claims to have recruited heavily because of its highly vocal opposition to incomes policies. Its success in opposing the results of such policies is, however, open to doubt. The union has tended to avoid open confrontation with incomes policies and, given the unwillingness or inability of many of its members to take effective industrial action, the Association has looked for alternative ways of overcoming them. Reviewing the period of the Conservative Government's incomes policies, 1972-3, Jenkins and Sherman declared:

> Only trade unions showing the greatest ingenuity, the greatest determination and the greatest understanding of the legislation have been able to provide their members with a service worthy of the name; this has been reflected in their membership growth or decline (1977, p.19).

However, the ingenuity, determination and understanding was not used to encourage membership action against incomes policies, it was used to render such action unnecessary. Centre stage, once again, is the team of profesional negotiators:

> With the intrusion of such legislation it becomes an exercise in Machiavellian policies and only unions with good, intelligent negotiators, backed up by a first class research and legal service managed to offer their members an adequate service (Jenkins and Sherman, 1977, p.21).

The emphasis here was on finding loopholes in the legislation. Later, when a Labour Government introduced sanctions against companies which broke its income policy, the Association's tack was to instruct that all settlements above the limit were to remain secret.

Not fundamentally challenging incomes policies meant that successes were bound to be confined to a minority of companies and ensured that the fight against them was restricted to local, and often unknown, initiatives. More particularly, the tactics were totally inappropriate for dealing with the effects of incomes policies on ASTMS's public sector membership. National negotiations with publically accountable bodies ruled out local evasion. The only possibility of gaining settlements over and above the limits laid down in government policy seemed to be through industrial action. This, however, the union leadership has been anxious to rule out: 'kamikaze' tactics should not be adopted because 'Governments know they can win in the public sector and are willing to take workers on there', Clive Jenkins told the Annual Delegate Conference in 1978. Instead the Association instructed its officers to compare public and private sector pay with a view to a series of Fair Wage claims under Schedule 11 of the Employment Protection Act. Such a move was never likely to succeed but the Association had no alternative other than to seek legal and political redress, once industrial action was ruled out.

The way in which the disquiet of its public sector members has influenced very directly the political stance of the Association can be seen in the support given to a document that was drawn up by the Economic Committee of the

147

TUC and the Labour Government in 1978 as the basis for a 'concordat'. In explaining support for it and his disappointment at its eventual rejection by the trade union movement Jenkins stated:

> Very important, it could have given new comparative exercises for the public sector, with special reference to the NHS, Universities and the low paid in Local Government, and thus further leverage in efforts to put right the quite scandalous mistreatment of our members (<u>ASTMS Journal,</u> November/December, 1978).

There is no simple option available to unions with low-paid public sector members. Merely to stress the necessity for industrial action ignores the very real problems of achieving it. The absence of the production of surplus value, the saving of money by local authorities and hospitals during many disputes, and public hostility to industrial action, all conspire to deter a powerful and confident trade union movement in this sector. In addition to these general problems, ASTMS also has supervisory and management grades in membership in the public sector who would be unlikely to regard industrial action favourably, even in situations more conducive to success. The need to solve the problem of low pay at the level of political action and pressure is therefore doubly reinforced in the case of the Association. ASTMS has been quite adept at political lobbying; what it has not been able to do - indeed has not attempted - is to build sympathy and solidarity with its public sector membership across its own heterogeneous membership. Yet it is only with such solidarity and wider public support that it seems sufficient political pressure can be mounted to rectify the anomaly of low public sector pay.

ASTMS's failure may not be principally caused by the class nature of its membership, but that membership and the basis on which it is recruited, make a solution that much more difficult.

Recognition
Despite the preparedness of the Association to accommodate itself to the function of capital performed by many of its members this has not avoided all employer hostility towards recognising the union. Employer resistance to the independent organisation of managerial and supervisory employees, together with the Association's probably correct calculation that many potential members would join only if the route to union recognition avoided industrial action, has led to the union supporting various proposals making recognition a legal right rather than a result of collective organisation and strength. In other words, the Association

has been drawn towards various political solutions to compensate for its inability to force recognition at workplace level.

In some respects ASTMS could be regarded as a victim of its own earlier success. Not only did its forerunner, ASSET, secure a recognition agreement from the Engineering Employers Federation in 1944, largely because of state pressure, but a major obstacle to its growth, the Foremen and Staffs Mutual Benefit Society, also changed its rules in 1969 to allow into membership trade unionists as the direct result of the introduction into Parliament of a private bill by ASTMS. As a consequence 'the union became convinced that relatively unorthodox but highly sophisticated tactics could be made to work' (Jenkins and Sherman, 1979, p.35). What this meant in practice was that the Association would spare no effort in publicising the difficult problems it faced gaining recognition from obdurate employers and in particular arguing and supporting various mechanisms 'by which we [the Association] can petition in some way or other for our union' (ASSET, 1967, p.2282).

It was the search for alternatives to industrial action to secure recognition that led the Association to register under the Conservative's 1971 Industrial Relations Act in order to gain access to the recognition provisions. It was the same reasoning that later saw ASTMS an enthusiastic supporter of the Labour government's 1975 Employment Protection Act, which gave to the Advisory, Conciliation and Arbitration Service (ACAS) an influential role in determining recognition claims. But, as ASTMS was to discover, ACAS did not smooth the path to widespread recognition and by 1977 the Association became disenchanted and critical:

> We have lodged 90 separate claims for recognition with the Advisory, Conciliation and Arbitration Service under the law. Unfortunately, the delays are very great indeed . . . In Michelin and IBM very backward employers are digging in, in defence of their world-wide anti-staff union policy. We are getting very impatient with the entire situation (ASTMS Journal, January/February 1977).

The Association was not only critical of the slowness of the procedure, however. It was also critical of the decisions which emanated from it. It had also been particularly critical of the granting of certificates of independence to professional and staff associations under the 1974 Trade Union and Labour Relations Act, which allowed such organisations to make applications for recognition. The Association, therefore, through its ASTMS MPs, attempted a series of initiatives to amend the legislation to close off access to the procedures for recognition by non-TUC unions.

In doing so, once again, the Association reflected its unwillingness or inability to fight these organisations where it was most crucial - at workplace level. Where trade unions were well-organised the gaining of certificates of independence by rival non-TUC organisations proved of little use in gaining recognition because employers and ACAS feared recognition would result in retaliatory industrial action by the already entrenched TUC unions. But the fact that the Association was not confident that it could deliver such action is in part a reflection of the class composition of its membership. Despite its experiences therefore it continued to be drawn towards legislative solutions, believing that government aid was crucial to the achievement of its aims. The weakness of such an orientation became even clearer with the advent of the Conservative government in 1979 and the abolition of the procedures for recognition within the Employment Protection Act.

ASTMS AND THE LABOUR PARTY

So far, it has been argued that the projected image of ASTMS, its methods of recruitment and certain central policies, have all displayed the sensitivity of its leadership to the class situations and behaviour of its members and potential members. And yet ASTMS has enjoyed a continuing reputation of being a left-wing union, largely because of its relationship and involvement with the Labour Party. This gives rise to an apparently paradoxical position: for a largely passive and conservative membership has not just supported a leadership which has been closely identified with the Labour Party, but a particular current within it, the left-wing Tribune Group. The explanation for the coexistence of a conservative membership and a seemingly radical leadership has, in part, already been suggested. The inability or unwillingness of sections of the membership to take industrial action at the workplace tends to cause the projection of solutions into the political arena. Before elaborating on this tendency, however, it is necessary to sketch out the extent of ASTMS's policies and involvement.

A superficial look at the support of ASTMS's members for the Labour Party might lead to the conclusion that it was not inconsiderable. In particular, a growing political fund and an increased number of members affiliated to the Party throughout the 1960s and 1970s might be taken to imply that the members and leaders were united in a common political strategy. In 1975, for instance, ASTMS affiliated 185,000 members, or 57 per cent of its total membership to the Labour Party. The growth of the political fund and the growing numbers affiliated, however, masked a diminishing level of membership commitment to the union's political orientation.

In the same year the annual accounts reveal that fewer than 50,000, or 16 per cent of the membership, had actually paid the full political levy. The discrepancy is accounted for by the fact that the union charged a much higher political levy than the amount needed to affiliate members to the Labour Party and used the surplus income to pay for extra affiliations. By 1985 the Association estimated that one third of its membership, or 130,000 members, paid the levy. Once again the accounts show that less than thirteen per cent, or 50,000 members, paid the full amount. The point is that the leadership is committed to increasing the union's political involvement despite the lack of positive support from the membership.

The 1970s saw concerted attempts to get members elected to Parliament culminating in a record number of 38 Parliamentary Committee members in 1977. The number has declined to 31 in 1985, but this is to be explained more by the poor showing of the Labour Party at the last election than by any change of union tactics. Nor is the reduced number any less active. The ASTMS Parliamentary Committee holds regular meetings, produces regular reports and is open to all ASTMS MPs. It organises Parliamentary lobbying, meetings with Ministers, the asking of questions in the House of Commons and the sponsoring of Private Members Bills.

The importance the union places on the activities of the Committee reflects, and reinforces, the lack of self-activity amongst large sections of the membership. Just as the union places emphasis on the ability of its professional negotiators rather than organisation and the determination of its members to settle workplace problems, so MP's are presented as higher level representatives of the union who are willing to take up and solve problems at the very centre of power. Sections of the membership with major problems, for instance, redundancies, frequently grasp the opportunity to send delegations to Parliament and lobby Ministers rather than take strike action. The Parliamentary Committee normally facilitates such visits. This can be illustrated by the response of the NEC to a complaint that only one of the Association's MPs turned up to support a delegation to a Minister. The reply by the President of ASTMS pointed out that there had only been one other occasion when the representation of MPs had been inadequate and that generally union deputations to Ministers included a high percentage of MPs (NEC Minutes, July 1977). Rather than the actions of the Parliamentary Committee being contradictory to the conservatism and passivity of the members it is therefore complementary to it.

The leadership's pursuit of increased political involvement by the Association is then not wholly a matter of political idealism but a necessary means of achieving a solution to problems faced by the union. In consequence, its involvement has tended to be of a highly opportunist nature. Richter, who made a study of the political involvement of ASSET, commented on the role of the General Secretary:

> Close observation . . . of Mr Jenkins' work . . . indicated that a major and perhaps preponderant share of his time and energy on and off his job was devoted to political operations designed to enhance ASSET's bargaining position as well as Mr Jenkins' prestige and authority. In a variety of political activities, Jenkins had a reputation of being a left-winger; in his ASSET Parliamentary Committee role, however, he was distinctly eclectic and opportunistic. He limited himself to strategies that would yield organisational and bargaining involvements (1973, p.182).

Richter's observations are still pertinent, even if his explanation for the strategy of political involvement was in some respects simplistic. He argued that 'the basic reason for the genuine commitment of this union to parliamentary techniques was simply that as a fledgling union fighting resistant employers, as well as TUC rivals, it needed political allies to legitimise and strengthen its bargaining role in many heterogeneous and fragmented labour markets emcompassed by the areas of organisation it had staked for itself (1973, p.182). Such an explanation suggests a declining commitment to the strategy as the union progressively established itself in those labour markets. On the contrary, however, the growth of membership from 58,000 when Richter made his study in 1967 to well over 400,000 in the late 1970s witnessed an increase in parliamentary representation and involvement.

There is no doubt that the Association's parliamentary strategy is subordinated to the aim of increasing its bargaining role, although the complexion of the present government restricts any very serious influence. But the explanation for the necessity of the strategy rests, not as Richter suggested, with organisational weakness but with the class composition of much of the membership and with the leadership's (probably correct) assessment that the preparedness to take industrial action to support demands does not exist. In forcing ASSET into a model of unions resorting to political involvement during the early, weak stages of unionism, and abandoning that involvement as they grow stronger Richter ignored the class nature of the membership. But this model, however appropriate it is for manual unions, does not hold for ASTMS. Nor can the Association's strategy be explained by reference to the importance of its public sector membership. The central positions taken up by the union in Parliament - for a legal right of recognition, for free collective bargaining, for the extension of the National Enterprise Board (NEB) and for import controls (see below) - are much more relevant to its private sector members than to its, in any case, relatively small public sector membership.

While the lack of industrial weight of the Association encourages attempts to secure political support it also lessens the likelihood of that support being delivered. Cultivating the favours of the powerful can prove frustrating, as ASTMS has found to its cost. In 1964, for instance, 'the focal activity of the entire full-time staff in the General Election was on behalf of "Brother Wilson", the Labour Party Leader and potential Prime Minister' (Richter, 1973, p.185). In addition, Wilson's constituency Labour Party received from ASSET the largest cash contribution to any constituency as well as the use of some office equipment, and this was even though it was far from being a marginal constituency. At the same time, the Association gave only token contributions to the general election fund of the Labour Party because, in the words of one executive member, 'we've got to put it where it counts for us' (Richter, 1973, p.183). There were, however, no visible dividends for the assistance given to the in-coming Prime Minister. Wilson's membership of ASSET notwithstanding, the Government refused to act to outlaw the rules of the Foremen and Staff Mutual Benefit Society which discriminated against trade union members, and showed no sign of legislating on the matter even after recommendations from the Donovan Commission.

The Parliamentary Committee may have given union members a route to those considered powerful and created the appearance of union activity and concern with their problems, but there are definite limits to the gains which have been achieved. For instance, although ASTMS's delegations protested about aspects of the working of the Employment Protection Act, they failed to stir the Labour government to anything more than vague statements about making future amendments (NEC Minutes, January 1976). Nor is it likely that any future increase in the number of ASTMS MPs will prove a solution because, if ASTMS's involvement with Parliament and the Labour Party has been opportunist, so too has the commitment of many MP's to the Association. While a small group have had close relations with the union and have shared its perspectives, a sizeable number have taken union membership simply because it aided their ambitions within the labour movement. As Richter commented on ASSET:

The personal reward for the Labour candidate for Parliament - and some sitting members as well - was that ASSET offered to many of them the most feasible union connection to people of their professional and business ties. And, of course, such a union membership remains vital for winning the nod from Labour Party selection conferences (1973, p.188).

This opportunism on the part of some Labour Party MP's has meant that any ties with the Association can be soon loosened, especially perhaps when they become Ministers.

Situations have arisen, where ASTMS MPs and members have found themselves on opposite sides of a conflict. In 1975, for example, ASTMS members joined the one-day strike called by the Works Council at Ebbw Vale Steel Works. This was against closures that had been proposed in a report by Lord Beswick, then Minister of State for Industry and an ASTMS member. In the same year, the No 15 Divisional Council submitted a resolution stating:

> In the light of the refusal of Dr David Owen to pay wages owing to Medical Laboratory Technicians, members of ASTMS, arising from dispute action, this D.C. calls upon the NEC to report the matter to the Investigating Committee . . . In the view of this DC explusion of Dr. David Owen is justified in the light of his actions (NEC Minutes, June 1975).

The NEC replied to the above resolution in terms that mirrored the Association's respect for managerial functions – no action could be taken against Owen when he was acting in his Ministerial capacity, however wrong his actions might be. The Association was not prepared to jeopardise the continued membership of MPs by exerting trade union discipline.[1] Other complaints against ASTMS MPs, particularly Ministers, illustrate the distance between them and sections of the membership. That such a gap has opened up is not surprising but the tone of the above resolution does reflect the expectations of union activists – that MPs should act as ASTMS members in Parliament – and it also indicates the extent to which Divisional Councils have been convinced by the strategy of the leadership.

The Association has used its MPs within Parliament as direct representatives of its immediate and sectional interests. The role of the Parliamentary Committee is presented to its members as de-politicised and ASTMS MPs are presented as a group of specialist members, 'experts', who can 'give a new dimension to ASTMS case presentation' (All About Our Political Fund, no date). If this were the whole picture, however, it is difficult to understand the union's refusal to consider requests from Conservative ASTMS members that the Committee should be broadened to include Conservative MPs (Financial Times, 2 December 1977). Conservative MPs could equally function as specialist members and, with the present government, would be more likely to influence events. The explanation for the leadership's hostility to such proposals stems from the fact that ASTMS's political involvement functions at two levels: behind the pragmatism and opportunism ASTMS has strongly supported a coherent political position which is deeply hostile to Conservatism. So while the Association has in membership Labour MPs who cover the whole spectrum of Labour opinion, it has been closely identified with a small but important group of MPs around the <u>Tribune</u>. Until 1977, for example, three Tribunite MPs sat on the NEC. Elected to national and regional seats of the NEC they were virtually unaccountable to the membership and constituted therefore a direct ideological component of the NEC. The most prominent of these was Ian Mikardo whose relationship with ASTMS was long-standing. Other important figures connected to the union have included Brian Sedgemore, Arthur Lewis, Jeff Rooker, Martin Flannery, Stan Thorne, Jo Richardson, Ron Thomas and Stuart Holland. Together, these MPs have formed an important component of the support for what has become known as the Alternative Economic Strategy, comprising import controls, an end to the role of sterling as a reserve currency, price controls and incomes policy, increased powers to the National Enterprise Board, industrial democracy, public ownership of financial institutions, and the maintenance of Labour's social programmes (Sedgemore, 1977, pp.30-1).

With the exception of an incomes policy, the Association has adopted policies similar to those above, which raises the question why, even if members have supported the political representation of their immediate interests, they have tolerated support for what would be widely considered a very left-wing industrial programme. The explanation is two-fold. Firstly, many members have remained untouched and unaffected by what they regard, quite correctly, as rhetorical declarations of little practical import. Secondly, and more significantly, where Association members work in ailing industries, such as footwear, electronics and engineering, the demands for Government intervention have been welcomed. The lack of confidence in their own ability to deal with the power of capital produces a hope that the government will intervene on their behalf. ASTMS's advocacy of a more active role for the NEB found sympathy amongst the membership not because of any very strong anti-capitalist ideology, but rather because it was seen as the only alternative to industrial action to save jobs. In response to cutbacks in the telecommunications industry, for example, the Association set up a Telecommunications Co-ordinating Committee which, in 1977, published an analysis of the industry arguing for its restructuring to enable the transition to new electronic technology and more effective competition with foreign companies. The union wanted a unified company created from the telecommunications divisions of Plessey, GEC and STC with a majority public share holding through the NEB. The Association made similar proposals to solve the same sort of problems in the power engineering industry.

This approach of encouraging state intervention into industry, while transferring the response of the Association from organising industrial action in defence of jobs to the political arena, has not been without dangers for members even when a Labour Government has accepted the invitation to gain control of companies. The experience of intervention is that it is aimed at modernising and rationalising sectors of industry and is invariably accompanied by productivity increases and redundancies. Public investment in International Computers Limited illustrates these dangers to union members. The company received substantial amounts of capital from the government up to 1976, which was used to build up a range of new computers, but this support and healthy orders books did not safeguard its workforce which was cut by 22 per cent from 1969 to 1976.

Underlying the Association's policy is the belief that the state is neutral and that Labour Governments are highly responsive to trade union pressure and will further the interests of the working class. As in the other areas of its political involvement the Association's assumptions are as questionable as its experiences are disappointing. The main impact of Labour's industrial intervention was to speed up the process of rationalisation and concentration of production. Given the restricted domestic and international market in the mid 1970s this inevitably meant fewer jobs. ASTMS, having posed the involvement of the NEB as the solution to the problems faced by its members, risked embarrassment when the consequences of the involvement became apparent. Referring to the closure of British Leyland's factory at Speke, for example, one Assistant General Secretary informed delegates at the 1978 Conference that all the union could do in such situations was send a representative to the funeral.

The political orientation of ASTMS has complemented and reinforced the weakness and passivity of much of the membership - with the notable exception of the insurance and banking membership. As a consequence of working in a stable and profitable part of the economy and not yet having had to face a wholesale threat to their jobs, members took exception to their leadership's support for the nationalisation of finance and insurance companies. Rather than nationalisation representing a promise of security (even if an empty one) they regarded it as a threat to their already fairly secure position. (Here it should be noted that the most highly unionised section of the workforce in insurance are those occupying male career positions, rather than the more lowly paid, and typically female clerical workers: see Crompton and Jones, 1984.) Fears of nationalisation led the insurance membership to mobilise within the union to reverse the Association's policy. Faced with this mobilisation against a central plank of the Alternative Economic Strategy the leadership support for it collapsed.

CONCLUSION

It has been a common criticism of writers on the new middle class who came to prominence in the 1970s that they had little or nothing to say about the politics of the class. Yet more particularly they had little or nothing to say about white collar (or other) trade unions and what their class composition might mean for what sociologists and industrial relations writers have called union 'character' (Lockwood, 1958; Prandy, 1965; Blackburn, 1967; Bain et al., 1973). An inspection of ASTMS might seem to suggest one good reason for this silence. At first glance, there are several respects in which the union's policies would seem to render inadequate on analysis which took as its point of departure the class composition of its membership. Most obviously, ASTMS organises its members against the power of employers. Its role in bargaining for better pay and conditions for its members appears therefore to be little different from the role of any other union. It is hardly surprising that this role spills over into the realm of politics, again as with most other unions. And although ASTMS organises managerial and supervisory employees it can point to rules about their conduct in industrial disputes which are designed to ensure that they neither undertake the work of strikers nor supervise 'blackleg' labour. In addition to appearing to function in the main no differently from unions with a much different social composition, it is also the case that the policies of the Association are the product of a number of contradictory pressures. The state of the economy, for example, affects sections of the membership unevenly, particularly as between those in the public and private sectors. Moreover, large numbers of ASTMS members are unambiguously working class: technicians, radiographers and test engineers, for instance, are fully rooted in a labour process and their expectations and demands on the union are a considerable influence on policy-making. It might be thought misguided, therefore, especially in view of ASTMS's militant reputation, to seek to link the union's distinctive character to its middle class composition.

On the other hand, it is equally possible, as this study shows, to point to a number of ASTMS policies, such as its support for differentials and opposition to incomes policies, which are directly linked to the middle class nature of its membership. Important as these policies are, however, it was never the intention of this contribution simply to reduce the policies and functioning of the union to an expression of its class composition. Rather, the argument is that the varied and complex processes which create policies are mediated by the leadership's concern not to alienate and jeopardise the membership of middle class labour. This orientation to examining the Association necessitates looking beyond its formal policies to its practice. Taking up the question of the union's militancy, for instance, it is the case that the leadership has on occasion been happy to adopt or accept radical policies. But the policies have for the most part been incidental to the interests of large sections of its membership and certainly have made no demands on the membership to take action. Nothing better illustrates this than the Association's close ties with the Labour Party. Because of passivity and lack of interest in the affairs of the union, the membership tolerates these ties even though it is fairly certain that the majority of the members vote Conservative. The leadership of the union have attempted to make the links with the Labour Party acceptable by emphasising the role of the Parliamentary Committee as a professional service of the union, which will take problems out of the hands of the membership and deliver them from the need to act on their own behalf. And even the left-wing industrial policy supported by the union, the Alternative Economic Strategy, emphasises increased state involvement as the solution to Britain's industrial decline and requires no action by members, an orientation not unwelcome to ASTMS members facing closures and redundancies but nevertheless having no faith in industrial action to change their situation.

ASTMS has said much in its propaganda to make it abundantly clear that its model of trade unionism encroaches little upon the individualistic aspirations of middle class employees. Frequently, because of their managerial and supervisory roles, its members' attitudes will also include hostility to the actions of the other trade unionists. The union clearly stops short of representing and reinforcing this hostility but it does not seek directly to challenge it, or the roles which engender the hostility. There are rules covering the conduct of its members during industrial disputes, for example, but there are definite limits to these rules which acknowledge the roles of its membership: members may not undertake work normally outside the terms of their employment - unless to safeguard plant, equipment and valuable materials; members are encouraged to co-operate with unions involved in disputes - 'as far as their terms of employment permit' (ASTMS Rules, 1977, p.105), a qualification with possibly overriding significance for managerial employees.

Elsewhere the Association's respect for the managerial functions of a large number of its members is more explicit.

For example: 'It is not part of the function of a union representing managers to seek to control their operations as managers. We have always accepted that it is their job to manage. The Union cannot and does not wish to interfere with that managerial function' (ASTMS Journal, July/August 1981). The union of necessity therefore has had to create a structure which allows almost complete autonomy to managers and ensures that they are not subject to decisions made by subordinate employees. Managerial members are not expected and cannot be instructed to come out on strike even in support of fellow ASTMS members. It is not that the Association does not want to see solidarity displayed by its membership - there is nothing in the rules to prohibit it - but simply that the union does not feel confident enough in the membership's reactions to insist upon it. Or, in the Association's own words, 'unless a union is willing to come to terms with this need [for managerial autonomy] there is little point in seeking to recruit and represent managerial staff' (ASTMS Journal, July/August, 1981). The nature of ASTMS policy is not decided voluntaristically by the leadership but results from a number of influences, central to which is the influence of the social relations of the people it seeks to organise. Any union organising members of the new middle class will reflect the same problems.

NOTES

1. It is important to note that David Owen is no longer eligible for the Parliamentary Committee because of his defection to the Social Democratic Party. This demonstrates that the leadership's own party political sympathies do affect union policy, a point expanded below. The general argument remains, however, that both the union's policies and its structure have been constructed in ways that are in practice compatible with the interests and aspirations of its new middle class membership.

Chapter Six

ENGINEERS, TRADE UNIONISM AND TASS

Chris Smith

This chapter explores the impact of changes in the occupational structure of technical jobs on TASS, the major trade union for technical staff in British engineering. In particular it examines how the union responded to and was shaped by the decline in draughtsmen, their traditional base, and the growth of graduate engineers and managers. It is argued that the decision to change the class base of the membership had important implications for the policies pursued by the union in the 1970s.

In chapter three I indicated that 'other technicians' and 'engineers' represented the main areas of growth for technical occupations and consequently technical trade unionism from the mid 1960s. Changes in the training of engineers, the decline in the value of qualifications obtained on a part time basis and the growth of degree-holding engineers has pushed Britain towards the situation that exists in the USA (Whalley, 1984). But whereas in other countries qualifications have been used by engineering unions and professions as a closure mechanism for the occupation, in Britain employers and the State have consistently blocked moves towards credentialism along professional lines (Armstrong, 1984; Whalley, 1984; Smith, 1985). Employers have insisted on controlling the allocation of technical labour according to the needs of the market or the division of labour, rather than by professional criteria endorsed by statute or laid down by a professional institute (Abercrombie and Urry, 1983). Whalley and Armstrong both argue that the open access and domination of professional institutes by employers has prevented the professionalisation of engineers along the lines of other occupations. The employer's resistance to this type of occupational control is nicely illustrated by the failure of the United Kingdom Association of Professional Engineers (UKAPE) to utilise the growing graduate status of engineers as a way of securing autmy from non-graduate or qualified technical staff. At C. A. Parsons for example, the management insisted that:

160

There [was] no identifiable level of jobs which [could] be regarded as the 'new graduate entry level' . . . There is no level of post in . . . which only employees with prescribed qualifications are employed . . . Management's policy [was] to appoint the most suitable candidate available and in making a choice academic qualifications and membership of a professional institution, though important factors, are only two of the several considerations which are taken into account (CIR, 1972, p.18).

Employers' resistance to professional control does not mean that they do not ulitise qualifications on their terms to differentiate and divide technical labour. In general technical labour is today more educationally structured, between graduates and non graduates and this has blocked mobility between the drawing office and design department (Roberts, Loveridge and Gennard, 1972; Smith 1982). It has formalised and fractured the division of labour in the technical area and served to 'solidify the social gap between engineers and the shop floor' (Whalley, 1984, p.127). Nevertheless as I argued in chapter three the breakup of a craft tradition for engineers is not in itself evidence of a change in their class position if they are located in non-supervisory, technical functions not directly engaged with quantifying the labour of other workers. Moreover, whereas when we examine the preparation of technical labour power we can see a major shift away from craft, towards indirect systems, the British legacy of 'learning by doing' or 'experience' is still significant. Whalley (1984, p.127) notes that even UKAPE, which has promoted professionalism, insisted in reports to the Finniston inquiry into the status of engineers on the 'absolutely vital' place of shop floor experience for engineers. While this is evidence of the employers' penetration of such organisations, something discussed later, I also found a strong emphasis amongst the engineers I interviewed on the importance of experience, and the disadvantages of a closed or rigid demarcation between mental and manual labour. The inability of engineering institutions, for whatever reasons, to establish an autonomous base for engineering in Britain, which is cut off from, superior and dominant over craft or experience, is a legacy that structures any discussion of professionalism or unionism amongst engineers (Ahlstrom, 1982; Glover, 1983; Smith, 1985). Unfortunately, as I will now show, it is a legacy not given sufficient attention by those examining organisation amongst engineers.

The conventional way of examining collective organisation amongst higher white collar groups is through the debate about professional associations versus trade unions. It has also been long recognised that for engineers such a dichotomous model is ambiguous (Kleingartes, 1969; Prandy, 1965; Roberts, et al., 1972). Where a professional association is functioning effectively in controlling the labour supply, wages, conditions and method of occupational evaluation then a dichotomy between unionism and professionalism may be appropriate. With engineers this is not the case. When engineers were only recruited in small numbers through the conventional channel discussed below, a stable elite or status consciousness within the technical division of labour was maintained. The growth in employment and the concentration of engineers within large organisations challenged the stability of such a situation. In 1972, at what is now NEI Parsons, engineers constituted 20.5 per cent or 345 of the 1695 technical staff (CIR, 1972). At the end of the 1970s qualified engineers at C. A. Parsons alone represented 27 per cent of TASS's 789 membership.

At the end of the 1960s the concentration of engineers, with increased insecurity due to mergers, rationalisations, redundancies and squeezed wage differentials, plus changes in the conditions of employment, converged to stimulate a need for effective organisation amongst engineers. The appearance of UKAPE in May 1969 has been strongly associated with these changes (Dickens, 1972). Relatedly, other so-called professional unions, the Association of Professional Scientists and Technologists (APST), 'UKAPE's sister body on the science and technology side' appeared because of similar forces (Gill, Morris and Eaton, 1977). But these 'professional unions' did not exist in a vacuum but in an arena in which white collar-unions like TASS and ASTMS were growing. The tension between unionism and professionalism in the 1970s took place within the organisational form or structure of 'trade unionism'. Obvious as this is to the protagonists, some sociologists continue within the terms of debate established by writers like Prandy and argue that professional unions and professional associations are 'two modes of occupational organisation' which should be 'seen as complementary alternatives' (McLoughlin, 1982, p.587). Such a view has not taken on board the irrelevance of professional associations to graduate engineers' wages and conditions. Neither does it take seriously the origins of UKAPE, which was promoted by Engineering Institutes not to compete with them but with established trade unions. What it also ignores is that in terms of industrial policy, political practice and ideology, UKAPE was seeking to accommodate engineers interests' with those of employers and establish separate, elite and 'third force' politics inside British engineering. And this, as I will now show, was a form of 'trade unionism' that was in marked contrast to TASS at the time, and their policy towards engineers.

TASS AND ENGINEERS: THE CONTEXT

The Association of Engineering and Shipbuilding Draughtsmen (AESD) was established by draughtsmen in 1913. Membership was only 200 in 1913, but grew rapidly during the First World War, stimulated by the transfer of craftsmen into the drawing office because of dilution (Mortimer 1960, Roberts et al, Smith 1982). Membership peaked at 14,500 in 1920 and declined throughout the inter-war period until rearmanent in 1935. AESD appeared with the Association of Scientific Workers (AScw) and the Association of Supervisory Staffs, Executives and Technicians (ASSET) - now ASTMS. They grew together and they declined together until 1935. Unlike some other white collar unions AESD survived the depression, largely by paying unemployment benefit. In 1939 the membership was 23,600 and in 1945 it stood at 44,158 - again stimulated largely by manual dilutees entering the drawing office in large numbers. Between 1945 and 1967 the average annual growth was around 2,000. As with ASTMS and APEX growth took off in the late 1960s, rising from 75,754 in 1968 to 127,362 in 1974 and only slowing down, stagnating and declining with the onset of the deepening depression in manufacturing in the late 1970s. Membership today is around 300,000. Growth was not as spectacular as ASTMS, largely because membership is concentrated within engineering which has suffered disproportionately to the service sector in terms of unemployment.

AESD was built on draughtsmen. The title of the union changed to the Draughtsmen and Allied Technicians Association (DATA) in 1960, but recruitment still relied upon draughtsmen and the expanding area of 'other technician'. The amalgamation with the AEF in January 1971 saw the name change to the Technical and Supervisory Section of the AUEW. This changed in 1973 to Technical, Administrative and Supervisory Section. TASS moved from a solidly technical base to a general white collar identity, although because of the existence of APEX - which could not be persuaded to join the AUEW in 1974 - and the density of unionism in engineering, it remains an overwhelmingly technical, not clerical or supervisory union. In 1981 TASS took over a small craft union to gain procedure agreements for manual workers[1]. In 1984 it merged with the sheet metal workers union, NUSMWCH and DE (the National Union of Sheet Metal Workers, Coppersmiths, Heating and Domestic Engineers) and established a manual group directly to compete with the AUEW and TGWU especially in the area of greenfield sites. This change reflects the failure of the TASS/AEU amalgamation, which wained from the mid 1970s and appeared to collapse completely in 1985. Nevertheless the craft exclusiveness of DATA has gone from the policy of the union, although the General Secretary often lambasts members for their craft sectarianism, which it is claimed has inhibited recruitment of deskilled white collar workers and supervisors (Smith 1982).

In recruitment documents aimed at engineers, discussed below, the union has consistently argued that there is no incompatibility between belonging to a professional institute and TASS. This not only reflects the union's accurate assessment of the irrelevance of the institutes to the wages, terms and conditions of engineers located in large industrial bureaucracies, but echoes the 'learned society' activities and craft practices of the old AESD. The union had a technical publications department from 1919 and members and others produced pamphlets and books on such things as a 'Resume of modern gunnery' and 'Design of overhead crane structures'. The union produced over 400 such publications between 1919 and 1960 (Mortimer 1960, pp.449-457.) Several attempts to regulate the supply of draughtsmen, through a 'control scheme', a characteristic of craft unions, occurred during the 1920s but came to nothing. Rising unemployment 'made it impossible to insist the drawing office staff should be recruited only through the medium of the AESD' (Mortimer p.90). However the union operated successful control of labour supply through the weekly publication of a Vacancy List in which employers paying union wage rates could advertise freely and those undercutting wages or conditions could be publically blacklisted. This paper later incorporated into TASS News, only ceased publication in the mid 70s. Through such measures TASS achieved a high density of unionism amongst drawing office staff, including designers and engineers who frequently retained their TASS card on promotion into a qualified engineer status or position. The union's effectiveness, craft nature and tradition made sharp differentiations between professionalism and craft hard to sustain in the era of the non-graduate engineer. But with engineers increasingly entering engineering without a craft apprenticeship, the organic unity and union density amongst technical staff began to decline. In addition the common class background began to change. Whalley in a study of 110 engineers found 60 per cent of engineers with HNC's had a working class background, while only 38 per cent of degree holding engineers had working class family backgrounds, although in a questionaire to 30 office representative at C. A. Parsons I found seven of the 30 with degrees as likely to come from a working class as petty bourgeois background.

The amalgamation between DATA and the AEF has been identified by some writers as a response to the reduction in the recruitment base of the union (Undy, Ellis, McCarthy and Halmos, 1981). The authors note the 168,550 draughtsmen in 1961 was down to 149,500 in 1971, a loss of eleven per cent in potential members. It is also true that DATA, as well as having a lower growth rate when white collar unionism 'took off' in 1967, only recruited 20 per cent more members between 1955-1964 relative to a 75 per cent growth rate for the AScW, 103 per cent for ASSET and 42 per cent for CAWU, later APEX. The same authors also claim, on evidence from a TASS official, that during the 1955-64 period, DATA 'drew approximately 50 per cent of its recruits from members of the AEU newly promoted to the drawing office' (Undy, et al p.194). While I agree with the above authors that draughtsmen were declining, to argue that the AEU could have moved upwards into technical areas or retained those individuals transferring into technical departments is to misunderstand the traditional relationship between the two groups. It was the practice for craftsmen to form the main recruiting base and therefore union base for DATA. To draw attention to union transfers, without stressing the normality of this situation, is to invent a threat that did not in reality exist. At least job territory was not in dispute at this time. The main forces towards amalgamation were political. The authors are correct to point out the significance of 'the replacement of [right wing] Carron with [broad left] Scanlon' inside the AEU. But they ignore the importance of the creation of ASTMS and its movement into engineering design, and secondly the employers' offensive against DATA's guerilla style industrial tactics. Lock outs and victimisations meant heavy costs to a union committed to supporting the industrial struggle of the membership with very high dispute pay. The craft tradition and the historical purchase in the idea of one union for engineering, were also emphasised by the DATA leadership in the run up to the vote on amalgamation (Smith, 1982).

But in many ways, closer association with manual workers and craftism was objectively flying in the face of the dynamic areas of occupational growth in the technical field. To emphasise the links between the technical and manual areas was a risky growth strategy for the union to take when for increasing numbers of higher technical workers the craft route was becoming irrelevant and anachronistic. For this reason, I think it is confusing to interpret the amalgamation through the perspective of recruitment, or to see dangers from the AEU moving up into the technical area as a real threat to DATA at the end of the 1960s. Much more important were the political considerations mentioned above. The choice of the AEU reflected, as Undy et al emphasise, the failures to team up another white collar union and more positively the craft and occupational affinity between the two unions. Most DATA members were ex-toolmakers or had close ties with manual workers (as indicated in chapter three) and at the end of the 1960s the overwhelming majority of DATA members were in middle range technical occupations.

The amalgamation represented the consolidation of occupational association for these groups and in certain instances, where joint shop steward committees existed between DATA and the AEU e.g. in parts of North London, unity signified a formalisation of these organisational links.

This is not the place to explain the degeneration and break up of the amalgamation at the national level, what interests me here is how stronger association with manual workers affected TASS's recruitment policy towards qualified engineers. I hope to show that in the early 1970s TASS's approach to engineers can be characterised by an emphasis on their status as technical wage labourers, akin to other parts of the union's membership and the working class as a whole. This follows the politics and militant industrial practice the union built up during the 1960s (Roberts et al., 1972; Smith, 1982). This policy changed during the mid 1970s due to the growing class heterogeneity within the membership itself and organisational imperatives to expand recruitment at a faster rate to pay for the enlarged official bureaucracy created under the guise of transforming the union from a craft to a general white collar union. The impact of these changes on the recruitment of engineers, and later managers, was to allow the growing hierarchy and elitism within the division of labour in the technical area to be reflected, accommodated and reinforced in the union's structure and ideology. The decision to recruit management, a different class of membership to technical staff, necessitated organisational and political adjustments to the union policy and structure. For engineers, instead of attempting to incorporate them into general union membership, recruitment policy located their interests with those of manager's as a special category of member, cut off from the activities of other technical workers. TASS policy began to relate to engineers as new middle class labour not as members of the working class, and then sought to build alliances between the different classes of membership. The impact of this policy is not confined to recruitment, but permeates the style and industrial practice at all levels of the official union apparatus. New non-craft engineers and new middle class managers remain a minority class within, TASS. Through the union leaderships method of recruiting and retaining them, however, their influence on policy has been significant. I later show the effect of this strategy on union consciousness and militancy at the workplace level.

TASS, ENGINEERS AND RECRUITMENT STRATEGIES

DATA conferences and publications during the 1960s registered the long term decline in draughtsmen and growth in the 'other technician' and technologist/engineer areas. It

166

was not, however, until the late 1960s that a national recruitment drive was aimed primarily at engineers. TASS had local agreements for senior design staff, and it was, as mentioned earlier on, common for those promoted into designer status to retain their TASS card. The union achieved national bargaining rights for weights, standards and spares engineers in 1968, but this still left largely untouched the growing volume of graduates entering design and production engineering. Up until the mid 1970s it had been the practice within TASS to organise professional engineers into the main body of members, with the same negotiating rights as the rest of the membership. This policy changed during the mid 1970s when separate bargaining units were established at plant level, and from 1977 separate branches were created to attract and accommodate professional engineers and later managers. The BAe Management Branch, established in 1977, was the first in TASS.

The politics and ideology of the early period is illustrated by a pamphlet entitled Which Way Forward for Professional Engineers (TASS 1971). It summarised the union's policy towards the recruitment of professional engineers through an analysis of their social, economic and class position in the engineering industry. It appeared in response to UKAPE's attempt, under recognition from the Industrial Relations Act, actively to recruit graduate engineers. UKAPE hoped to take advantage of the growing economic insecurity within the higher end of technical employment. The first edition of this TASS pamphlet sold out within four weeks and was reviewed in the following terms: 'A powerful attack on status conscious professional organisations' (The Times); 'A strongly worded attack on "quasi-unions" ' (The Engineer); 'TASS criticises "status conscious" professional organisations as diversions which are often employer dominated' (Express and Star Wolverhampton).

The pamphlet was a defence of trade unionism, collective bargaining, industrial action and left politics and an attack on status consciousness, neutrality in industry and the right wing politics of UKAPE. Divided into three sections, part one charts the history of TASS to show that the professional 'illusions' of the early draughtsmen were dropped after experiencing employers' opposition to their organisation. It emphasizes the class divisions at the heart of industry and the importance of taking sides. It explains that employers have consistently attempted to divide white collar and manual unions, while the labour movement has sought unity. It charts the fight for TASS's affiliation to the TUC, the CSEU and Labour Party and the amalgamation with the AEF. The style is not apologetic about the political and militant image of TASS, stressing the importance of both for strong trade union organisation. Part two draws largely upon thirteen separate sociological studies to demonstrate that white collar workers <u>are</u>, and should be, in workers' organisations. It claims that the reason professional engineers are suffering squeezed differentials is because they have shunned trade unionism. The goals of professional associations are not seen as incompatible with TASS membership, indeed TASS is said to be better able to pursue the goals of professional associations for improved recognition for engineers through its collective strength. Part Three concentrates on the background, emergence and character of the professional 'unions', in particular UKAPE, APST and the Association of Supervisory and Executive Engineers (ASEE). UKAPE, set up by the Engineers Guild in 1969 as a negotiating arm for 'improving the conditions of professional engineers' was the greatest threat to TASS and received the most attention.

The pamphlet explains the employers' influence inside UKAPE, quoting the chairman of the Engineers Guild on the 'professional' orientation of UKAPE:

> We, as professionals, do not like to see our salaries determined by methods of blackmail, but by methods which give a fair reward for responsibility such as will ensure the continued supply of recruits to our position.

The chairman's business connections are exposed in order to challenge the validity of such professional independence. The pamphlet also quotes from two articles by the Vice-President of UKAPE. In one he says UKAPE does 'not identify with one side of industry rather than another', and in the second article he claims:

> UKAPE is a fully registered union under the Act in the same way as is DATA. It acts for its members in just the same way.

The TASS pamphlet ridicules UKAPE's claims simultaneously to promote closer association between employers and employees, remain independent from both groups and yet be commited to employees against employers. The pamphlet also attacks UKAPE's claims to political neutrality by pointing out its involvement and connections with the right wing Monday Club. The chapter ends by denying the necessity for any duality between professional associations and trade unions:

> The 'conflict' only arises when professional employees try and hark back to the old direct client-professional fee paying relationship. If they build on the illusion that they are neutral between employer and employees or even that, like the Engineers Guild and UKAPE, they represent both at once, then they cannot fail to be, at best, ineffective and at worst positively harmful to

their membership.

In the pamplet TASS denies the idea of there being any middle or neutral ground between employers and workers, and rejects, as the union has always done, the 'third force politics' of professionalism:

> As a union we know there is a continual conflict in industry between the employers and the employee. We do not see any necessary conflict between employees, whether 'professional' white collar or 'blue collar'. If it develops it can only benefit the employer and any growth of new status conscious, employer–dominated professional associations can only have the same effect.

The pamphlet ends with an expose of the undemocratic structure of UKAPE, its inflated membership figures and its strong links with employer's organisations.

I have described the pamphlet in detail because it firmly rejects the professional aspirations of engineers in favour of a trade unionism based on a clear recognition of the divided interests of workers and employers. 'Status consciousness' was attacked as both naive and employer orientated. Trade unionism was seen as the only realistic response to a society divided by class, where only the power and resources of organised labour can counter the strength and organisation of employers. Accompanying the pamphlet was a recruitment leaflet which circulated in technical departments between 1971-1973. The leaflet echoed many of the arguments already examined, in particular the importance of professional engineers needing to take industrial action to give credibility to their bargaining position - something that was strongly denied by UKAPE (Dickens, 1972). Issues of status and strong workplace organisations are not seen as opposites (Prandy), but as complementary:

> If the status of the engineering profession is to reflect the importance of its role in industrial development then engineers must be prepared to take part in tough collective bargaining. They will only reach this position if they are organised in a strong trade union.

The overall impression of the leaflet is that 'naive professionalism' or neutrality in industry should be rejected and strong trade unionism adopted. The leaflet deliberately tackled the thorny issue of strike action, defending its use as a legitimate method of struggle. By contrast, a leaflet put out by ASTMS for professional engineers in the aerospace industry at the same time, played down the use of industrial action. The leaflet took the form of questions and answers.

It asked, 'Can we be instructed to strike?' and replied:

> The ASTMS Rules are specifically designed to prevent this. No full time officer from the General Secretary down has the power to instruct in this way. Quite the reverse. Our Rules provide that members themselves seek permission from the National Executive to strike if they feel so disposed. In other words, it's the members who request such permission. No officer can instruct.

Both leaflets acknowledge the reservations professional engineers have about strike action, but TASS defends its use and importance, and ASTMS (as Carter's comments in chapter five would lead one to expect) denies its significance by not locating the use of strike action within an industrial context, but the organisational structure of the union. I will later argue that such a clear line cannot be drawn between the two unions today.

A change in the basis for recruiting professional engineers was evident from a recruitment document circulating in 1976 and 1977. The leaflet was written by Ken Gill, General Secretary of TASS, from a reprint of an article 'Engineers in an Integrated Union' that appeared in Electrical Review (Gill, 1976). The document made no concession to organisational independence for professional engineers, and their integration into a broad industrial band of technical workers was emphasized. This policy changed a few months after this leaflet was produced. The leaflet divided into two parts. The first examines the importance of engineering standards to TASS. The second argues the case for 'vertical trade unionism'. In part one, Gill only mentioned strike action in relation to TASS winning recognition as a trade union with the Engineering Employers Federation. He quotes from Wigham's (1973) history of the EEF on 'how well run and disciplined TASS is'. The second part of the leaflet argues quite forcefully for a united approach in bargaining and that professional engineers were in a far weaker position, if organised 'occupationally' rather than 'industrially':

> Collective bargaining is organised around industrial function not around qualifications. Each occupation, each grade, each function, has, of course, its own separate interest. But these separate interests are catered for within TASS's highly flexible structure. It is of the greatest benefit, when bargaining collectively, if one organisation can integrate these interests and present united demands to an employer who would otherwise be only too ready to play off one union against another.

This is a cogent attack on the concept of autonomous bargaining groups, which within a few months of this leaflet appearing actually became union orthodoxy. The leaflet stresses the importance of integration within the whole technical spectrum of occupations in addition to establishing unity with manual workers, through the AUEW. The AUEW was held to offer the advantages of 'size, pooling of resources, sharing of services and close associations, both in industrial action and political representation'. But Gill went on to argue:

> In any event, the traditional descriptions of blue and white collar are changing, and we should remind ourselves that the original boundaries were largely created by the employers. The AUEW does, however, recognise that staff conditions are different and require special and expert attention which TASS is organised to provide. TASS has complete autonomy to deal with all matters affecting staff employment and professional issues.

Less than two months after this article appeared TASS policy underwent a total turnaround on the issue of organising professional engineers. From emphasing the integration of engineers in an industrial union (after all the article had been called 'Engineers in an Integrated Union'), TASS started to emphasize their autonomy within the structure of the union. The article that signalled the policy change, and the move towards recruitment through autonomy, appeared in the January 1977 edition of the TASS News and Journal. Professional and managerial staffs were now encouraged to 'form separate bargaining groups', later this also included separate branches. This about-turn took place between conferences, the article preparing the ground for Conference 'endorsement'.

Conference did not create a blanket policy of management branches until 1978, with Coventry being the only area to voice serious opposition to the policy. The immediate reason for this sudden change had been the decision of the Association of Supervisory and Executive Engineers (ASEE) to amalgamate with the Electrical Power Engineers Association (EPEA) in January 1977, to form the Engineers and Managers Association (EMA) to recruit outside power engineering (Gill and Eaton, 1981; Taylor, 1980). Unlike UKAPE, the EPEA had industrial experience negotiating for power station engineers going back to 1913. In December 1977 the 1612 members of the Shipbuilding and Allied Industries Managers Association (SAIMA) transferred engagements to become one of the four groups that eventually composed the EMA. TASS had fought unsuccessfully to obtain sole bargaining rights for shipbuilding engineers and managers against SAIMA. So the decision of SAIMA to join EMA was threatening. TASS's early concession of a management branch to managers in BAe reflected the leadership's view that the EMA judged aerospace to be a key entry route into engineering. This belief was later vindicated by the decision of two BAe Staff Associations to join the EMA in 1979 (EMA, 1979).

The TASS leadership was perhaps justified in seeing the EMA as a much greater threat than UKAPE. However it would be inaccurate to explain the change of policy as solely the result of external competition. Internal changes at TASS, in particular the enlargement of the bureaucracy, are also important. Between 1971 and 1977 Divisional Organisers increased by over 100 per cent, although membership growth only rose by 60 per cent (Smith, 1982). At the same time the amount of subscription income returning to the membership as dispute pay declined from 49 per cent in 1970 to 27 per cent 1972; 15.4 per cent in 1974; 8.1 per cent 1976; 5.4 per cent 1978 (Smith, 1982). Full-time officials and staff salaries as a percentage of subscription income rose from 17.3 per cent in 1970 to 27.3 per cent in 1979. There is an inverse relationship between the rising claims of salaries on subscription income and declining percentage directly returning to the membership as dispute benefit. To pay for the growth in full time officials the TASS leadership began to look at recruitment as the most important issue inside the union. External pressures, competition and the recession in engineering were slowing union growth so the strategy of recruitment through militancy and integration was dropped. Militancy was more costly in dispute pay, the Parson's struggle, as I later show, lasted nearly five years and involved two major lock outs. But politically and ideologically militancy and industrial activity were also increasingly considered counter productive when recruiting engineers and managers. Ways of 'appealing' to engineers by changing TASS's militant image and association with manual workers were discussed before the formal appearance of the EMA in April 1977.

At the 1975 Conference a motion was submitted calling for a change in the title of the organisation to get away from the craft connotations of TASS. TEAM (Technical, Executive, Administrative and Managerial) and TEAMS (Technical, Executive, Administrative, Managerial and Scientific) were both suggested but rejected. Other motions at the 1975 conference called on the EC to pay more attention to recruiting scientific and managerial staffs. In 1976 the Recruitment and Publicity Sub-committee was changed to the National Recruitment Office, directly responsible to the Industrial Sub-committee - indicative of the growing importance attached to recruitment. Towards the end of 1976 TASS began buying advertising space on buses, and in streets in certain towns. This 'blanket advertising' indicated the broadening of the recruitment net. In 1979 the EC report to conference mentions, for the first time, the appearance of national officials on television (i.e. really only one official, Ken Gill) and says 'this has aided recruitment'.

I have examined the conference reports between 1968 to 1980, and towards the end of the 1970s the General Secretary began to introduce the Executive Committee (EC) report on recruitment, emphasizing the importance of growth regardless of economic conditions, or area:

> Blaming lack of recruitment on 'objective circumstances' was merely saying that there were problems. There were always problems to be solved in the trade unions (TASS, 1980).

Greater effort was continually stressed in an almost Stakhanovite fashion, indeed in the mid 1970s league tables and divisional competition were encouraged.   This all flowed out of decisions on the structure and policy of the union developed before the emergence of the EMA.   In contrast to ASTMS, TASS initially allowed separate management negotiating committees or branches for exceptional circumstances e.g. the West Midland Supervisory Branch was transferred as an autonomous unit out from the Engineering Section as a result of the amalgamation.   At the 1976 Conference a Coventry delegate criticised a recruitment leaflet that seemed to be endorsing separation as general policy, not one suited to particular conditions.   The leaflet spoke of 'management staff having rights to determine their own affairs [and] special interests [in] separate organisational structures and arrangements' (TASS, 1976).   The delegate argued that such leaflets 'were no help in the essential job of involving management staff in the organisation with the same benefits and responsibilities as other members' (TASS, 1976).

The leadership replied to such criticism in rather confused terms by, on the one hand, saying it was not 'TASS's policy to argue for separate organisations' and yet recognising that 'special arrangements were necessary . . . if the union was to expand into management grades not previously organised'.   Integration, it was suggested, 'might involve special provisions' (TASS, 1976).   Such ambiguity and hesitancy indicated that the policy change did signify a real break with past traditions and politics.   As management branches multiplied, however, multi-level unionism became accepted policy.[3]

The EMA decision to recruit in engineering acted as a catalyst on those inside TASS who wanted to drop integration or what they viewed to be the 'purist pursuit of unity' in favour of a policy of organisational autonomy in the interests of rapid union growth.   A TASS national spokesmen interviewed in the early 1980s justified the change in terms of quantitative union growth, although he also saw the question of unionisation leading to integration:

> . . . in terms of bargaining requirements these groups
> of staff demand separate rights. That's the stage of
> development they're at, there's not much point in
> arguing from the outside that they are wrong. The only
> thing you can do is to get them in, and hopefully
> experience will teach them over a period of time the
> value of having a joint bargaining unit.[4]

This view expresses two aspects of the ideology of the TASS
leadership. Firstly a view that while managers are different
from other technical workers, these differences are
ideological not structural, and will eventually be
transformed through the experience of union membership. In
other words an orthodox Marxist perspective on class.
Secondly, there is an assumption that managers and engineers
will have no political or ideological influence on TASS
policy, but that the determination of change will be one way,
from the non-managerial elements in the union. This view is
wrong for managers on both counts. To suggest that this
category of staff 'demands separate rights' is only to
acknowledge, in different words, that they are a different
<u>class</u> to non-managerial staff. Moreover, in contrast to the
policy of recruitment through militancy, when the mass of
technical staff exerted a powerful influence on the
unionisation of engineers, with managers this social conflict
between the two classes is negated through an organisational
accommodation based on the principles of 'special interests'
and separation. The unionisation is passive with little
engagement between technicians and managers. This has
exercised a major influence on union policy. Under the
impact of growth through autonomy TASS has become more of a
servicing agency to all categories of members. A 1980
recruitment leaflet aimed at professional engineers and
managers illustrates this drift towards projecting the union
as a servicing agent rather than an industrial force for
organised labour:

> TASS recognises that Professional Engineers particularly
> those with managerial and supervisory functions, occupy
> a special position in the industry. TASS therefore
> offers such members a specialised service.

Top of the list of what TASS offered professional engineers
were: salary differentials; separate and autonomous
bargaining groups; separate management and senior staff
branches; 40 full time officials; computerised information;
national recognition by the EEF to represent and negotiate
for professional engineers in the industry. References to
the role and history of trade unions were now removed as too

were allusions to the centrality of industrial struggle to trade unionism. The impression thereby created is that joining a trade union requires very little effort on the part of the member: no activity, no involvement and no sense of joining a wider movement committed to working class politics. The passivity of membership is emphasized.

In 1978 TASS submitted a report to the Finniston Committee of Inquiry into the Engineering Industry. At the end of 1978 TASS published the full text to use for the recruitment of professional engineers. The pamphlet, Qualified Engineers: The Way Forward (TASS, 1978) is in marked contrast to the 1971 document previously examined. TASS is presented as an expert, professional body concerned with the smooth running of industrial relations in British engineering. TASS is concerned with the status, responsibility, salary differentials and training standards of professional engineers. The pamphlet makes an effort to emphasize the autonomy of engineers from the struggles of other TASS members:

> Within TASS professional engineers determine their own collective bargaining priorities and need not be involved in the industrial problems faced by other groups of TASS members . . . Support a union which opposes salary restraint and fights for adequate and acceptable differentials for skill and responsibility. JOIN TASS – the union which defends British Engineering.

The slogan at the bottom began to appear on all TASS propaganda from 1977. TASS has a history of firm committment to economic nationalism, but this coexisted with a strong class based industrial practice. What begins to emerge in the mid 1970s is a corporatism without class politics or industrial militancy. The corporate appeal to professional engineers and managers is the main ideological element in the pamphlet. The propaganda gives the impression of a union integrated into society, the State and bodies concerned with British industry. The pamphlet proclaims that TASS has:

> Representation where it counts. TASS is directly represented on the TUC General Council, the E.C. of the European Metal Workers Federation, the Engineering Industry Training Board, the Technician Education Council, the Business Education Council, the Industrial Scholarship Scheme, and all major Sector Working Parties of the National Economic Development Council.

Another 'brochure' (they ceased to be pamphlets in 1980) aimed at management staff was entitled: Professional and Managerial Staff in Engineering (TASS, 1980). Unlike the 1978 pamphlet engineers do not appear as a separate group, but as professional staff bracketed very closely with management. But like the earlier document the stress is on their autonomy from the majority of TASS members:

> Within TASS managerial and professional staff enjoy complete industrial autonomy. They and only they determine the issues which concern them collectively. They, and only they, decide whether or not they have grievances in common with TASS members they supervise. They and only they decide whether or not to take industrial action against an employer.

The brochure claimed that TASS has '35,000 members who occupy senior positions in industry'. In 1976 TASS claimed 10,000 senior members, in 1978 30,000, approximately 15 per cent of their national membership. They were however, as Ken Gill explained in the Forward to the pamphlet, 'the fastest growing sector of our membership'. In fact managers were the only area of significant growth inside TASS at the time.

The brochure considers managers central to 'British engineering' and to TASS policy in industrial and political areas. Management's role in industry is exclusively identified with the national interest. The division of society into social classes and the accompanying inherent struggle between classes, which had coexisted with economic nationalism in earlier propaganda, is now eliminated. Corporatism and the generation of policy statements not industrial action, is strongly emphasized in the document:

> Since becoming a major union for management staff, TASS has been able to make a much greater impact in the task of winning support for an expanding and prosperous engineering industry in Britain. Our campaign had its ups and downs against the background of employer neglect, and the inadequate industrial policies followed by successive governments. But at the <u>policy level, TASS managers have made a very valuable contribution.</u> Their knowledge of, and commitment to, the industry has been invaluable to the union in drawing up the policies necessary to defend and expand the industry in which all our members work. Their expertise must be harnessed by the British engineering industry if it is to remain competitive [my emphasis].

The function of management, their identification with capitalist rationality, with profit, with the exploitation of labour, is not considered. Managers are another group of employees with special skills and responsibilities. Their skills are making decisions, and these 'skills' are being increasingly devalued by the bureaucratic control of senior management, and their remoteness from middle managers. TASS can help managers regain their 'skills', shore-up their authority and responsibility, on the one hand, and make management more democratic on the other.

In the 1960s TASS refused to organise ratefixers and foremen on 'trade union grounds', as they exercised supervisory functions in relation to manual workers and were judged to be the 'direct agents of management' on the shop floor (TASS, 1963, p.52). Today, TASS claims that the unionisation of managers will restore their confidence and ability to manage. Managers are not situated within the capitalist enterprise, but the neutral sounding 'engineering industry', or in 'modern industry' or the 'British engineering industry'. Profitability is a legitimate managerial goal because it is directed against foreign-competition. The pamphlet says:

> Managers need the power to manage. They need a bigger say in the way their company is run. In modern industry this can only be achieved if managers are prepared to unite in powerful independent trade unions. Paradoxically, managers can only manage effectively in modern industry if they are part of the trade union movement. Only in this way can they play their full part in decision making. Only in this way can they win wider acceptance of the <u>crucial role that management skills play in building a successful engineering industry. Such developments are central to the future prosperity of Britain</u> [my emphasis].

Economic nationalism and corporatism became the central ideological plank of the union in the mid 1970s. With this the value of industrial militancy - the hallmark of the union in the 1960s - has been rejected in favour of industrial policy and sloganising. The General Secretary remarked at the 1978 Conference that: 'The slogan "TASS fights for British engineering", was gaining TASS a wide reputation in industry, and was a proud and ambitious one'. To make it effective, he said, 'TASS must extend its influence, enhance its power, ensure trade union unity, in the most important trade union in Britain - and must grow fast'. Anthony Frodsham (1979) the former Director General of the EEF, remarked in an article in <u>The Engineer</u> on unions in engineering that: 'senior staff consider that an influx of senior recruits to these unions (ASTMS, AUEW-TASS) would, itself, have an effect on their policies and industrial attitudes' (Frodsham, 1979). On the evidence from a comparison between TASS literature in the early and late 1970s it appears that managers have had a definite effect on TASS policy.

The policy of the earlier period was that engineers, as another section of technical employees, should be fully integrated into TASS. The approach towards all unorganised technical sectors was that recruitment was always more successful, and made for a better and more stable membership, if it was tied into a wage campaign or a struggle over conditions, holidays, or whatever. The thinking behind this strategy of 'recruitment through militancy' was that an active union made for an active membership, and presented those new to trade unionism with a clear demonstration of its rewards and benefits. It was also believed that 'struggle changes consciousness', and the elitism of professional engineers could only be challenged by their direct engagement in trade union militancy (Wooton, 1961). The status consciousness of professional engineers was attacked as being antiquated, while the need to maintain engineering standards and skills was stressed through TASS's commitment to skill differentials. Professional engineers were not recruited in a vacuum, but in competition from UKAPE, and the contrast between UKAPE and TASS was marked. UKAPE was portrayed as employer-dominated, right-wing and ineffective. TASS was presented as militant, progressive and strongly committed to labour against capital. In the later literature, the competition from EMA and UKAPE was criticised from a purely organisational and narrow industrial relations perspective. TASS sided with the EEF, CSEU and ACAS in claiming there were 'too many unions in engineering' therefore the EMA should be denied recognition:

> All parties recognise that there are already too many unions in the industry. The CSEU unions . . . seek to extend collective bargaining in an orderly fashion, building upon the established framework (AUEW-TASS, 1980).

There has been no adequate critique inside TASS as to exactly what function management perform. From my research they were clearly in a contradictory and vulnerable position. TASS depicts the 'skills' and 'functions' of managers as neutral ones in order to promote the idea of shoring up their authority, power and separation from other technical workers. TASS wants 'managers to manage', but the question of control, hierarchy and authority, and the relationship between managers and capital, is not discussed. The conclusion must be that the TASS leadership is now only concerned with giving managers more control and authority. This is in sharp contrast to the earlier period when the prejudices and elitism of professional engineers were openly recognised and seen to stand in the way of organisation and therefore needed to be challenged. 'Recruitment through autonomy' leaves these prejudices untouched. The very deep anti-unionism of managers, again evident from research at BAe, is something TASS does not openly discuss. And unlike professional engineers and other technical workers, managers have largely joined TASS under the involuntary pressures of Government policy. In Aerospace, TASS's biggest concentration of management staff, recruitment only began after nationalisation (Smith, 1982, chapter seven).

It is one thing to examine union policy through official publications and debates at annual conference. It is quite another however to look at that policy in practice in the workplace. There is a disjuncture between the two, but also a relationship. To explore the policy in practice I will now examine the unionisation of senior staff, chiefly engineers at C. A. Parsons in the early 1970s. I say chiefly because the TASS leadership at Parsons also wanted to organise 'above the line' in the areas of management staff, against EEF and company policy which sought at the time to maintain a managerial barrier between unionised and non-unionised staff (CIR, 1973). The organisation of engineers and managers at BAe Filton will then be studied to illustrate the practice of the policy of recruitment through autonomy in the late 1970s. The question of whether autonomy and the granting of separate bargaining agreements were necessarily the only way to organise managers will be dealt with in the conclusion. The case studies are also illustrative of the key role of union leadership at factory level.

MILITANCY AND AUTONOMY AS MODES OF RECRUITMENT

Recruitment through militancy: C. A. Parsons

The fight between TASS and UKAPE at C. A. Parsons is well known (CIR, 1972; Woodley, 1973; Smith and Sawbridge, 1976). In what follows, what has already been written about the dispute is supplemented with interview material and documentation from leading [5]TASS members in the plant, a source ignored by other writers.

C. A. Parsons was part of the Reyrolle Parsons group of companies producing turbo generators. In 1976 Reyrolle was absorbed into a larger conglomerate, Northern Engineering Industries (NEI). NEI comprises large companies such as C. A. Parsons, International Combustion, A. Reyrolle, Clarke Chapman, John Thompson, Bruce Peebles and a host of other subsidiary and associated groups. In 1965 after a major reorganisation in the industry, there were only two companies in England producing turbo generators - Parsons and GEC. GEC entered the large turbo generator field in the late 1960s by acquiring English Electric and AEI to become Parsons' only rival in Britain. In 1965 Parsons acquired GEC turbo generators, gaining a Turbo factory in Erith, Kent and a section of the GEC complex at Wilton, Birmingham, which manufactured generators. The merger between A. Reyrolle and Co. Ltd., and C. A. Parsons, took place in 1968 and was a direct result of merger between GEC and AEI.[6]

C. A. Parsons produced a highly technical product and employed a large number of technical and craft workers. In 1972 the Heaton site employed 7,500 of whom 65 per cent were craftsmen or apprentices, and 24 per cent technical and engineering staff. Up until the Second World War, trade unionism was discouraged at Parsons. In 1947 the first full-time convenor was appointed. Smith and Sawbridge say the recognition of white collar unions followed that of manual ones. This is true for clerical and supervisory grades, but DATA or the old AESD, had been established at Parsons amongst draughtsmen since 1918 (CIR, 1972). Indeed Parsons formed a key group of the AESD membership in the North East during its formative years. A membership agreement dating from January 1918 arose out of a threat of strike action by forty draughtsmen. Terry Rogers, Chairman of the TASS Negotiating Committee at Parsons, and TASS member since the 1940s explains the union's history in the plant:

> There is a story about them attempting strike action after the 1914-18 war. The story goes that they put in a claim for increased wages which wasn't granted so they all packed up their gear on the Friday night and they were in the process of taking strike action when the company conceded. But they still took the Saturday off to demonstrate their point. . . TASS has got an organisational tradition yet the company as a whole has had a low level of trade union organisation. It was only during the last war they they got any sort of organisation going amongst the manual workers. It's not very militant now, but at least they've got a 100 per cent closed shop.

By 1968 TASS were negotiating for more than draughtsmen. The national agreement in 1968 extended the procedural groups to various types of technical staff who in most large companies were already in TASS membership: planning engineers, estimators, weight engineers, standard engineers, spares engineers, technical authors and illustrators. However the national agreement and most local agreements did not apply to 'chiefs, assistant chiefs and those of comparable status', i.e. to managers. TASS nationally launched a 100 per cent membership campaign in the late 1960s. Inside Parsons TASS decided vigorously to pursue this recruitment drive: Terry Rogers:

> We were in a position where we had about 40 to 50 per cent of the technical staff in membership, but we were negotiating conditions and wages for virtually everybody.

TASS concentration was in the traditional technical areas, mentioned above, but:

> The other part of the technical side, the technologist areas, were the expanding ones. So we were becoming smaller and smaller in our relative position. So we decided to do something about it and started this massive 100 per cent membership campaign.

TASS began the campaign in 1968:

> The starting point was when we negotiated an agreement which was supposedly a productivity agreement. We said to the company that we can't guarantee that the non-members in the company will abide by the productivity clauses. And we want the agreement to be confined to members. The Company were horrified at this.

Vindication of TASS's claim that they negotiated for the entire technical staff, despite having only fifty per cent membership, came from the personnel manager who said, on being informed that TASS wanted the agreement confined to members only: 'We always pay TASS rises to all technical staff'. The Company eventually responded to TASS demands by recommending staff to join TASS. According to TASS activists at Parsons this was a very luke warm recommendation, only made under pressure from the union, but it did allow TASS members to address departments in company time. At this time, 1968, TASS was the only union in the technical area, but despite limited company approval, and the absence of competition, recruitment was not easy:

> One of the problems was that we suffered from the reputation of our militancy. People who were outside the union decried us and didn't want to join for all sorts of reasons, some of them personal.

Before the company's tacit support for unionisation, they had discouraged membership and had:

> Given them [the higher grades], the impression that it wasn't in their interests to join the union, and if they joined the union it would effect them in terms of merit reviews, which take place annually, and their wage position and promotion prospects. So the company always discouraged them from joining up until this point in time. So in order to justify this position they always used to slander us in terms of our militancy, our unreasonableness and always having strikes and upsetting everything. So we suffered from this sort of thing.

It was as a consequence of this that when pressure to join TASS was applied, engineers and others began looking around for an alternative to TASS, and this was when ASTMS entered the scene.

It is important to understand the clear-cut choice technical staff were being offered. TASS had a justifiably militant image at Parsons as they had been involved in strikes, overtime bans and work to rules on many occasions during the 1960s. There was no attempt on the part of the Negotiating Committee of the Joint Office Committee (JOC) to 'water down' that image. They wanted to demonstrate that it was the company who were 'unreasonable', to stress the legitimacy of their actions, and to correct the inaccuracies of their image. When they tried to recruit foremen it was this militancy that prevented recruitment and they eventually ended up in ASTMS:

> The militancy of the technical staff was a factor that prevented the foremen coming into TASS. We had this reputation [laughter]. It didn't do us any good in recruiting terms. It made life very difficult. There was also a lot of mythology about the way we operated. People actually believed that we rigged general meetings, for example. People slandered us in that way. It was something totally impossible to do. We have very open general meetings. But we suffered from that sort of thing.

The approach of ASTMS in this situation can best be described as 'opportunistic'. TASS were suffering from their militancy, so ASTMS emphasized their moderation and professionalism. Their answer to TASS's general wages policy was salary scales; their response to the status consciousness of higher grades was to offer them separate negotiating rights. They 'pandered' to status consciousness. The differentials between draughtsmen and designers/senior staff were narrowed by TASS's flat rate £80 agreement in 1968. This was exploited by ASTMS who said it was a 'taste of things to come'. TASS was identified as being the leveller of differentials - pushing the majority of technical staff up, and holding back senior staff. ASTMS spoke as 'the voice of the professional' and recruited about 60 people in the technical area, and this formed the base of what they called their 'office group'. This had declined to 22 in the early 1970s (CIR, 1972, p.28). They had four separate groups in all, their biggest concentration was amongst foremen. The ASTMS office group produced several 'Bulletins' during the period attacking TASS and promoting their own organisation as a moderate professional union to cater for professional engineers. Bulletin No 3, May 1969, was entitled: <u>Resistance</u>

<u>to TASS Recruiting</u> and said:

> We, as professional staff, should not be misled into
> thinking that it is in our interests to join TASS either
> because of threats, or of bribes or because we feel we
> can rely on TASS's goodwill.   There is certainly no
> <u>evidence</u> for the goodwill.   They have shown that they
> are not out to promote the best interests of the
> professional staff and logically as draughtsmen must
> always be in the majority they ought not to do so.

The Bulletin accused TASS of trying to improve the status of
its membership by incorporating higher technical workers in a
minority position.   It also said TASS wanted to get
intertransferability between draughtsmen and designers and
develop the idea of parity between them.   The ASTMS office
group concentrated on separating the two and improving the
differentials of designers.   The decision of the TASS
conference to ballot on amalgamation was carried in an ASTMS
Bulletin in the following terms:

> <u>STOP PRESS</u> At their National Conference last week TASS
> has agreed to amalgamate with the AEU - this completely
> ruins any credibility in their claim to be the union to
> represent professional staff.

The Bulletin, of only two sides, made 15 references to
'professional staff', 'professional ASTMS' and seven
references to 'differentials'.
So prior to the appearance of UKAPE, ASTMS was trying to
recruit in the higher technical grades by emphasising
differentials, status differences and autonomy, <u>against</u> what
they saw as the militant integration policies of TASS.
Between December 1968 and May 1970 DATA fought for its 100
per cent membership agreement.   In November 1968, the
personnel manager issued a memo to TASS to say that the
company could not allow them sole negotiating rights as this
woud be in breach of a national agreement between the EEF and
the CSEU, of which ASTMS was a member.   DATA imposed
sanctions and the company at first recognised TASS's claim on
technical areas, but later returned to its position regarding
national agreements.   In response to union sanctions,
management locked out DATA members for ten weeks in what
Terry Rogers described as a 'very bitter dispute'.   Following
this action management conceded to a DATA agreement, which
gave the union sole negotiating rights for all technical
staff 'below the line' (non-managerial staff).   This was in
May 1970.   It meant that the bulk of graduate engineers were
expected to join DATA and for those 'above the line' the
union was given a verbal assurance that DATA was their
appropriate union.   Following the dispute, the intervention

of the TUC and Department of Employment, ASTMS eventually withdrew its claim for negotiating rights for its 'office group'. All new employees were required to join TASS as a condition of employment, and other non-unionists were given one year to take up membership or leave the company.

It was within this context that UKAPE entered the scene and attempted to recruit designers, engineers and managers. They focussed on the same themes as ASTMS and tried to place a wedge between designers and draughtsmen, professional engineers and middle grade technical employees. They projected a purer image of moderation and professional unionism together with an exclusiveness which ASTMS, with membership in production areas, lacked. Before the May settlement they distributed leaflets advertising UKAPE as an anti-strike, moderate, professionals-only union. This image, in the context of TASS's militancy and projected amalgamation with the AEU, made UKAPE attractive to qualified engineers. The current secretary of TASS at NEI Parsons, himself a graduate engineer, had joined the company in the late 60s and became an office representative in a design department during UKAPE's emergence:

> Everybody could become a UKAPE member in the design areas. UKAPE were suggesting that the design engineers' proper bargaining group was with management and that UKAPE should straddle managers and design engineers, and this was their area of common interest. It wasn't design engineers with draughtsmen. And UKAPE did make a bit of headway with that.

TASS, today, would concede the designers' professional demands for autonomy and separation from draughtsmen and other technical staff. But at that time, with the policy of integration and a militant stand against a right wing unionism, TASS stood firmly against professional autonomy. Bob Murdock:

> UKAPE had about 50 members in the design area at the time and more were watching to see the way things would go . . . There was the 100 per cent membership agreement and there was a lot of bad feeling and high emotional temperature around the place. The department was split about half and half and there wasn't any room for playing around at it, you know, you had to be quite positive, quite hard and you had to argue incessantly. One bloke who played it both ways [i.e. paid TASS and UKAPE subs.], he used to come in in the mornings and he used to harangue people and get the weaker types all worked up and worried. Talk about agitation, far better than me at it, you know [laughter]. He would come in and, you know, I'd play it fairly cool, thinking that he

was alienating people, but eventually half an hour of this and I couldn't stand it any more. And we used to spend our working day arguing and everybody was listening. There was no way round it, you had to argue like mad. I was involved up to my eyeballs.

Dickens (1972) argues that UKAPE were chiefly blocked by employers' opposition and their support for established unions. At Parson's management were pushed through activity and the threat of further action into opposing UKAPE. However, inside the departments where UKAPE built up support, ideological argument about whether engineers were technical workers or managers (a more meaningful distinction than today) reigned. The membership of UKAPE in July 1972 was 82, 17 of whom also held TASS cards (CIR, 1972, p.31). The company also supported UKAPE in certain departments by promoting engineers 'over the line' into assistant management posts to avoid TASS membership claims (CIR, p.21). This was further evidence of the ambiguous position the company had towards TASS.

After the deadline for remaining staff passed with a 'hardcore' of UKAPE members outside of TASS the company issued 38 dismissal notices. UKAPE challenged this through the courts and in the Court of Appeal Lord Denning made a ruling on the dismissal notices that allowed the Company to get round TASS by handing out dismissal notices to come into effect on the 29th February 1972, one day after the Industrial Relations Act, which outlawed closed shops, became operative. The scene was now set for a major confrontation between TASS and the company over UKAPE, which having registered under the Act used the National Industrial Relations Court as an arena to establish negotiating rights at Parsons.

These developments were compounded by the company decision, under the influence of a new managing director, to announce a series of redundancies in different sections of the Parson's group. Sanctions began to be operated against the company by TASS, while UKAPE issued statements condemning TASS's strike action, and supporting the company's rationalisation policy which they saw as necessary for safeguarding future jobs.

29 February arrived and the dismissal notices on the 38 non-members were rescinded in accordance with the IRA. The matter was referred to the Commission of Industrial Relations. On the 1 March 1972 resignations from TASS came in. About 60 resigned after the February deadline although only one had resigned before then. Events were now set for Parsons to become the first 'test case' under the Act. This gave the dispute a national political signficance inside the TUC beyond the issue of the TASS closed shop. In response to the resignations, which can be seen as evidence of the way

people were sitting on the fence, TASS instituted a policy of non-cooperation and blacking by non TASS members 'below the line'. This meant two sets of sanctions were being simultaneously applied. While some engineers opted to leave TASS when circumstances allowed, most remained. Bob Murdock argued that the polarisation introduced by the two events crystallised the choices available to engineers. This was particularly true of UKAPE approval of redundancies, and TASS's opposition:

> We were involved in a redundancy dispute and because of the IRA the company withdrew notices to people who were to be sacked because they wouldn't join the union. So we blacked their work and that led to sackings, suspensions and all the rest of it. . . Lots of people lost a lot of nervous energy on that one, it was very close. But it threw up a lot of questions; it's a bit hard to be explicit now, but on the relationship with the manager for instance, UKAPE were saying 'you've got a common interest with him' and he was dishing out redundancy notices. You were getting UKAPE members dishing out redundancy notices to UKAPE members. This was the position. And this clarified a lot of minds about what the nature of the process was.

At one stage 704 TASS members had been suspended for blacking non-union work. Eventually the company withdrew these redundancy notices and TASS agreed to await the outcome of the Court of Industrial Relations recommedations. In line with TUC opposition to the NIRC, TASS refused to attend or submit evidence to any hearings (CIR, 1972). The company, as indicated at the start of this chapter, refused to concede to the principle of qualifications determining work although behind this stand lay the proven strength of TASS opposition to any deal with UKAPE. The CIR report was eventually published on 18 October 1972 and came down in favour of recognising TASS's claim to be the sole bargaining agent for those 'below the line' in technical areas. The 'above the line' position was left in the air, and is still disputed by TASS today, which is the dominant union in both areas. In the aftermath of the acceptance of the CIR report TASS membership grew. Terry Rogers:

> A lot of people came back into TASS after the battle was over - they had fought the battle then the Industrial Relations Court had ruled that TASS was the proper organisation to represent them. And for some reason, even though they didn't actually have to join (because we didn't win 100 per cent at that time, what we did win was that new people would have to join even though there was an Industrial Relations Act), . . . virtually

everybody came into line within a couple of years after that.   People who'd been actively against us, they joined.   They became office reps [laughter].   They collected the subs.   Quite sincere people you know, that was the side they were on at the time, but when it was possible to change sides without losing face, I think they did so, they accepted the argument in the end.

UKAPE at Parsons were evenly spread in the design area although with small pockets of support in two departments, where the manager exerted a strong influence in favour of UKAPE.   Because of the spread they were unable to gain a total control in any one group of departments.   There were always TASS members there to harass them.   When I examine the situation at BAe this difference will be brought out.   UKAPE also identified the interests of professional engineers with management, and recruited both middle managers and professional engineers.   When UKAPE managers handed out redundancy notices to both TASS and UKAPE members, TASS could argue that they were doing the company's job and were not genuine trade unionists at all.   The redundancy issue did not cloud the fight for the closed shop, it clarified the issues and differences between the two organisations.   Smith and Sawbridge argue that because the company supported TASS they were bound to win out, but this underestimates the process of struggle and action associated with unionisation, and the role of the State which could have provided UKAPE with springboard into the technologist field.   According to those in leadership positions inside TASS the dispute was very finely balanced in design areas where graduate engineers had resisted voluntary and involuntary pressures to join TASS. According to Bob Murdock, UKAPE had a general appeal in the Design Department at Parsons amongst: a. those who identified the interests of workers directly with those of the employer, and b. those who saw themselves as a craft grouping with skills that placed them in a different category from draughtsmen and technicians:

These positions were exploited by UKAPE (and ASTMS prior to the 100 per cent membership agreement of 1970). Obviously people who are not 'professional engineers' also fall into these categories.   The fact that UKAPE misjudged the trade union instincts of workers probably lay in the assumption that professional engineers were exclusively in the (a) group whereas there were many who professed support regarding the 'elitist craft position' and yet expected a hard line with the employer.   In fact there were people in this group who had come from the shops, done degree equivalent courses and had become senior design engineers without ceasing to be working class in their outlook.

This conclusion reinforces my earlier comments about the legacy of the craft tradition, but it probably underestimates the importance of trade union leadership at Parsons and the national policy of TASS dedicated to the active pursuit of unionisation and the elimination of UKAPE. The five year period of struggle for the 100 per cent membership agreement was both costly for the national union and demanding on the commitment of the membership at the factory level. The process of unionisation was not a passive experience and the choices between TASS and rival organisations were presented in polarised terms that related to questions of class in a clear way. This, I will now argue, was absent from unionisation at BAe in the second period of TASS's recruitment policy.

Recruitment through autonomy: British Aerospace

> We're not a lot of sheep, we're all intelligent people. Like when we have a mass meeting, if anybody stands up and says 'Good afternoon brothers', that'll cause a riot. They will not be called brothers. You've got a lot of what you might call conservative people in the union, they joined the union because of the good it can do them, they're not like British Leyland workers (Colin Luck, Draughtsmen, Jig and Tool Design, Machine Shop, BAe).

The trade union tradition inside the technical area at BAe was weak compared with C. A. Parsons. The JOC at Parsons has been influenced by members of the Socialist Workers Party for over a decade. There was a stable core of political leaders who played a key role inside TASS, the joint staff-manual Corporate Committee, and an industry-wide combine. By contrast, outside of three waves of redundancies which had involved sanctions but no all-out strike action, the only significant dispute TASS members had been involved in was during a pensions dispute in 1973. It was the only dispute people recalled when I interviewed them in the late 1970s. The legacy of the dispute was not a positive one as the uneven eight week lock out across the technical field ended in defeat, with none of the original TASS demands for representation on a pensions committee being conceded (Smith, 1982). The leadership of TASS at BAe were acutely aware of this dispute which acted as a negative demonstration of the efficacy or feasibility of involving the Filton members in a mass strike. In addition, it did not exactly promote the value of TASS membership to graduate engineers and UKAPE members at BAe. Whereas at Parsons varied and successful industrial action against redundancies promoted unionism, at BAe the reverse was the case. The importance of **efficient** as well as active trade unionism should not be underestimated.

Another contrast with the TASS position at Parsons lay in the absence of support for disputes at other sections of BAe or with workers in Bristol and nationally. There were trade union networks, which assisted the transfer of work, but little joint industrial activity. At Parsons alongside the tradition of militancy and activity inside the plant, solidarity action with other parts of the NEI empire had also taken place. There had been levies for disputes at Reyrolle Parsons in Newcastle and a smaller plant in Scotland. There was also a tradition of collecting for other workers in struggle and joining local disputes and picket lines, e.g. picketing a local hospital threatened with closure.

I was unable to obtain details of membership concentrations at BAe for the late 1960s and early 1970s. The activists I spoke to said TASS was confined to drawing offices and planning departments. When I was interviewing, it was the Drawing Offices and Planning departments that held longstanding TASS members. In some of the newer departments, e.g. N.C. Programming, unionisation by TASS had been relatively recent. By coincidence one of the people on the Negotiating Committee at C. A. Parsons had earlier in his career been a designer in the Engineering Design Organisation (EDO) at BAe. He left in the late 1960s. His recollections were quite revealing:

> TASS organisation after I left BAC was confined to the Drawing Offices and the Development Labs. There was only one member in the Design Area where I worked. There was, however, some evidence of change. Communications meetings (with managers) were being held which I attended as a rep. and these were handled so stupidly that trade union organisation was becoming seriously talked about, so it was an embryonic thing towards the end of my stay. There was some influence possibly from Rolls Royce where the organisation was known to be harder and where the unionisation of design staff was already being projected. Another influence was the erosion of the merit payment system. Shortly before I left I was told that any increases were likely to be TASS negotiated. This could lead only to one conclusion! Finally I think it was becoming apparent that improvements in wages and conditions were no longer applied directly from manual workers to staff.

According to Bob Murdock there was little opposition to trade unionism in the design area, it was simply that it hadn't been put to them. There had been no serious campaign to get Design into TASS.

I had nothing against joining, it's just that I'd never

been asked and there was no union there, no one to represent us. I think that's the difference (between being organised and not), that even with a rotten trade union structure you've got <u>something</u> for people to join. And it was so bad that one of the technicians I knew (I knew him a bit later), he approached me and suggested that if I joined I could get on the Negotiating Committee, you know [laughter]. With absolutely zero base in the design area, it was totally unthinkable. That's how bad it was. They wanted people in the leadership.

It was difficult to establish when UKAPE appeared at BAe, but it was sometime after 1969 and before 1973. They were initially concentrated in three departments in the EDO, electrodynamics, stress and weights, all areas with a high graduate entry. In 1981 they had over 100 members and throughout the 1970s they had maintained between 100-250 engineers across the Filton site. During the 1973 pensions' dispute TASS blacked the work of those in electrodynamics, central records, the drawing library, print room, weights, stress and data editing group. It can be assumed that UKAPE were active in most of these departments.

There was no action against UKAPE members along the lines of disputes at C. A. Parsons. This, I think, reflects the trade union leadership in the two plants. At BAe, UKAPE did not gain 'formal' negotiating rights, but the existence of the organisation throughout the 1970s, and its concentration in several departments meant it acted as a strong informal voice for engineers. It also solidified professionalism and acted as an alternative ideological counter to TASS. The way TASS dealt with UKAPE in the late 1970s reveals the influence of the national policies on a plant with a weak trade union tradition.

The creation of the Bristol Management Branch in 1977 could have solved the problem of the one hundred and sixty members of UKAPE. If middle managers had actively recruited in the EDO area they could have absorbed UKAPE members. But the management branch was not brought into existence by the activity and struggle of the managers, but out of a sense of resignation that they 'had to join a TUC affiliated union' because of the nationalisation of BAe. Besides which, the managers wanted to be on their own, without non-managerial supervisors or professional engineers, a sense of exclusiveness borne of the method of recruitment. In 1977 TASS would have had to impose sanctions, and forced a dispute in the UKAPE areas to polarise engineers towards TASS, because of the entrenched ideological opposition to TASS. This was something TASS policy no longer endorsed, and the TASS organisation at BAe had never risen to it.

Early in 1980 UKAPE merged with the EETPU. Following

this UKAPE made a claim for membership agreement with BAe. On 10 September 1980 the company met TASS representatives from No.3 Branch and the Management Branch on the question of recognition of UKAPE members. The company told TASS that it had no intention of recognising UKAPE: 'just because they jointed the EETPU there was no guarantee that they would be recognised'.

In a circular between the EETPU and the TUC about the question of EESA/UKAPE recognition at BAe Bristol, they claimed in April 1981 that the membership at BAe was 41 in the Dynamics Group and 162 in the Aircraft Group. These figures were, however, exaggerated. According to a Bristol Divisional Organiser, the EETPU take-over of UKAPE nationally had angered UKAPE members at BAe. The new organisation did not produce negotiating rights in the region, and severely weakened the UKAPE claim to professional exclusiveiness.

During 1981 the Management Branch set up a committee to investigate ways of solving the 'UKAPE issue'. A circular ('The Problem of Representation [by TASS] in Areas Where UKAPE is Present at BAe Filton') was discussed in May and June 1981 and the recommendations and approach of the report is very revealing relative to the experience of fighting UKAPE in the early 1970s. I will use the report to indicate the changes in policy in TASS during the 1970s.

Starting with the distribution of UKAPE members, the Report revealed both a concentration of UKAPE membership and a wider spread than previous estimates that had been given to me suggested. They were located in ten departments, not three, and considering that the average size of technical departments was about 14, they represented a significant body within seven of the ten departments, and a strong majority in four of the ten. The total UKAPE membership mentioned in the report was 104, although lower than the EETPU claim of 162 (April 1981) it was still significant. The spread of membership meant TASS members were either in a minority or absent from ten departments on the Filton site. TASS Management Branch members were also weak in some of the departments, with UKAPE exercising such a strong influence as to maintain the loyalty of management staff.

The existence of UKAPE through the 1970s and early 1980s weakened TASS overall, the presence of an elite alternative structure acting as a mobilising point for separation amongst higher technical group. When I discussed the position of the professional engineers in TASS with young graduate engineers UKAPE acted as a reference point for expressions of elitism. Had TASS eliminated UKAPE, this consciousness of a serious alternative to TASS would have been set back.

TASS membership was firmly based on the older technical occupations, and also older technical workers. The average age was 53 in the main design area. The TASS convenor told me that the high average age of the TASS members meant 'pensions' often took priority over wage struggles. Although TASS had unionised the new middle range technical areas - computer programmers, NC part programmers - technologists and graduate engineers were largely unorganised. These groups lacked the trade union traditions of the craft-based technical jobs, and therefore their unionisation was not aided by borrowing trade union consciousness from manual areas. The only way they could be organised was directly by TASS activity. There was a certain 'craft hostility' towards graduate engineers amongst the majority of technical workers, and this had, in part, prevented a serious attempt to organise in these areas. At Parsons TASS's defeat of UKAPE meant a rapid expansion in the non-craft based technical areas, and the leadership used the skills, qualifications and graduate status of engineers to successfully drive up wages across the board. They kept detailed records of the educational background of the membership and used this in wage bargaining. When I asked the convenor if TASS kept any such records, he said: 'most graduates have to forget 90 per cent of what they've learnt when they come in here' - a throwaway remark that reflected a general attitude towards graduate engineers.

The report by Bristol Management Board claimed that the solution to the question of UKAPE would be to change the eligibility criterion in the Management Branch to absorb non-managerial professional engineers. 30 of the UKAPE total were managers anyway, 49 were graduates and would have fulfilled the revised criteria of membership. That would have left 25 members within the EDO not able to join the BMB, and they would have had to join Bristol No.3. The BMB were therefore proposing a graduate cut-off point between the two TASS branches, something UKAPE argued for and lost at C. A. Parsons. That TASS members were now proposing solutions that were previously UKAPE policy indicates the ideological shift that had taken place within the union.

The reasons for these changes are not straightforward. The broad left inside TASS had been built up during the 1960s through an emphasis on industrial struggle and the encouragement of membership activity. Dispute pay was initially set at 100 per cent of net pay, this later falling to 80 per cent and 60 per cent (Smith, 1986). The employers' offensive against TASS and the growth of lockouts in response to sanctions pushed the union towards amalgamating with the AEU but also forced the leadership away from a strong commitment to workplace action funded and supported by the national union (Wigham, 1973). The failure of the amalgamation to integrate the two major constitutents, TASS and the Engineering Section, together with the difficulty of establishing combine committees and closer links in the workplace between the two sections, was not helped by the low priority attached to integration at this level, and pushed the TASS leadership towards building closer links in the 'staff area'. Recruitment was given increased importance as the amalgamation broke down in the mid 1970s, and the two main sections began to compete with each other for members. In TASS, as mentioned above, the expansion of the official structure needed funding. Given the density of unionisation in engineering and the leadership's reluctance to diversify into other sectors, rapid growth, outside of greenfield developments, could only come from the unorganised sections of management and senior staff. The experience of the early 1970s in factories like Parsons had indicated the benefits but also the risks and costs of the militant integration of engineers. For management the earlier strategy was considered not only unnecessary, but actually counter-productive. Militancy, an emphasis on the importance of worker unity and <u>common</u> not <u>special</u> interests, may have forced management into resisting union advances. A passive, moderate, 'professional' approach appeared to engender a fateful acquiescence to union membership amongst the managers I interviewed. To unionise management the TASS leadership removed what, in the 1960s, had been considered the 'trade union qualities' of the union. That a Communist Party dominated broad left controlled the official machine meant, on the question of recruiting managers, the kind of intellectual somersaults noted earlier in the official literature. That the Bristol Management branch should adopt the argument of UKAPE is not surprising given these changes in the official line.

A graduate entry was clearly a 'professional' cut-off point, a way of deliberately excluding other technical workers. It represented a conscious attempt to accommodate TASS to the elitism of professional engineers. The BMB were not acting on their own, the report received the unanimous approval of the TASS Divisional Council and Divisional Organiser. The report even acknowledged the difficulty of defining 'professional', and yet remained locked within UKAPE's categorisation:

> The main problem here is the difficulty of defining 'professionally qualified', a problem which defeated UKAPE. A Professional shall, in this context, be any person employed by the British Aerospace Weybridge-Filton Division, at the Filton site, and engaged in an occupation for which he/she holds a recognised Graduate or equivalent qualification, together with a minimum of five years experience in that occupation.

Even though the report argued that by simply changing the eligibility of membership the 'problem' of UKAPE would be cleared up, it did not foresee any full integration between engineers and managers in the BMB. The report said there would be two negotiating sub-committees, for the two groups, and the possibility of a single sub-committee representing both groups on 'matters of common interest'. Not only did the TASS policy of recruitment through autonomy generate a mood of passivity in recruitment, it also fragmented TASS organisation in the factory. Had the report been accepted by the company, there would have been three TASS negotiating committees instead of two.

The report listed the advantages of its proposals in terms of increasing TASS membership, eliminating 80 per cent of UKAPE, endorsing 'TASS HQ' policy, and clearing up the 'problem' of UKAPE for the company. The disadvantages were said to be that Bristol No.3, Branch may not approve of the management branch 'poaching', and the management branch may object to a 'dilution' of their status by allowing in non-managers. Neither of these two disadvantages stopped the proposals, as the company refused to allow the changes, and TASS refused to even contemplate action to enforce their recommendations. The report had said: 'the company (whose agreement is essential at the outset) would most likely welcome a solution to the UKAPE problem.' When the company did not agree, the proposals were shelved.

The tone of the BMB report was extremely conciliatory towards the company and UKAPE and there was no suspicion that the company might actually benefit from having a division of union forces in the EDO. The report saw the difficulties chiefly coming from the two TASS branches, not the company. It abided by the company's power to decide which groups should be represented by the BMB and the Bristol No.3 branch. It was considered perfectly normal that the company should have the authority to determine trade union membership. This and other aspects of the response to UKAPE were in marked contrast to both the policy of TASS in the early 1970s and the struggle for unionisation at C. A. Parsons.

CONCLUSION

TASS policy on the best way to recruit professional engineers should be seen against the different political backgrounds of union organisation and tradition within the two plants. However the policy itself produced certain consequences and posed certain solutions. I have argued that in the early 1970s, TASS nationally backed a 'hard unionism' to recruit and integrate engineers as workers into the general membership of the union. The action encouraged by this policy challenged the ideology of professional autonomy and the independence of engineers from the labour movement as a whole. The action at C. A. Parsons, although led by people who were to the left of the Communist Party dominated

Executive Committee, was nevertheless supported financially and politically by the official structures of TASS. The JOC at Parsons were clearly seen to be carrying out national policy. In the mid 1970s the policy shifted towards accommodating the separatist and elitist view of engineers and from 1977 towards locating engineers' interests with those of managers, who were encouraged in join TASS by the services and autonomy the union provided. At BAe all the managers I interviewed were opposed to unionisation and had only joined TASS after nationalisation and because it offered them a separate branch (Smith 1986). There had been little change in the consciousness of managers brought about by this effortless unionisation. This is in contrast to the recruitment of engineers in the earlier period where the thinking behind the policy was aimed at making unionisation a 'radicalising' or political experience. The victory of TASS over UKAPE demonstrated to the leadership within Parsons that engineers had been drawn towards unionism and the working class. Bob Murdock:

> It related to the basic argument about whether design engineers are part of management and therefore part of the bourgeoisie, or whether they are workers and part of the working class. It was very clear, because you had this group of design engineers and there were forces pulling them both ways at that time and we won, we won.

While it is possible to criticise the essential voluntarism of such an argument (that struggle alone changes class location) the actual experience at Parson's generated, through a polarisation of opposites and clear cut resolution in favour of TASS, a sense in which engineers had 'changed sides' or 'class identities'. Because the process concerned non-supervisory engineers, rather than management staff, the struggle did engender significant ideological changes. But whatever transitory gains it achieved in terms of changing consciousness, a longer term achievement was the elimination of UKAPE as an organisational option for engineers. Ideas of elitism and exclusiveness are endemic to their place in the division of labour, but so too can be the values of cooperation and unity. By destroying UKAPE the former beliefs remained atomised, while the active trade union values of collective militancy and solidarity were allowed organisational embodiment and expression. Within the context of Parsons at the time TASS clearly 'embodied' ideas of social class, while ASTMS and UKAPE represented ideas of professionalism and status. But it would be wrong to conclude that this set of arrangements was immutable, as it strongly depends on trade union leadership and the type of policies pursued by the national union and the conditions inside the economy and labour movement as a whole (Smith,

1986).

My analysis of TASS has revealed that far from embodying a single ideology, the union held together competitive ideas of craftism, class solidarity and professional autonomy during the 1970s. It seems reasonable to conclude, however, that the changes in the union stance which began to appear in the mid 1970s were in effect an attempt by the leadership to recruit and retain a membership with a different class base. The definite shift towards exclusiveness and professional autonomy meant that, in unionising managers, the TASS national policy was on the one hand emphasising the employee status of the manager, while simultaneously projecting their class separation and differentiation from the rest of the TASS membership. When the conference set up management facilities in the TASS structure, this was considered necessary in order 'to provide management staff with their own identity and the facility to meet their own problems and needs' (TASS, 1978). There was no questioning of the value of recruiting managers if they had not consciously opted for trade unionism or been forced through industrial struggle into joining. Everything was designed to accommodate TASS to management. Terry Rogers questioned the value of effortless unionism in his own plant:

> There's no evidence that if we recruited these people (certain middle managers), they'd make a positive contribution to the organisation . . . Obviously it would be different if they got organised and brought forward grievances and we had a dispute with the company in relation to their problems. In areas where they've done that they've changed their whole attitude towards the company.

The TASS convenor at Rolls Royce in Coventry also told me that the recruitment of management weakened TASS's links with the shop floor unions. While the 'process' of recruiting engineers and the structure they are accommodated within does have a bearing on their ideology, with departmental managers, who form the first rung of the managerial hierarchy, their functional location is not simply infused with a contradictory ideological practice, but definite functions of capital. They are in a different class position to other technical staff, however grey the boundaries may be in many technical settings where overt supervision is not a necessary or feasible control strategy. This class division inside the membership has not been recognised but it is possible to see, as I have shown, how the craft practices and militancy of the draughtsmen shaped the approach to engineers in the early period, but was negated in the second period when such signs of working class consciousness were removed from the policy of recruiting managers.

The relative ease of unionising managerial grades can be seen as symtomatic of the underlining affinity between technical staff and management. Conversely, the difficulty of establishing stronger bonds with the shop floor through the amalgamation could also be seen as indicative of a class barrier between the two groups. These views ignore the differentiation between technical staff and management demonstrated in this chapter, and underestimate the craft links between technical and manual workers discussed in chapter three. However, given the class heterogeneity of TASS today, and the threats to craftism previously outlined, it seems that, objectively, technical staff and manual workers are further away today, organisationally, than they were in the early 1970s.

NOTES

1.   The Union was the National Union of Gold, Silver and Allied Trades, a skilled manual union with 3,000 members in 1981.

2.   See Mortimer (1960) for a discussion of third force politics inside engineering in the 1920s.

3.   Interview with TASS national spokesman who wished to be anonymous. Interviewed 17.3.82.

4.   TASS had separate committees for managers in the following plants before the formation of management branches: Lucas Aerospace, Bradford; Churchill Gears, Newcastle-upon-Tyne; Fords, Halewood; and Westland Helicopters, Yeovil. Fourteen branches appeared between 1977 and 1980, mainly geographical not industrial branches.

5.   Interviews with Terry Rogers, Chairman of NEI Parsons and TASS Negotiating Committee; and Bob Murdock, Treasurer, NEI Parsons and TASS Negotiating Committee 13.12.79. and 26.7.81. I also corresponded with Bob Murdock on details of the TASS organisation at NEI Parsons.

6.   Information on C. A. Parsons from above and TASS News and Journal, December 1978.

7.   The Bristol No.3 TASS Branch represented Technical Staff at BAe Aircraft Group and was referred to as 'TASS Ordinaire'. This differentation came about after the establishment of the Bristol Management Branch in 1977. Inside the factory this was known as 'Super TASS'.

BIBLIOGRAPHY

Abercrombie, N. and Urry, J. (1983) Capital, Labour and the Middle Classes, London, Allen and Unwin.

Adams, R. J. (1975) 'The recognition of White Collar Unions', British Journal of Industrial Relations, 13, 1.

—— (1977) 'Bain's Theory of White Collar Union Growth: a Conceptual Critique', British Journal of Industrial Relations, 15, 3.

AESD (1963) Report of Proceedings of AESD Representative Council Conference, Richmond, Surrey, AESD.

Ahlstrom, G. (1982) Engineers and Industrial Growth, London, Croom Helm.

Albu, A. (1980) 'British Attitudes to Engineering Education: a Historical Perspective' in K. Pavitt (ed.) Technical Innovation and British Economic Performance.

Allen, V. (1977) 'The Differentiation of the Working Class' in A. Hunt (ed.) Class and Class Structure.

Amin, A. (1983) 'Restructuring in Fiat and the Decentralisation of Production in Southern Italy' mimeo., Curds, University of Newcastle.

Armstrong, P. (1984) 'Competition Between the Organisation Professions and the Evolution of Managerial Control Strategies'. Paper presented to the Aston/UMIST Conference, Organisation and Control of the Labour Process, Aston University, March.

ASSET (1967) Minutes of Evidence 53, Royal Commission and Trade Unions and Employers' Associations, London, HMSO.

ASTMS (1969) Resistance to DATA Recruitment, C. A. Parsons ASTMS.

AUEW-TASS (1971) Which Way Forward for Professional Engineers? Richmond, Surrey, AUEW-TASS.

—— (1976) Report of the Proceedings of AUEW-TASS Representative Council Conference, Richmond, Surrey, AUEW-TASS.

—— (1978) Qualified Engineers: The Way Forward, Richmond, Surrey, AUEW-TASS.

—— (1980) Professional and Managerial Staff in Engineering, Richmond, Surrey, AUEW-TASS.

—— (1980) Report of Proceedings of AUEW-TASS Representative Council Conference, Richmond, Surrey, AUEW-TASS.

Bain, G. S. (1970) The Growth of White Collar Unionism, Oxford, Oxford University Press.

Bain, G. S., Coates, D. and Ellis, V. (1973) Social Stratification and Trade Unionism, London, Heinemann.

Baldry, C. and Connolly, A. (1984) 'Drawing the Line–Computer Aided Design and the Organisation of the Drawing Office'. Paper presented to Aston/UMIST Conference, Organisation and Control of the Labour Process, Aston University, March.

Banks, J. (1978) 'A Comment on Rosemary Crompton's "Approaches to the Study of White Collar Unionism" ', Sociology, 12.

Bannan, L., Barry, U. and Holst, O. (eds) (1982) Information Technology: Impact on the Way of Life, Dublin, Tycooly International Publishing Ltd.

Batstone, E. (1979) 'Systems of Domination, Accommodation and Industrial Democracy' in T. Burns, (ed.) Work and Power.

Behrend, H. (1957) 'The Effort Bargain', Industrial and Labour Relations Review, 10.

Berthoud, R. and Smith, D. J. (1980) The Education, Training and Careers of Professional Engineers, London, Department of Industry.

Bettelheim, C. (1976) Economic Calculation and Forms of Property, London, Routledge and Kegan Paul.

Blackburn, R. M. (1967) Union Character and Social Class, London, Batsford.

Blyton, P., Nicholson, N. and Ursell, G. (1981) 'Job Status and White Collar Members' Union Activity', Journal of Occupational Psychology, 54, 1.

Booker, P. J. (1963) A History of Engineering Drawing, London, Chatto and Windus.

Bowey, A. (1983) 'The Changing Status of the Supervisor', British Journal of Industrial Relations, 4, 3.

Bowley, M. (1966) The British Building Industry, Cambridge, Cambridge University Press.

Braverman, H. (1974) Labor and Monopoly Capital, New York, Monthly Review Press.

BIM (1976) The Front Line Manager, London, British Institute of Management.

Burns, T. (ed.) (1979) Work and Power, New York, Sage Publications.

Carchedi, G. (1977) On the Economic Identification of Social Classes, London, Routledge and Kegan Paul.

Carter, R. (1979) 'Class, Militancy and Union Character: a Study of the Association of Scientific, Technical and Managerial Staffs', Sociological Review, 27.

——(1980) Managerial and Supervisory Workers: Class, Unionism and Union Character, unpublished Ph.D. thesis, University of Bristol.

——(1985) Capitalism, Class Conflict and the New Middle Class, London, Routledge and Kegan Paul.

Child, J. (1984) 'Managerial Strategies, New Technology and the Labour Process', Work Organisation Research Centre Working Paper Series, No.1, University of Aston.

Child, J. and Partridge, B. (1982) Lost Managers: Supervisors in Industry and Society, Cambridge, Cambridge University Press.

Child, J., Pearce, S. and King, L. (1980) 'Class Perceptions and Social Identifications of Industrial Supervisors', Sociology, 14, 3.

Clarke, S. (1977) 'Marxism, Sociology and Poulantzas' Theory of the State', Capital and Class, 2.

Cliff, T. (1970) The Employers' Offensive: Productivity Deals and How to Fight Them, London, Pluto.

Cohen, G. A. (1978) Karl Marx's Theory of History: A Defence, Oxford, Clarendon Press.

CIR (1972) C. A. Parsons and Co. Limited and Associated Companies, Commission on Industrial Relations Report, 32, London, HMSO.

—— (1973) Recognition of White Collar Unions in Engineering and Chemicals, Commission on Industrial Relations Study 3, London, HMSO.

CBI (1984) Attitudes Towards Employment, London, Confederation of British Industry.

Cooley, M. (1972) Computer Aided Design: its Nature and Implications, Richmond, Surrey, AUEW/TASS.

—— (1976) 'Contradictions of Science and Technology in the Productive Process', in H. Rose and S. Rose (eds) The Political Economy of Science.

—— (1980) Architect or Bee: The Human/Technology Relationship, Slough, Hand and Brain.

Cottrell, A. (1984) Social Classes in Marxist Theory, London, Routledge and Kegan Paul.

Crompton, R. (1976) 'Approaches to the Study of White Collar Unionism', Sociology, 10, 3.

—— (1979) 'Trade Unionism and the Insurance Clerk', Sociology, 13.

Crompton, R. and Gubbay, J. (1977) Economy and Class Structure, London, Macmillan.

Crompton, R. and Jones, G. (1984) White-Collar Proletariat: Deskilling and Gender in Clerical Work, London, Macmillan.

Crozier, M. (1964) The Bureaucratic Phenomenon, London, Tavistock.

Cunnison, S. (1966) Wages and Work Allocation, London, Tavistock.

Dahrendorf, R. (1959) Class and Class Conflict in an Industrial Society, London, Routledge and Kegan Paul.

Dalton, M. (1949) Men Who Manage, New York, John Wiley.

Daly, A., Hitchens, D. M. W. N. and Wagner, K. (1985) 'Productivity, Machinery and Skills in a Sample of British and German Manufacturing Plants', National Institute Economic Review, 111, February.

Dickens, L. (1972) 'UKAPE: a Study of a Professional Union', Industrial Relations Journal, 3, 3.

DATA (1965) Report of Proceedings of Draughtsmen and Allied Technicians Representative Council Conference, Richmond, Surrey, Draughtsmen and Allied Technicians Association.

Dunkerley, D. (1975) The Foreman: Aspects of Task and Structure, London, Routledge and Kegan Paul.

Dunkerley, D. and Salaman, G. (eds) (1979) International Yearbook of Organisational Studies, London, Routledge and Kegan Paul.

Edwards, R. C. (1975) 'Social Relations of Production', in R. C. Edwards, M. Reich, and D. M. Gordon, Labour Market Segmentation.

———(1980) Contested Terrain, New York, Basic Books.

Edwards, R. C., Reich, M. and Gordon, D. M. (1975) Labour Market Segmentation, Lexington, Mass., D. C. Heath.

Elsheikh, F. and Bain, G. S. (1980) 'Unionisation in Britain: an Inter-Establishment Analysis Based on Survey Data', British Journal of Industrial Relations, 18.

EITB (1984) Economic and Industry Monitor, 17, November.

EMA (1979) The First Years 1977-79, Surrey, Engineers' and Managers' Association.

EAPM (1979) Management Unionisation in Western Europe, European Association for Personnel Management.

Farnham, D. (1977) 'Can Managers Collect Their Strength?' Management Today, February.

Friedman, A. (1977) Industry and Labour: Class Struggle at Work and Monopoly Capitalism, London, Macmillan.

Frodsham, A. (1979) 'Engineers' Unions Row: EEF Turns Down Debating Challenge from AMPS Chief', The Engineer, 8 February.

Frost, P. (1980) 'The Representation of Managerial Interests', in M. Poole and R. Mansfield (eds) Managerial Roles in Industrial Relations.

Giddens, A. (1973) The Class Structure of Advanced Societies, London, Hutchinson.

Giddens, A. and MacKenzie, G. (eds) (1982) Social Class and the Division of Labour, Cambridge, Cambridge University Press.

Gill, C., Morris, R. S. and Eaton, J. (1977) 'APST: the Rise of a Professional Union', Industrial Relations Journal, 8, 1.

Gill, K. (1976) 'Engineers in an Integrated Union', Electrical Review, 26 November.

Glover, I. (1983) 'How the West Was Last? The Decline of Engineering Manufacturing in Britain and the United States', mimeo., Dundee Technical College.

Goldman, P. and Van Houten, D. A. (1979) 'Bureaucracy and Domination: Managerial Strategy in Turn-of-the-century American Industry', in D. Dunkerley and G. Salaman (eds) International Yearbook of Organisational Studies.

Goldthorpe, J. H. (1982) 'On the Service Class, its Formation and Future', in A. Giddens and G. MacKenzie (eds) Social Class and the Division of Labour.

Goldthorpe, J. H., Lockwood, D., Bechhofer, F. and Platt, J. (1969) The Affluent Worker in the Class Structure, Cambridge, Cambridge University Press.

Goldthorpe, J. H., Llewellyn, C. and Payne, C. (1980) Social Mobility and Class Structure in Modern Britain, Oxford, Clarendon Press.

Gorz, A. (1976) 'Technology, Technicians and Class Struggle' in A. Gorz (ed.) The Division of Labour.

Gorz, A. (ed.) (1976) The Division of Labour, Hassocks, Harvester.

Gould, A. (1980) 'The Salaried Middle Class in the Corporatist Welfare State', Policy and Politics, 9.

Gouldner, A. W. (1954) Patterns of Industrial Bureaucracy, New York, Free Press (also Routledge and Kegan Paul, 1955).

Gramsci, A. (1957) The Modern Prince and Other Writings, London, Lawrence and Wishart.

Grant, A. (1983) Against the Clock, London, Pluto.

Hall, S. (1977) 'The "Political" and the "Economic" in Marx's Theory of Classes', in A. Hunt (ed.) Class and Class Structure.

Hartman, H. (1974) 'Managerial Employees: New Participants in Industrial Democracy', British Journal of Industrial Relations, 12.

Heritage, J. (1980) 'Class situation. White Collar Unionisation and the "Double Proletarianisation" Thesis: a Comment', Sociology, 14.

Hill, S. (1973) 'Supervisory Roles and the Man in the Middle', British Journal of Sociology, 24, 2.

Hopflinger, F. (1981) 'White Collar Unions in Switzerland', Industrial Relations Journal, 12, 4.

Hunt, A. (ed) (1977) Class and Class Structure, London, Lawrence and Wishart.

Huws, U. (1984) The New Homeworkers. New Technology and the Changing Location of White Collar Work, London, Low Pay Unit.

Hyman, R. and Brough, I. (1975) Social Values and Industrial Relations, Oxford, Blackwell.

Hyman, R. and Price, R. (eds) The New Working Class? White Collar Workers and their Organisations, London, Macmillan.

IDS (1982) CAD Agreements and Pay, IDS Study 276, October, London, Incomes Data Services.

Irvine, J., Miles, I. and Evans, J. (eds) (1979) Demystifying Social Statistics, London, Pluto.

Jenkins, C. (1965) 'Tiger in a White Collar?' in Penguin Survey of Business and Industry, Harmondsworth, Penguin.

——— (1973) 'Is Personnel Still Underpowered?' Personnel Management, June.

Jenkins, C. and Sherman, B. (1977) Collective Bargaining, London, Routledge and Kegan Paul.

———(1979) White Collar Unionism: the Rebellious Salariat, London, Routledge and Kegan Paul.

Johnson, D. (1982) (ed.) Class and Social Development A New Theory of the Middle Class, London, Sage Publications.

Johnson, T. (1971) 'What Is To Be Known?' Economy and Society, 6, 2.

———(1977) 'The Professions in the Class Structure', in R. Scase (ed.) Industrial Society, Class, Cleavage and Control.

Jones, B. (1982) 'Destruction or Redistribution of Engineering Skills? The Case of Numerical Control', in S. Wood (ed.) The Degradation of Work.

Katz, F. E. (1973) 'Integrative and Adaptive Uses of Autonomy: Worker Autonomy in Factories', in Salaman, G. and Thompson, K. (eds) People and Organisations.

Kelly, M. P. (1980) White Collar Proletariat: the Industrial Behaviour of British Civil Servants, London, Routledge and Kegan Paul.

Kleingarter, A. (1969) 'Professionalism and Engineering Unionism', Industrial Relations, 8.

Kocka, J. (1980) White Collar Workers in America 1890-1940, London, Sage Publications.

Lockwood, D. (1958) The Blackcoated Worker, London, Allen and Unwin.

———(1966) 'Sources of Variations in Working Class Images of Society', Sociological Review, 14, 3.

Loveridge, R. (1982) 'Occupational Change and the Development of Interest Groups Amongst White Collar Workers in the UK', British Journal of Industrial Relations, 10, 3.

McLoughlin, I. (1982) 'Misunderstanding the New Middle Class', Sociology, 16, 4.

Marchington, M. (1982) Managing Industrial Relations, New York, McGraw-Hill.

Marx, K. (1969) Theories of Surplus Value, London, Lawrence and Wishart.

———(1976) Capital, 1, Harmondsworth, Penguin.

Marx, K. and Engels, F. (1967) The Communist Manifesto, Harmondsworth, Pelican.

Massey, D. (1984) Spatial Divisions of Labour, London, Macmillan.

Meiksins, P. F. (1984) 'Scientific Management and Class Relations', Theory and Society, 13.

Melling, J. (1983) 'Supervisors and Innovation in British Industry with Reference to Engineering Production 1870-1914', mimeo., Kings College, University of Cambridge.

Merton, R. K. (1968) Social Theory and Social Structure, New York, Free Press.

Mills, C. W. (1953) White Collar, New York, Oxford University Press.

More, C. (1980) Skill and the English Working Class 1870-1914, London, Croom Helm.

Mortimer, J. (1960) A History of the Association of Shipbuilding and Engineering Draughtsmen, Richmond, Surrey, AESD.

Murray, F. (1983) 'The Decentralisation of Production: the Decline of the Mass-Collective Worker', Capital and Class, 19.

Nichols, T. (1969) Ownership, Control and Ideology, London, Allen and Unwin.

—— (1979) 'Social Class: Official, Sociological and Marxist', in J. Irvine, I. Miles and J. Evans (eds) Demystifying Social Statistics.

—— (1986) The British Worker Question, London, Routledge and Kegan Paul (forthcoming).

Nichols, T. and Beynon, H. (1977) Living With Capitalism, London, Routledge and Kegan Paul.

Nicholson, N., Ursell G. and Blyton, P. (1980) 'Social Background, Attitudes and Behaviour of White Collar Shop Stewards', British Journal of Industrial Relations, 18.

Noble, D. (1978) 'Social Choice in Machine Design: the Case of Automatically Controlled Machine Tools, and a Challenge to Labour', Politics and Society, 6, 3 and 4.

Parkin, F. (1979) Marxism and Class Theory: A Bourgeois Critique, London, Tavistock.

Pavitt, K. (ed) (1980) Technical Innovation and British Economic Performance, London, Macmillan.

Poole, M. and Mansfield, R. (eds) (1980) Managerial Roles in Industrial Relations, Aldershot, Gower Press.

Poulantzas, N. (1975) Classes in Contemporary Capitalism, London, NLB (also Verso, 1978).

Prandy, K. (1965) Professional Employees, London, Faber.

Prandy, K., Stewart, A. and Blackburn, R. M. (1974) 'Concepts and Measures: the Example of Unionateness', Sociology, 4, 3.

—— (1982) White Collar Work, London, Macmillan.

—— (1985) White Collar Unionism, London, Macmillan.

Price, R. (1983) 'White-collar Unions: Growth, Character and Attitudes in the 1970s', in R. Hyman and R. Price (eds) The New Working Class? White Collar Workers and their Organisations.

Rader, M. (1982) 'The Social Effects of Computer Aided Design: Current Trends and Forecasts for the Future' in L. Bannan, U. Barry and O. Holst (eds) Information Technology: Impact on the Way of Life.

Rader, M. and Wingert, B. (1981) Computer Aided Design in Great Britain and the Federal Republic of Germany, Karlsruhe, Abteilung für Angewandte Systemanalyse, Kernforschungszentrum.

Read, A. J. (1980) The Division of Labour in the British Shipbuilding Industry, 1880-1920 with Special Reference to Clydeside, Unpublished Ph.D. thesis, University of Cambridge.

Reynaud, J. D. (1983) 'An International View' in R. Hyman and R. Price, (eds) The New Working Class? White Collar Workers and their Organisations.

Richter, I. (1973) Political Purpose in Trade Unions, London, Allen and Unwin.

Roberts, B. C., Loveridge, R. and Gennard, J. (1972) Reluctant Militants, London, Heinemann.

Roberts, K., Cook, F. G., Clark, S. C. and Semeonoff, E. (1977) The Fragmentary Class Structure, London, Heinemann.

Roethlisberger, F. J. (1945) 'The Foreman: Master and Victim of Doubletalk', Harvard Business Review, 23.

Rose, H. and Rose, S. (eds) (1976) The Political Economy of Science, London, Macmillan.

Roslender, R. (1981) 'Misunderstanding Proletarianisation: a Comment on Recent Research', Sociology, 15, 3.

Ross, G. (1978) 'Marxism and the New Middle Classes: French Critiques', Theory and Society, 5, 2.

Runciman, W. G. (1967) Relative Deprivation and Social Justice, London, Routledge and Kegan Paul.

Sabel, C. (1982) Politics and Work, Cambridge, Cambridge University Press.

Salaman, G. and Thompson, K. (eds) (1973) People and Organisations, London, Longmans.

Scase, R. (ed.) (1977) Industrial Society, Class, Cleavage and Control, London, Allen and Unwin.

Scullion, H. (1981) 'The Skilled Revolt Against General Unionism: The Case of the BL Toolroom Committee', Industrial Relations Journal, 12, 3.

Sedgemore, B. (1977) The How and Why of Socialism, Nottingham, Spokesman.

Smith, C. D. (1982) Technical Workers: Class, Work and Trade Unionism, unpublished Ph.D. thesis, University of Bristol.

—— (1984) 'Managerial Strategies: Capital and Labour. A Reply to John Child and an Alternative Model Part One', Work Organisation Research Centre Working Paper Series, No.2, University of Aston.

—— (1985) 'Design Engineers and the Capitalist Firm', Work Organisation Research Centre Working Paper Series, No.6, University of Aston.

—— (1986) Technical Workers: Class, Work and Trade Unionism, London, Macmillan (forthcoming).

Smith, R. and Sawbridge, D. (1974) 'Professional Associations, Trade Unions and Industrial Conflict', mimeo., University of Durham.

Spoor, A. (1967) White Collar Union: 60 years of NALGO, NALGO.

Spybey, T. (1984) 'Traditional and Professional Frames of Meaning', Sociology, 18, 4.

Stewart, A., Prandy, K. and Blackburn, R. M. (1980) <u>Social Stratifications and Occupations</u>, London, Macmillan.

Taylor, F. W. (1947) <u>The Principles of Scientific Management</u>, New York, Harper and Row.

Taylor, R. (1980) <u>The Fifth Estate: Britain's Unions in the Modern World</u>, London, Pan Books.

Titmuss, R. M. (1958) <u>Essays on the Welfare State</u>, London, Allen and Unwin.

Undy, R., Ellis, V., McCarthy, W. E. J. and Halmos, A. M. (1981) <u>Change in Trade Unions: The Development of UK Unions since the 1960s</u>, London, Hutchinson.

Wainwright, H. and Elliott, D. (1982) <u>The Lucas Plan: A New Trade Unionism in the Making</u>, London, Allison and Busby.

Weir, D. (1976) 'Radical Managerialism: Middle Managers' Perceptions of Collective Bargaining', <u>British Journal of Industrial Relations</u>, 15, 3.

Westergaard, J. and Resler, H. (1975) <u>Classes in a Capitalist Society</u>, London, Heinemann.

Whalley, P. (1984) 'Deskilling Engineers? The Labour Process, Labour Markets, and Labour Segmentation', <u>Social Problems</u>, 32, 2.

Wigham, E. (1973) <u>The Power to Manage: A History of the Engineering Employers Federation</u>, London, Macmillan.

Wood, S. (ed.) (1982) <u>The Degradation of Work</u>, London, Hutchinson and Co.

Woodley, M. (1973) <u>TASS: A Trade Union During a Period of Change</u>, unpublished M.A. thesis, University of Durham.

Wooton, G. (1961) 'Parties in a Union Government: the AESD', <u>Political Studies</u>, 9.

Wray, D. E. (1949) 'Marginal Men of Industry: The Foreman', <u>American Journal of Sociology</u>, 54.

Wrench, J. and Stanley, N. (1984) 'Old Problems for New Workers: A Study of Changing Patterns of Shiftworking in the West Midlands', <u>British Sociological Association Annual Conference</u>, 2-5 April.

Wright, E. O. (1977) 'Class Boundaries in Advanced Capitalist Societies', <u>New Left Review</u>, 98.

——(1978) <u>Class, Crisis and State</u>, London, NLB (also Verso, 1979a).

——(1979b) 'Class, Occupation and Organisation' in D. Dunkerley and G. Salaman, (eds) <u>International Yearbook of Organisational Studies</u>.

——(1979c) <u>Class Structure and Income Determination</u>, London, Academic Press.

AUTHOR Index

Abercrombie, N. 6, 11-13, 15, 25, 160, 199
Adams, R.J. 113, 119
Ahlstrom, G. 161, 199
Albu, A. 100, 199
Allen, V. 19, 199
Amin, A. 104, 199
Armstrong, P. 106, 160, 199

Bain, G.S. 19, 111, 112, 113, 114, 117, 120, 121, 157, 199, 202
Baldry, C. 103, 199
Banks, J. 114, 200
Bannan, L. 200, 205
Barry, U. 200, 205
Batstone, E. 34, 200
Bechhofer, F. 20, 202
Behrend, H. 38, 200
Berthoud, R. 121, 200
Bettelheim, C. 8, 200
Beynon, H. 23, 205
Blackburn, R.M. 13, 19, 20, 21, 111, 112, 113, 115, 119, 120, 157, 200, 205, 207
Blyton, P. 118, 119, 200, 205
Booker, P.J. 81, 200
Bowey, A. 119, 200
Bowley, M. 82, 200
Braverman, H. 21, 22, 26, 43, 44, 45, 79, 94, 116, 132, 200
Brough, I. 145, 203
Burns, T. 200

Carchedi, G. 1, 3, 5, 6, 20, 21, 23, 27, 34, 45, 46, 47, 64, 114, 132, 200
Carter, R. 1, 10, 21, 74, 116, 118, 121, 170, 200
Child, J. 19, 21, 22, 43, 76, 119, 120, 121, 200
Clark, S.C. 20, 120, 206
Clarke, S. 8, 201
Cliff, T. 75, 201
Coates, D. 19, 111, 113, 117, 199
Cohen, G.A. 4, 201
Connolly, A. 103, 199
Cook, F.G. 20, 120, 206
Cooley, M. 100, 102, 201
Cottrell, A. 6, 10-11, 201
Crompton, R. 13, 19, 20, 21, 23, 110, 114, 115, 116, 119, 132, 156, 201
Crozier, M. 32, 201
Cunnison, S. 26, 201

Dahrendorf, R. 2, 201
Dalton, M. 31, 201
Daly, A. 54, 201
Dickens, L. 162, 169, 185, 201
Dunkerley, D. 40, 201, 202, 207

Eaton, J. 162, 171, 202
Edwards, R.C. 22, 29, 117, 202
Elliot, D. 99, 207
Ellis, V. 19, 111, 113, 117, 164, 199, 207
Elsheikh, F. 114, 202
Engels, F. 4, 204
Evans, J. 203, 205
Farnham, D. 118, 119, 202

Index

For Product Safety Concerns and Information please contact our EU
representative GPSR@taylorandfrancis.com
Taylor & Francis Verlag GmbH, Kaufingerstraße 24, 80331 München, Germany